# FROM SUNDOWN
# TO SUNUP

# THE AMERICAN SLAVE:
## A COMPOSITE AUTOBIOGRAPHY

# THE AMERICAN SLAVE:
# A COMPOSITE
# AUTOBIOGRAPHY

## 1

## FROM SUNDOWN TO SUNUP
### The Making of
### the Black Community

GEORGE P. RAWICK

Contributions in Afro-American and
African Studies
Number 11

GREENWOOD PUBLISHING COMPANY
WESTPORT, CONNECTICUT
1972

Library of Congress Cataloging in Publication Data

Rawick, George P        1929–
    From sundown to sunup.

    (The American slave: a composite autobiography,
v. 1) (Contributions in Afro-American and African
studies, no. 11)
    Bibliography: p.
    1. Slavery in the United States--History. I. Title.
II. Series: Contributions in Afro-American and
African studies, no. 11.
E441.A58 vol. 1      301.451'96073      71-105986
ISBN 0-8371-6299-8

*Library of Congress Catalog Card Number: 71-105986*

*ISBN 0-8371-3314-9 (Set)*
*ISBN 0-8371-6299-8 (Vol. I cloth)*
*ISBN 0-8371-6747-7 (Vol. I pbk.)*

*Volume I first published 1972*
*second printing 1973*
*third printing 1974*

*Paperback edition  1973*

*Greenwood Publishing Company*
*A Division of Greenwood Press, Inc.*
*51 Riverside Avenue, Westport, Connecticut 06880*

*Printed in the United States of America*

FOR MICHELLE YUFFY GOLDMAN
AND MY SONS
JULES DANIEL AND CHE CALLE

# CONTENTS

# ACKNOWLEDGMENTS

The influence and assistance of many people made this present work possible, although I am, of course, solely responsible for the judgments and for the execution of the work. The work extended over a decade and there were many more influences upon its creation than I will be able to acknowledge. The many students and friends with whom I have discussed this work or who indirectly aided in its conception and execution must go unnamed, but ultimately I owe much to them for their questions and comments. In a wider sense, this work owes a great deal to the black community itself, which during the years in which I worked on this project was astonishing the world with its militant challenge to its own continued oppression.

However, certain people must be mentioned, for my debt to them is so great that I can only here discharge it in some small measure. As an undergraduate at Oberlin College in the 1940s, I learned what historical research was about and what it was for from Professors Harvey K. Goldberg and Thomas LeDuc. In graduate school at the University of Wisconsin, Professor Merle Curti taught me American history. My gratitude to him is great. At Wisconsin I also worked under Professor Hans H. Gerth, who taught me how to think sociologically and to transcend the American intellectual horizon.

Anthropological and ethno-historical interests were enriched by my friend and colleague Professor Robert K. Thomas of Monteith College of Wayne State University. From him I learned that "culture" was a process—not a sterile repetition of the behavior of the past, but the creative transformation by people of that past. His comments on the manuscript of this book were most useful.

For most of the twentieth century, C. L. R. James of Trinidad, Europe, and the United States has left a profound mark on both political and cultural work. His writings and lectures on history, politics, and culture, with their profound insight into the activities of ordinary people, were before me throughout my work. I cannot overstate my debt to him.

The evidence of the influence of Martin Glaberman appears throughout this work. His personal encouragement was of great importance at many crucial points; his reading of the final manuscript was the most recent of his many acts of aid to this work. He has been friend, colleague, and mentor.

I am also appreciative of the work on slavery of William Gorman.

A number of other friends must be mentioned as having particularly aided me in my work. I can only acknowledge in a small way my gratitude to Daniel and Mary Ann Clawson, Stuart House, Dianne Luthmers and Albert Luthmers, Barry Thompson, Preston Schiller, William Watson, and Robert Wicke.

Two people helped in the preparation of the manuscript. I wish to thank Penelope Dexter and Mary Peters for their intelligent and generous assistance.

My sociological and ethnographic interests and skills were broadened and deepened during the year 1957–1958 which I spent at Cornell University under the auspices of a Social Science Research Council postgraduate fellowship in sociology and anthropology. I hope that the SSRC will accept this work as the final report which I have owed them for over twelve years.

The Faculty Research Grant Committee of Oakland University made a series of grants that greatly facilitated the work. The staff of the Schomburg Collection in New York City rendered their usual intelligent aid and assistance. Secretarial help partially provided by the Department of Sociology of Washington University made possible the completion of the manuscript.

Professors Eugene Genovese and Sidney Mintz read sections of the manuscript at various stages and helped clarify and deepen many points. Professor Norman Klein saved me from significant errors in my discussion of West African development. Professor John Szwed volunteered many helpful suggestions and I am grateful to him. I am also grateful to Julius Lester for taking time from a very crowded schedule to read my manuscript and for his most helpful comments. Of course, they are neither responsible for any errors that may be found in the book nor, necessarily, for any of my judgments.

Material from Harold Courlander, *The Drum and the Hoe: Life and Lore of the Haitian People*, originally published by the University of California Press, is reprinted by permission of the Regents of the University of California.

The encouragement and help of my publisher, Herbert Cohen of Greenwood Publishing Company, made the total work possible. His patience and hard work has been in the finest tradition of book publishing. Elisabeth Krabisch and Linda Weinraub of Greenwood Publishing Company saved me from disaster at one crucial moment and made important contributions in the preparation of the final manuscript.

In the deepest intellectual and personal way this work was made possible by the aid, encouragement, hard-headed criticism, and suggestions of Michelle Yuffy Goldman. This book is dedicated to her and to my two young sons, Jules Daniel and Che Calle.

# INTRODUCTION

Black history in the United States must be viewed as an integral, if usually antagonistic, part of the history of the American people. Without understanding the historical development of black society, culture, and community, comprehension of the totality of America's development is impossible. Slavery was a fundamental part of the history of the whole American people, just as its aftermath continues to pose a fundamental question for our national life.

Most discussion of American development has ignored, sidestepped, or treated as a minor theme slavery and its aftermath. Emphasis has been placed, instead, upon geographic conditions, upon technological achievements and the organization of industry, upon ideological uniqueness, and upon governmental practice and constitutional theory. The history of American society has been subordinated to the history of the American state; the reality of the American people to ideologically determined abstractions. The history of the American people has been subordinated to the history of industrial technology, of capitalism, and of related values and institutional arrangements.

There has been as a consequence very little written social history of the American people, and what there has been has usually avoided discussion of either class conflict or the subordination of blacks to whites. Thus, for example, labor historians have usually focused upon the institutional development of trade unions, rather than upon the activities of working people. No one has written a "Making of the American Working Class," but there have been many serious works on the institutional history of particular trade union organizations.

If white workers have rarely appeared in the annals and chronicles of the American people, blacks have appeared hardly at all. And the black slave himself has been virtually absent from the written history other than as the victim of white aggression or the recipient of white paternalism.

The black slave usually has been portrayed as the victim who never enters his own history as its subject, but only as the object over which abstract forces and glorious armies fought. Historians have justified this absence of slave voices in the history of slavery and the American people by insisting that, after all, the slaves left no records, accomplished little that was "noteworthy," and therefore did not have much of a history. In an article in the influential popularizer of American history, *American Heritage* magazine, Peter Chew wrote:

> A subjugated people, reduced to and held in a condition little better than that of domestic animals, is not likely to make much history . . . . As uneducated slaves, blacks were obviously in no position to lead noteworthy careers: they could not become doctors, lawyers, military leaders, architects, engineers, statesmen.[1]

While slavery has left an indelible mark on American life, the slaves themselves have rarely been heard telling their own stories. The masters not only ruled the past in fact; they now rule its written history. Like the rest of the population which did not lead "notable" lives, the slaves appear usually only as faceless and nameless people murmuring and mumbling offstage. At best, only the loud and demanding voice of an exceptional slave, such as the great black abolitionist leader Frederick Douglass, is heard, and then only above the din of the speeches of politicians, statesmen, and ideologists of all persuasions. The history of black Americans has been treated by most historians as a specialized, exotic subject, not as a central focus for the study of the development of the American people.

But it is not enough to assert that the history of black people has never been made integral to the history of the American people, or that the voices of the slaves have rarely been heard. There must be sources that demonstrate that white society cannot be understood without seeing its symbiotic relationship to black society, sources in which the slaves speak for themselves. But we have been told very often that slaves were illiterate and therefore left no records. And even those historians most interested in finding the slaves' own accounts have so far depended upon those books left by occasional, and exceptional, runaway slaves.

Yet there is a large body of previously untapped material which directly expresses the views of slavery held by those who had been slaves. It is largely upon these records that this work is based, selections from which comprise the collection of materials that this work introduces. What are these sources?

First, there were the scores of slave autobiographies published before the Civil War or shortly thereafter.[2] While they are of uneven quality, they are at least no less significant than the special pleadings of the slaveowners and white abolitionists whose writings historians always have dealt with seriously. Further, there were thousands of interviews with ex-slaves recorded in the 1920s and 1930s by several groups of investigators, by private scholars, and under the auspices of the federal government, all of which have received only scant attention by historians.[3]

There were at least eighty published slave narratives which appeared before the Civil War and probably many more. These fell generally into three types: those which were written by former slaves who had made their way to freedom; those obviously written by an amanuensis but clearly and accurately reflecting the experiences of the narrator; and those which were either thoroughly ghostwritten by a well-known abolitionist or were outright forgeries. While there were examples of the last type written by such men as John Greenleaf Whittier and Richard Hildreth, most of the slave narratives were clearly of the first two types.[4]

In addition to the narratives published before the Civil War, there was a thin but steady stream that followed in the four decades after the war. These often were written by black ministers as fundraising devices for themselves and their churches; consequently, they tend to be very moderate in their views of the slave experience, reflecting the required ideological posture blacks had to assume in order to get money out of whites.

Of the interviews, the outstanding ones are the Slave Narrative Collection of the Federal Writers' Project of the Works Projects Administration compiled during the years 1936–1938. This collection consists of over 10,000 pages of typescript, containing over 2,000 interviews with ex-slaves.[5] The Federal Writers' Project interviews were the culmination of several independent efforts during the late 1920s and early 1930s to preserve the life stories of ex-slaves.

The first two major projects were begun in 1929 at Southern University in Louisiana and at Fisk University in Tennessee, both outstanding black institutions. At Southern, under the direction of the historian John B. Cade, interviews were taken which culminated in the publication of an article entitled "Out of the Mouths of Ex-Slaves" in *The Journal of Negro History*.[6] Cade did another collection of interviews of some 400 ex-slaves from thirteen states; these have never been fully published. The two volumes of the Fisk University study are reprinted with the permission of Fisk University as Volumes 18 and 19 in the second series of the present project.

In 1934, Lawrence D. Reddick, then a member of the faculty of Kentucky State College, who had worked on the Fisk University project, presented a proposal to the Federal Emergency Relief Administration which would employ 500 black white-collar workers to interview ex-slaves. In 1934 some 250 interviews were taken in Indiana and Kentucky. These also have never been published.[7]

The culmination of these various independent efforts to preserve the life stories of ex-slaves was the comprehensive program of interviewing inaugurated and carried through under the auspices of the Federal Writers' Project of the Works Projects Administration during the years 1936 to 1938.[8] For a brief but crucial period, the outstanding American folklorist John A. Lomax was director of this enormous project, which ultimately produced over 10,000 pages of typescript containing over 2,000 interviews with ex-slaves.[9] Out of this project came such varied activities as the publication of *These Are Our Lives*—a series of life histories of inhabitants, mostly white, of the southeastern United States, as well as the slave narratives whose publication is the central focus of the project this volume introduces.

The actual inauguration of the slave narrative project in the Writers' Project series began on the local and regional level. Only after there had been a number of independent pilot studies, significantly projects in Georgia and Florida, did Lomax inaugurate a systematic national project.[10]

The interviews were taken in seventeen states and were then deposited in seventeen volumes in thirty-three parts in the Rare Books Division of the Library of Congress from which they have been available on microfilm. There has been a highly selective printing of parts of these interviews, organized not as full-length indi-

vidual narratives, but as information about topics, edited by B. A
Botkin, who himself had been one of the administrators of the origi
nal project. A hardcover edition of his book appeared in 1945
and a paperback edition in 1958.[11] Selections from the Virginia
narratives were published, carefully edited, and the original interviews are deeply buried under the interpretive material; the
Louisiana narratives were used in the preparation of a book on
Louisiana folklore, and the Savannah Writers' Project put out a
book based on the narratives. In 1968, Julius Lester, former Field
Secretary of the Student Non-Violent Coordinating Committee,
published a book of selections from the slave narratives and other
related material.[12]

I am indebted to Norman Yetman for his careful study of the
background of the slave narrative collection which appeared both
as an article in the *American Quarterly* in 1967 and in a slightly
different form in his recent volume, *Voices from Slavery*. Professor
Yetman's selections in this volume of 100 of the WPA narratives,
while excellent, also have been edited. At times, in order "to improve
readability and continuity," he has rewritten sentences and deleted
others; he has eliminated the different "dialect" spellings in "an
attempt to achieve some uniformity"; he has eliminated "those comments . . . that concerned the informant's situation when interviewed"; and he has usually deleted all the material included in
the interviews that deal with events that occurred after the Civil
War.[13]

In order to allow the full benefit of the items that Professor
Yetman has deleted, I have left the interviews exactly as they were
recorded, thus permitting future scholars to handle the narratives
as they see fit. Often the informant's situation at the time interviewed has considerable bearing on his personal memory of slavery.
For example, old people living in poverty in the midst of the Great
Depression of the 1930s very often looked back upon slavery with
some positive glances, because at least under slavery they had
enough to eat.

I have also retained all the editorial marks; often, these marks
reveal the differences among the interviewers, in terms of style
and bias. In addition, I have retained the attempts at rendering
regional black speech dialects; no matter how inept these attempts
may have been, they are evidence of a matter of considerable importance: the development of American speech. Moreover, I have left
in all the references to events after the Civil War because oral

history records, if they are to have scholarly use, must not be altered. They are documents about the entire life of the individual being interviewed, including his situation at the time interviewed.[14]

I am struck, moreover, by the fact that many ex-slaves clearly did not distinguish between the experience under slavery and that after abolition. The plantation system did not change drastically for most ex-slaves after the end of slavery, and many continued to live and work on the same plantations where they formerly had been slaves. Indeed, when interviewed in the 1930s some were still living on the same plantation or very near to it, even though they might have owned the portion of the plantation they worked. I believe that evidence of this important continuity between slavery and freedom must be made available if we are to understand the depths of the system of American racism.[15]

Approximately 2 percent of the total ex-slave population in the United States in 1937 were interviewed. (There is room for a considerable margin of error in this figure, based as it is on estimates derived from 1930 census figures.)[16] Almost all those interviewed had experienced slavery within the states of the Confederacy and still resided there; very few had been freedmen before the Civil War. The slave holdings of the ex-slaves' owners varied considerably, ranging from over a thousand slaves to situations in which the informant was the only slave owned by the master.

However, there is very little about the sample that is random, and it would be unwise to make statistically precise calculations about the material. The method of selection of the ex-slaves interviewed was by pure happenstance, which not only does not assure randomness, but introduces self-selection as a factor. It is clear from the interviews themselves that very often the ex-slaves being interviewed were either volunteers or were known previously by the interviewer.

This does not mean, however, that there is no use for these materials, particularly if methodologies are devised to utilize them. They are essentially no different from any other oral history collection in which both self-selection and selection by the interviewer, rather than randomness, was the principle of selection. If we carefully avoid drawing conclusions that demand precision from these materials, they can be very useful.

If a collection of materials not readily available before and certainly rarely used is placed before the public, it is primarily because these materials can become the basis for a new understanding of the significant and usable past. This collection of slave narratives and interviews is no exception. The value of such narratives and interviews does not generally lie in their descriptions of great historical events. While we might learn something from them of the politics of the antebellum South, of the economic development of the nation, and of its intellectual life, such information does not dominate these works. Instead, they reveal the day-to-day life of people, their customs, their values, their ideas, hopes, aspirations, and fears. We can derive from them a picture of slave society and social structure and of the interaction between black and white. We can see in them the outlines of the slave community, that network of communication systems whereby people were enabled to live. And we can study through them the development of the community. From these materials we can see how the black slave, forced to abandon his African past and its institutions and to adapt himself to being a slave under white masters in a new land, formed an Afro-American way of life that combined the thought patterns of the African heritage with the social forms and social conditions of the new land. Rather than becoming "deculturized," the slaves used what they brought with them from Africa to meet the new conditions; they created new social forms and behavior patterns which syncretized African and New World elements under the particular conditions of slave life in the United States. In the narratives we can find ways of understanding and dealing with the slaves' daily accommodations to their conditions and, as well, with their resistances and rebellions. We can learn a great deal about the treatment of the slaves and the consequences of such treatment.

The emphasis throughout this work will be on the creation of the black community under slavery, a process which largely went on outside of work relations. Up until now the focus in the discussion of American slavery has been on what went on from sunup to sundown. It is hoped that this work will shift the emphasis to the full life of the slaves, to those aspects of their reality in which they had greater autonomy than at work. While from sunup to sundown the American slave worked for another and was harshly exploited, from sundown to sunup he lived for himself and created the behavioral and institutional basis which prevented him from becoming the absolute victim.

Our task is primarily sociological and ethnological. Only the combined methods of historians, sociologists, and anthropologists can help us develop these materials in ways that illuminate black American society, community, and culture. This present essay is a first attempt to use these materials in this way. Its primary function is to raise questions, to make what will eventually probably be seen as crude attempts to develop an appropriate methodology for such work, and to present a general outline of American slave society, community, and culture. There is no claim that what will be presented is a total picture of slave life in the United States.

Intellectual life, if it is to be at all fruitful, is ultimately a collective undertaking. If this work will act as a catalyst in the development of a social history of the American people, then its writing and publication will be warranted, even if many or most of its specific conclusions will be rejected or modified by future work. Consequently, at times I have offered interpretations that go far beyond the data immediately available. I hope others will be encouraged to challenge, modify, or further these views. Only in this way will we begin to get a history of the American people that gives us a sense of life as it was lived from the bottom up.

## Notes

1. Peter Chew, "Black History or Black Mythology," *American Heritage* 20 (August 1969):7.

2. See the bibliography of primary sources of this book. There have been many recent reprints of some of these narratives, but the bulk of them have not been reprinted. There are two works which rely exclusively on the printed slave narratives for their accounts of slavery. For a very useful, straightforward account based on the published slave narratives, see Charles Nichols, *Many Thousands Gone: The Ex-slaves' Account of Their Bondage and Freedom.* For a well-meaning but patronizing and pedestrian utilization of the narratives, see Stanley Feldstein, *Once a Slave: The Slaves' View of Slavery* (New York, 1971).

3. The series which this volume introduces will contain at least two collections: the narratives of the ex-slaves interviewed by the Federal Writers' Project of the WPA in the mid-1930s and the two volumes of interviews collected at Fisk University in the 1920s and published in mimeographed form in 1945. Other similar material may eventually be added.

4. Richard Hildreth, *Archy Moore, The White Slave: or Memoirs of a Fugitive.* Charles Nichols, in *Many Thousands Gone,* p. xiii, writes of a book edited by the poet Whittier:

> *The Narrative of James Williams, An American Slave Who Was For Several Years a Driver on a Cotton Plantation in Alabama* was dictated to John Greenleaf Whittier and published by the American Antislavery Society in 1838. A short time after the narrative appeared, the editor of *The Alabama Beacon* asserted that no such plantation or planter as Williams mentioned was to be found anywhere in Alabama. It was then rumoured

that Whittier had been hoodwinked by a free Negro pretending to be a fugitive slave. By the time of the exposé, James Williams had gone to England, and the Antislavery Society suppressed the book.

5. These narratives will be referred to throughout as Federal Writers' Project, Slave Narratives, *A Folk History of Slavery in the United States from Interviews with Former Slaves.* In abbreviated form it will be FWPSN, followed by the state in which the ex-slave lived.

6. John B. Cade, "Out of the Mouths of Ex-Slaves," *The Journal of Negro History* 20 (1935):294–337.

7. See Norman R. Yetman, ed., *Voices from Slavery*, pp. 344–346.

8. Only the state of Louisiana did not participate directly in this project. However, somewhat later, narratives were collected in Louisiana, which were employed in the writing of Louisiana Writers Project, *Gumbo Ya-Ya.* The records of the Virginia project were used in the writing of Virginia Writers' Project, *The Negro in Virginia* (New York, 1940).

9. Yetman, ed., *Voices from Slavery*, pp. 350–351.

10. See Norman Yetman, "The Background of the Slave Narrative Collection," *American Quarterly* 19 (1967):534-553 and Yetman, ed., *Voices from Slavery*, pp. 339-355.

11. B. A. Botkin, ed., *Lay My Burden Down.*

12. Julius Lester, ed., *To Be a Slave.*

13. Yetman, ed., *Voices from Slavery*, p. 350.

14. The slave narratives written during the 1930s contain many interesting reflections on black life during Reconstruction and in the years of the Great Depression of the 1930s.

15. See Chapter 7 of this book.

16. Yetman, ed., *Voices from Slavery*, p. 2.

# PART I

# THE SOCIOLOGY
# OF SLAVERY IN THE
# UNITED STATES

# 1

# MASTER AND
# SLAVE

American Negro slavery was a human institution, albeit an exceedingly inhumane one. Yet rarely has the discussion of slavery in North America proceeded from this premise. Rather, almost all historians have presented the black slaves as dehumanized victims, without culture, history, community, change, or development.

This assumption that the slave was a total victim is at its heart elitist and untenable. What flows from it is the view that the slave could not help himself because he had no culture, history, community, or opportunity for change and development and that, consequently, he had to be liberated by those whose history had fortunately left them intact and thus in human terms better equipped to help him.

But if the slave had a history, then his behavior changed over time as he learned from the past and met new experiences. Men, however, do not move in their own behalf or make revolutions for light and transient reasons. Only when they no longer can stand the contradictions in their own personalities do they move in a sharp and decisive fashion. The victim is always in the process of becoming the rebel, because the contradictions demand this resolution.

As the German philosopher Hegel understood in the famous passage on master and slave in *The Phenomenology of Mind*, the slave fights against the master by wrestling with his own internal conflicts. The will of the master and the will of the slave both appear as a contradiction within the slave.[1]

3

We can see this process working in many accounts left by ex-slaves telling of their flight from slavery. Even when writing their stories as abolitionist propaganda, they indicate their fears, self-doubts, even guilt, about running away. The greatest of all abolitionist leaders, the ex-slave Frederick Douglass, indicates this ambivalence in his autobiography, *Narrative of the Life of Frederick Douglass: An American Slave*. "Slaves," he writes, "when inquired of as to their condition and the character of their masters, almost universally say they are contented, and that their masters are kind."[2] After attributing this in part to the fear of the presence of spies, he goes on to indicate an even more profound reason:

> I have been frequently asked, when a slave, if I had a kind master, and do not remember ever to have given a negative answer; nor did I, in pursuing this course, consider myself as uttering what was absolutely false; for I always measured the kindness of my master by the standard of kindness set up among slaveholders around us. Moreover, slaves are like other people, and imbibe prejudices quite common to others. They think their own better than that of others. Many, under the influence of this prejudice, think their own masters are better than the masters of other slaves; and this, too in some cases, when the very reverse is true. Indeed, it is not uncommon for slaves even to fall out and quarrel among themselves about the relative goodness of their masters, each contending for the superior goodness of his own over that of the others. At the very same time, they mutually execrate their masters when viewed separately. It was so on our plantation. When Colonel Lloyd's slaves met the slaves of Jacob Jepson, they seldom parted without a quarrel about their masters; Colonel Lloyd's slaves contending that he was the richest, and Mr. Jepson's slaves that he was the smartest, and most of a man. Colonel Lloyd's slaves would boast his ability to buy and sell Jacob Jepson. Mr. Jepson's slaves would boast his ability to whip Colonel Lloyd. These quarrels would almost always end in a fight between the parties, and those that whipped were supposed to have gained the point at issue. They seemed to think that the greatness of their masters was transferable to themselves. It was considered as being bad enough to be a slave; but to be a poor man's slave was deemed a disgrace indeed.[3]

Most of Douglass' book deals with the years of preparation that he went through in order to be ready to run away. At all times he was unsure of himself. Even after making his way to freedom in New York City he reports that shortly after arriving there,

> . . . I was again seized with a feeling of great insecurity and loneliness. I was yet liable to be taken back, and subjected to all the tortures of slavery. This in itself was enough to damp the ardor of my enthusiasm. But the loneliness overcame me. There I was in the midst of thousands, and yet a perfect stranger; without home and without friends, in the midst of thousands of my own brethren—children of a common Father, and yet I dared not to unfold to any one of them my sad condition.[4]

Douglass felt all of this probably even more keenly because in fact he never had had a home. His father had been a plantation owner with whom he had no relationship and he had seen his mother four or five times since infancy. Nevertheless, the ex-slave Frederick Douglass, without either mother or father, became a powerful, influential leader in the struggle against slavery.

But Douglass' achievement must be set into the context that while tens of thousands of other slaves, in tribute to human courage, did indeed follow the North Star to New England, the upper Midwest, and Canada, many thousands more either failed in their attempts to escape or never made the effort. After having examined the situation and themselves, many decided not to go. For thousands of others the thought of flight was more than could even be entertained.

Running away from slavery was objectively difficult. It entailed a journey of hundreds, even a thousand miles from the Deep South, on foot, with only the food one managed to get from the land, or an occasional slave, under circumstances in which virtually every white man, and even an occasional black, was a potential captor. The patrol system operated throughout the South and the patrollers and their bloodhounds were in fact in pursuit of runaways. Harriet Beecher Stowe's portrayal of a slave runaway in _Uncle Tom's Cabin_ was not particularly exaggerated, although not as interesting as stories of the hundreds of real runaways recorded in the slave autobiographies and narratives.

We get a picture of the magnitude of the task involved in running away in the autobiographical account of Solomon Northrup. Northrup, born a free man in New York State, was kidnapped and spent twelve years as a slave, almost all of the time in a relatively primitive, inaccessible area of the frontier territory of western Louisiana. In his volume *Twelve Years a Slave* he tells us that he made only one effort to escape and that that effort demonstrated to him that such an attempt was fruitless.[5]

The obstacles that the slaves had to overcome in making their way across the many miles to freedom were too great for most, particularly since these obstacles were both subjective and objective. Convinced of their desire to be free, they were nevertheless afraid of the consequences of reaching freedom. After all, when individuals change the conditions of their lives, they do not totally eradicate the residues which the past has left on their personalities. A slave must inevitably make some adjustment to his situation, an adjustment which must include some view that the condition of being a slave is the normal one for people such as himself. The mark that necessary adjustment left on Frederick Douglass was not the sense of being childlike but the much more poignant sense of being "lonely" when finding himself finally free.

Culture and personality are not like old clothes that can be taken off and thrown away. The ability of anyone to learn even the simplest thing is dependent upon utilizing the existing cultural apparatus. "New" cultures emerge out of older cultures gradually and never completely lose all the traces of the old and the past. Human society is a cumulative process in which the past is never totally obliterated. Even revolutions do not destroy the past. Indeed, at their best, they liberate that which is alive from that which stifles human progress, growth, and development. Culture is a historical reality, not an ahistorical, static abstraction. Thus, the process whereby the African in the New World changed in order to meet his new environment was dependent upon his African culture. While it is certainly true that the African under American slavery changed, he did so in ways that were recognizably African.

Coming for the most part from West Africa, these people, who had been stolen or captured and taken from their homes, *brought virtually nothing with them except themselves*. Coming from a large area of West Africa which was subdivided among dozens of distinct peoples, each with their distinct customs and religions, but united by a long period of continual interaction and consequent cultural borrowing, they were jumbled together on board the slave ships, "seasoned" by the "middle passage" across the Atlantic and then "seasoned" again in their first years in the New World. As slaves, not only were they prevented from bringing material objects with them, but they also could not even bring over their older social relations or institutions.

Such was not the case with the Europeans. They brought their churches with them. They brought their own foods with them and could continue to get supplies of specific items from the old country if need be. They brought their own dress with them and could choose to wear it or abandon it as they saw fit. They brought their own marriage customs, their own rites of passage, their own kinship system. The Europeans preserved their old customs for as long as they were needed and gradually modified them as they moved into the main society. While some met opposition for being foreigners, they were not stripped of their foreignness overnight.

But the African slaves could do none of this. Overnight they were transformed from merchants, or Arabic scholars, or craftsmen, or peasant farmers, or cattle-tenders into American slaves. They ate what they were given, not what they wanted. They dressed in the clothes that were given them, not those they had known in the past. African women were removed from a stable social order which gave them a specific place and function, which protected them with a traditional morality—and indeed exploited them in a traditional way—and made commodities, unprotected by a traditional morality, without specific places and functions, sexually exploited by the master and even deprived of a full relationship with their children.

The Africans had to give up their own languages and learn to express themselves through other media of communication. They had to give up their old kinship systems and create new ones. They had to give up almost all of their culture and become American slaves.

That was demanded of them. But on the other side, the slave could not really do any of these things, for he brought with him his past. He brought with him the content of his mind, his memory; he recognized as socially significant that which he had been taught from childhood to see and comprehend as significant; he gestured, laughed, cried, and used his facial muscles in ways that he had learned as a child. He valued that which his previous life had taught him to value; he feared that which he had feared in Africa; his very motions were those of his people and he passed all of this on to his children.

He faced this contradictory situation in a context which was complicated by the fact that while there were many similarities among West African peoples, there were also many differences. Each people had its own language, history, technology, and so forth. Moreover, in the United States (unlike the Caribbean), no single group dominated the slave market for any significant period.

Slaves in the United States had come from many different African cultures. They were thus faced with the difficult task of adjusting not only to their new environment and their new social relationships, but also to each other; they had as well to build a culture out of the interactions of Africans with other Africans. Therefore, while all Africans were slaves and slaves were supposed to act in a specific way, none knew what this way was. There was no model to follow, only one to build.

How was this contradiction between the denial of the right and ability of the slave from Africa to act out the content of his mind and memory and the fact that *he had to do this* resolved? What were the new forms created in the context of American slavery?

Out of the interaction of the men and women who carried a varied African heritage in their minds and memories along with the environment of a harsh plantation system based on slave labor, there emerged over time an independent black community. It showed the marks of the African experience while at the same time being insistently American.

This community took its form in the slave quarters of the plantations, among the dispersed but large numbers of slaves who lived on small farms and plantations and in the back alleys of the cities. It developed its own church, one designed to meet the needs of slaves and Afro-American freedmen in the New World. It had its own value system, reflective of the attitudes of African countrymen, but modified by contact with and the need to live with those of European origin. It employed modes of communication which, whatever their particular origins and forms, were neither African languages nor the same languages spoken by Europeans in their own countries—but new and different.[6] It had its own class system based on the division of labor on the plantation. It even had its own subordinate economic structure and activities and its own political system.

People take what they have and adapt and transform it to meet new ecological and social circumstances. The process involves choice, the adoption of tactics and strategies, although it must be emphasized that communities of people "adopt" such tactics and strategies by processes not primarily conscious. Analysis must both look backward to the complex sources of these responses to life and concrete circumstance and forward to the continuing manifestations of people adapting and changing in order to survive and improve their lives.

This stress on tactics and strategies helps insure that we do not proceed to a view of slavery as a "totalitarian" society. Stanley Elkins has argued that not only was slavery a totalitarian society, it was analogous to a concentration camp. In such a total institution the inmate has no living room within which to maneuver. There is something questionable about this view as an adequate understanding of the concentration camp. As a view of a whole society, it is inadequate and will not meet the test of empirical verification. After all, concentration camps, unlike plantations, could not be settings for enculturation, since successive generations did not grow up in them.[7]

We shall view slavery as an ongoing social institution in a developing and relatively open society in which a rough democracy and egalitarianism prevailed for the whites. In such a society there was room for maneuver, for tactics and strategies, for blacks as well as for whites. The conditions under which blacks lived were, of course, different from those of whites, but this did not mean that blacks were totally denied social space within which to struggle to meet the natural and social environment.

To reject the thesis of the slave as absolute victim, the slave as infantilized, slave society as totalitarian, and the plantation as a concentration camp, and to assert that there was room for maneuver is to argue that the slaves were not totally isolated. They were, in fact, in constant communication with free men, black and white; they were involved in constant interaction with masters and their families, with overseers, with poor whites, with white merchants, artisans, professionals, and laborers. The slave community was daily influenced by the white community. It was actively confronting the white world. For example, while slaves were often deliberately inefficient, it is also true that they took pleasure and pride in acquiring new technical skills as they came into contact with a new technology.

Above all the slave community was making itself. The patterns of communication set up by the daily and nightly exchanges of conversation, social activities, and fellowship were the most significant events that happened to the slave. The slave community was ultimately more important to the slaves than the nuclear family, because while the family could be—and was—regularly broken up, the individual slave could be taken to another plantation hundreds of miles away and become part of another community where he knew how to behave and where he would be accepted. This reality of community was the major adaptive process for the black man in America.

But more than that, the white community was influenced by the slaves through both imitation and reaction to the slaves' tactics and strategies. Not only did the slave community make itself, it also directly and indirectly helped make the white world.

The South was one single social system, one single society, with two communities, one white and one black. To assume that the slaves "borrowed" from and were influenced by the masters' behavior, but that the masters' actions were not in turn also related to that of the slaves, is to argue that there was no symbiotic relationship between the two communities and that there was no response to the slaves' struggles.

What were the possible strategies of the American slaves?

They could have worked as hard as required, disciplined themselves to accept the conditions of slavery, and lived out their lives, finding as much satisfaction as they could in the routines of daily life.

They could have accepted their lot as slaves in this world and, by having hope in another world to come and acting this out in religious practices, given themselves the necessary inner strength to meet the problems each day brought.

They could have presented a collectively contented face to the master class while individuals could and would get out of line and behave violently toward their oppressors.

They could have thought of themselves as inferior beings and accepted their lot, gaining as much satisfaction as possible from emulating and serving the master class.

They could have done their work but at the same time struggled through strikes and sabotage, actions which required some common community and some prior discussion among groups of slaves.

They could have supported individual acts of rebellion by protecting those of their number who acted violently toward a member of the master class or his agent, or who ran away and hid, or who tried to make it to freedom.

They could have supported the actions of those who ran off

into the woods or swamps and created communities or joined Indian groups.

They could have spent a great deal of time and social energy in adapting the West African cultures that they brought with them to meeting the new conditions of the United States.

They could have become revolutionaries, while waiting for the right time to strike.

And above and through all of these possible approaches was the ever-present, ever self-creating and -renewing strategy of building the slave community. The individual slave was never alone except when he ran away, and even then he often went from one community of slaves to the next, aided in his flight by his fellow slaves united into communities by the processes of slave production.

The slaves could have chosen any of these strategies. In fact they chose all of them and they all were interrelated. If any of these approaches had been abandoned, major transformations in the other strategies would have become necessary. This was the set of choices that faced an entire community and it was this total situation that dictated the context in which the community functioned, although certain individuals were socially specialized in particular approaches.

In order to understand this we have to view black slaves in America as people whose ancestors had come from somewhere, who in the American South lived in a particular kind of environment and social system, who out of the past and present—a present in which the majority of the population were of European ancestry— wove a future. Black slaves were descendants of West Africans; they were field-hands or house slaves or urban slaves in the American South's slave social system, one which was embedded in the matrix of world capitalism, despite the fact that slavery as a mode of production was itself different from capitalism.[8] And the slaves were to become free men as a result of struggles in which they themselves played important roles.

The slaves labored from sunup to sundown and sometimes beyond. This labor dominated part of their existence—but only part. Under slavery, as under any other social system, those at the bottom of the society were not totally dominated by the master class. They found ways of alleviating the worst of the system and at times of dominating the masters. They built their own community out of materials taken from the African past and the American present, with the values and memories of Africa giving meaning and direction to the new creation. They lived and loved from sundown to sunup.

## Notes

1. G. W. F. Hegel, *The Phenomenology of Mind* (London, 1910), I:183ff.
2. Frederick Douglass, *Narrative of the Life of Frederick Douglass, An American Slave*, p. 20.
3. Ibid., pp. 20–21.
4. Ibid., p. 106.
5. Solomon Northrup, *Twelve Years a Slave*, pp. 101–107. See p. 183 of the Northup volume for the following interesting statement:

> There was not a day throughout the ten years I belonged to Epps that I did not consult with myself upon the project of escape. I laid many plans, which at the time I considered excellent ones but one after the other they were all abandoned. No man who has never been placed in such a situation, can comprehend the thousand obstacles thrown in the way of the flying slave. Every white man's hand is raised against him—the patrollers are watching for him—the hounds are ready to follow in his tracks, and the nature of the country is such as renders it impossible to pass through it with any safety.

6. Of these languages, Sidney W. Mintz has written:

> Each slaving expedition brought together by force captives from one or more linguistic and cultural community; by the time such captives were transported and sold, they normally entered slave groups in the New World that were very heterogeneous in ancestral culture and in language. Thus, New World slavery created, among other things, a kind of Babel, within which the slaves had to discover how to understand, and how to be understood—in short, how to communicate symbolically, in the distinctive fashion of the human species and no other. The problem of discovering how to communicate, as expressed in the development of new linguistic forms, was also a problem in rediscovering oneself . . . .
> We know far too little about the process by which such creole languages emerged, but there is no doubt that these processes involved an expansion of each such language, and an enrichment of its sphere of expression, to make it adequate to everyday needs. It matters little, from one point of view, whether the origins of the lexicon, the morphology, the phonology and the syntax were European or African; for the processes involved were set in motion by the slaves themselves, and the languages were distinctively their own, though they sometimes came to be important media of communication, even for the master class . . . . Yet creole languages are surely one of the most significant cultural achievements of transplanted Africans, attesting both to the resourcefulness and creative genius of the slaves, and to the capacity of language systems to expand as necessary.

Sidney W. Mintz, "Toward An Afro-American History," *Journal of World History* 13 (1971):323, 325–326.

7. Stanley Elkins, *Slavery* (Chicago, 1958), pp. 103–133. While Elkins indicates that he is aware that the analogy between the Nazi concentration

camps and North American slavery was not precise and must be taken as suggestive rather than definitive, nevertheless the essential point that comes through is that the two "total institutions" had, in Elkins' view, virtually identical impact upon the personalities of their respective inmates.

8. See Eugene Genovese, *The Political Economy of Slavery*, and his *The World the Slaveholders Made*, for the development of an analysis that sees North American slavery as a noncapitalist social system embedded in the market relations of world capitalism. Karl Marx accurately described the capitalist epoch as one characterized by the fact that "labour-power takes in the eyes of the labourer himself the form of a commodity which is his property; his labour consequently becomes wage labour." Karl Marx, *Capital* I:189. However, while New World slavery was fundamentally not a form of capitalism itself, it is also clear that New World slavery was an essential part of the process of the emergence of modern capitalism. See Marx, *Capital*, I:260, and Eric Williams, *Capitalism and Slavery*, passim. It must be understood, however, that the degree to which slavery in the New World was embedded within the development of world capitalism varied over time and from place to place, and such differences had great consequences for the slaves. For example, Franklin W. Knight in his masterful *Slave Society in Cuba During the Nineteenth Century* presents a view of a particular slavery system in the nineteenth century that was more imbedded in world capitalist market relations than virtually any other.

# 2

## THE ROLE OF AFRICA
## IN THE MAKING OF THE
## AMERICAN BLACK PEOPLE

If we are to understand the development of Afro-American culture and community, then we must have some understanding of the role the African experience played in the making of the American black people. To do this, we need some adequate understanding of certain aspects of West African history, for it was out of West Africa that most of the slaves that were brought to North America came. This task is important particularly because the heritage of racism has nowhere more obscured reality than in this area of an image of the African past. While there is no need to argue that Afro-American behavior was "African," we must have some concept of a base line in order to comprehend the processes of change and adaptation that the slaves went through in the New World.

While there were crucial and major differences between European and African social structure and development both before the beginning of the Atlantic slave trade and after, there were certain similarities which are important to an understanding of the history of racism and slavery. For rural people in both Europe and Africa the pace of life was quite similar—and, of course, most people on both continents were country folk. Farming and grazing methods had not appreciably changed for thousands of years. Men smelted ore and worked iron with similar methods and tools. West African and European storytellers tapped similar and related folk sources for their themes. The forces of the universe were invoked by similar charms and spells. There was a thin veneer of literacy, in Latin in Europe and in Arabic in West Africa, but all but a small number of religious specialists were illiterate.

But while many useful parallels can be drawn between West European and West African development, we must not exaggerate the similarities. European achievements cannot become the yardstick with which to measure African achievements. As the Guyanese historian Walter Rodney has indicated, we must reject the view that the main criterion to be used when judging on a comparative basis the success of societies should be "the ability to bring together millions in a single political unit."[1]

There is little reason to believe that in the fifteenth century West Africa was necessarily developing analogous social institutions to those out of which European capitalism developed. Indeed, the social structures of West Africa at the beginning of the slave trade were quite different from those present in European society at the same time. For example, West African servility was very different from both American chattel slavery and European feudal serfdom. It was part of distinctly West African systems of social relations.

There were certain spheres of life in which West Africans had achieved much that contributed to meeting human needs and aspirations. The development of the social self, the creation of a rich, popular expression in music, dance, and the plastic arts, the development of life styles and resources that released potentialities of people at every age and stage of life, the elaboration of the customs and arts of hospitality, the humane treatment of the aged and the development of meaningful roles for them, and the creation of elaborate legal codes and court systems were among the creative advances of West African societies.

By the fourteenth century, West Africa had developed an elaborate productive system. In normal times, food, shelter, and clothing adequate to human needs were produced. In many areas there was a surplus which was traded as part of an elaborate system that linked West Africa with Egypt and Europe, although the needs of the market did not dominate even a sizeable portion of production. These marketing activities did require the creation of markets, merchants, and factors, caravan directors and agents, moneylenders and account-keepers. However, a fully developed urban economy did not arise.

There was even less sense of national unity in the fourteenth century in West Africa than in feudal Europe. Extended family groupings, villages, and clans in West Africa were bound together into units which believed in a common ancestry and which made descent the basis of association. However, the strength of the sense of unity in West Africa varied with the degree to which one group or another imposed its authority over areas inhabited by several peoples. National unity itself was constantly being destroyed by particularisms.

No single political and economic unification of all of West Africa, or even of a significant part, ever occurred. The largest political units of the fourteenth and fifteenth centuries in West Africa were military units which did not manage to maintain more than a loose hegemony over the adjacent population. While one group might create a town-based "empire" or "kingdom," there would likely be several others in the same area which were autonomous and even independent. The West African states before the beginning of the Atlantic slave trade were all inland military-political complexes which never managed to develop control over the trade routes, and new groupings were formed out of drifting individuals for the purpose of conquest. No group extended its power over a wide area for any length of time so as to legitimize its power. The city economy did not dominate the countryside. Side by side with city-states were stateless segmentary village societies. Local loyalties both in the towns and in the countryside were at all times more important than more universalistic and ideological claims.

The particular nature of West African economy was due primarily to geographic conditions. The desert on the north, the virtually harborless coast on the west, and the tropical rain forest to the south presented an environment that was hostile to the development of states that had as a central core some other authority beside force. In West Africa great armies or hordes could be raised which could sweep through the area and dominate the trade routes without at any time making it necessary—or finding it possible—to develop institutions permanently to garrison an area.

While Islam made significant inroads in West Africa and the military states of the Sudan were virtually all dominated by Islamized groups, the faith of the Prophet did not become the universal religion uniting the entire area. Even at times within a single people, such as the Fulani, the urban trading people were Muslim, and the rural pastoral and agricultural people were not. Without any great impetus from without or any support from a universal ideology, the Islamic chieftains of the Sudan often compromised with local belief and practice.

West African society never became city-dominated. Cities in West Africa were trading centers along the trade routes, they were usually quite small, and they were centers of some religion and learning. Above all, they were the capitals of chieftains who utilized them as much for defense as for administration and tax-collection centers. There is some evidence to suggest that at the time of the beginning of European penetration in Africa, successful attempts at creating permanent states were in the offing. The slave trade ended these.[2]

The basic unit of life in West Africa was the village. A village was composed of a number of family compounds in each of which a man, his wives, their children, his grown children and their families, and outsiders adopted into the family unit lived and worked fields or grazed animals. A man would usually get his wives from villages other than his own, but exogamy was not universal. Each one of the family compound units, often amounting to several hundred people, constituted the essence of a clan. Decisions in the village that affected everyone were made by the heads of family units. Villages were linked with each other by marriage ties and were made cohesive internally by the cooperative association of family compounds.

West African life was not particularly primitive in the stateless societies. In work arrangements and political behavior, large parts of West Africa had highly complex institutions which were important for the development of the social personalities of those who were to be transported involuntarily to the New World as slaves.

There were two basic work arrangements and accompanying work ethics in West African society. Work arrangements based upon a simple, frequently sexual division of labor within an extended kinship group corresponded with the stateless village societies, while work relationships based on cooperative institutions which transcended the extended kinship network and even at times went beyond the limits of individual villages existed in the more complex city-states, chieftaincies, and kingdoms. In some areas of West Africa there were both types of cooperative labor arrangements, while in others only that of the kinship system of the stateless societies existed. Many West Africans had developed complex work arrangements and an accompanying work discipline. Work was a relatively steady, continuous matter designed to produce both subsistence and a surplus.

The study of slavery in the New World has been confused by an inadequate view of West Africa at the time of the beginning of the slave trade and in the years that followed. Europeans and Americans of the nineteenth and early twentieth centuries, with their racist assumptions and beliefs in unilinear human progress, had no difficulty in projecting contemporary African reality into the past. Because the slave trade became important in eighteenth- and nineteenth-century West Africa, it was assumed that slavery had been an important social institution in fourteenth-century West Africa. Because human sacrifice and ritual cannibalism were found in nineteenth-century West Africa, it was assumed that such practices had been even more common in the past but had begun to disappear under the civilizing impact of the Europeans. None of this was the case.

Nineteenth-century Africa was as it was as the result of almost four centuries of the Atlantic slave trade and consequent harsh internal class conflict which altered African social structure. Entire African quasi-states such as Ashanti, Dahomey, Oyo, and Benin were developed, at least partially, on the basis of the slave trade and became what they became largely because of that trade.

While the origins of these quasi-states were in part independent of the slave trade, what they became (and what they did not become) was highly involved with their participation in providing slaves for the New World markets. While they made important advances in terms of power, they were wracked by internal conflict produced by forces unleashed by the slave trade upon which they had prospered. While they increased in wealth and prestige, they all eventually decayed and were picked apart by the European powers at the end of the nineteenth century, although not without putting up a significant fight. While the slave trade helped make them powerful, it eventually also destroyed them.

In the forest territories along the coast of West Africa, quasi-states had begun to emerge by the sixteenth century. These, particularly Oyo and Benin, developed somewhat further than those of the Sudan in terms of maintaining hegemony.

Oyo, the great center of the Yoruba people, was the earliest to emerge and it lasted longer than most of the others. Oyo's major towns were important centers by the fifteenth century. The governmental structure was based, before the eighteenth century, on a quasi-feudal system in which the Alafin, the ruler of Oyo, was the first among equals (i.e., of the other lords), but there was no manorial system of production. The powerful armies of the Alafin were raised in cooperation with the other lords.

Old Oyo city became the center of an important trade route across the western Sudan as well as to the east, a trade primarily in ivory, salt, iron goods, and kola nuts. In the fifteenth and sixteenth centuries a complex society emerged in which a considerable degree of individuation—the mark of urbanization—existed. It produced a remarkable artistic culture reflecting some secularization. The Benin ivory statues of human beings which had been originally created in Oyo, and which were taken by the British from Benin and placed in the British Museum, are strikingly secular in treatment and resemble more closely the art of the Italian and Flemish city-states of the early modern period than the so-called West African "primitive" art.

By the middle of the seventeenth century, Oyo had begun to participate in the coastal slave trade with Europe, and the rise of the power of the Alafin was the inevitable consequence of this development. The power of the Alafin rested in the Oyo cavalry which had been developed to ensure the safety of the slave caravans from Oyo and further east and north to the port of Ouidah in the vassal kingdom of Allada on the coast.

But the rise of the power of the Alafin led to the decline of Oyo in the nineteenth century. In order to protect the trade routes, the Alafin had increased the power and authority of local rulers and the councilors of state, the *Oyo Mesi*. In a cyclical movement, the local rulers began to break away from the control of the Alafin in order to get for themselves a larger share of the profits of the slave trade, which profits could then be used to obtain guns in order to further enhance their independent power.

The history of Benin to the southeast of Oyo in the same period was essentially similar. In the thirteenth century, Benin was conquered by armies from Oyo, and in the century or so that followed the Yoruba conquerors set up a dynasty of their own with its capital at Benin city. Benin became politically independent of Oyo, although culturally and spiritually recognizing its authority. A rich and handsome city emerged.

In the eighteenth and nineteenth centuries, the rulers of Benin, even more than those of Oyo, engaged in slave-raiding and the slave trade. As a result of these operations, the tyranny of the Oba, the king of Benin, increased in the early nineteenth century, while at the same time the geographical extent of his actual authority

dwindled. Indeed, the lessening of the Oba's authority and the increase of his tyrannical policies were related. The Oba's vassals'
authority had been increased by their growing control over the
slave trade, the support given them by the European slave traders
who wanted slaves but also wanted a weak Oba, and the general
breakdown of the central authority in Oyo. The Oba attempted
to defend his power by tyrannical means, including a great increase
in ritual human sacrifice, a symptom that reflected increasing instability (as it did, for example, in seventeenth-century New England
and twentieth-century Germany). This tyranny increased as central
authority was weakened by the transferral of the actual control
over the slave trade from the Oba to the town chiefs. Thus, when
Benin fell to the British in 1896, it had gone through a period
of increased tyranny and human sacrifice and greatly decreased
power. When the British entered Benin they found a city of which
large parts had been deserted years earlier and left to crumble.
The Benin state, having become primarily an instrument to make
war and capture slaves, was destroyed by that very process which
had been at one time the source of its greatest strength. Large
areas of the country had been left uncultivated for a long time
the people had fled to create societies elsewhere along the West
African coast, and there had been internal dissension in the army.

The history of the Ashanti in what is now northern Ghana is
also related to the slave trade. In the fifteenth century there had
been a number of city-states of the Akan people competing and
often warring with one another. By the beginning of the eighteenth
century these states, with one exception whose independence was
maintained until the early nineteenth century, had been absorbed
by one of the Akan groups into the large but somewhat loosely
organized Ashanti "empire."

The Ashanti Union succeeded in merging a number of distinct
Akan-speaking peoples into a single nation under the leadership,
in the eighteenth century, of the priest Anokye and the king Osei
Tutu. United by the myth of the Golden Stool of Ashanti, the
symbol of divine authority which was supposed to have descended
from heaven, and a conscious and well-planned campaign to give
everyone in Ashanti common lineage, thereby abolishing all separate
traditions, Ashanti expanded in the eighteenth century.

The Ashanti culture became rich and complex, and the economy,
partially through the slave trade, flourished. However, the Ashanti
were never able fully to centralize their rule and many peoples

resisted what they felt to be Ashanti imperialism. The independent power of local administrators was enhanced by the wealth and trading opportunities of each town. As a result there were always centrifugal tendencies in Ashanti.

The Fon kingdom of Dahomey came into its modern form in the 1720s when the Fon gained control of the ports in the so-called "Benin Gap," the savanna country that breaks down to the ocean between what are now southern Nigeria and southern Ghana. Because it had this combination, unique for West Africa, of direct access to the sea as well as control of the trade routes into the interior, Dahomey emerged as an entity somewhat approximating the unitary nation-state. Its port, Ouidah, controlled the trade with the Europeans, enabling the kings of Dahomey to profit while at the same time isolating the greater part of the country from European influence. Thus, as Basil Davidson asserts, "There was no scope here for sub-chiefs to break away from royal authority . . . and go into business on their own."[3]

Dahomey was organized as a military state in order to throw off the rule of Oyo. The Fon had been victims of the slave raids made by the rulers of the city-states of the Slave Coast for the first 150 years of the Atlantic slave trade. They gained their independence from Oyo by making alliances with the European slave merchants, thus capturing the coastal markets and gaining firearms. With a regular supply of firearms they could and did turn the tables on their Yoruba overlords. They who had been enslaved by the Yoruba of Oyo and the other Slave Coast city-states, enslaved the enslavers in turn.

Rodney summarized the impact of the slave trade on Dahomey:

> The Fon people of Dahomey were so devoted to the slave-trade that their state was organized with the main purpose of making war to obtain captives. Dahomey went so far as to set up a special battalion of female warriors, who were feared by all their opponents. Dahomey paid the penalty for paying attention only to warfare. Agriculture was neglected and famine took place in the late eighteenth century.[4]

While the history of West Africa would have been different from that of Europe even if it had not been for the introduction by Europeans of the slave trade, there is little question that the trade actively distorted and hampered the development of Africa.

African technology, always different from that of Europe, was effectively cut off in its development by the slave trade. We must be careful, however, not to give the impression that without the slave trade West Africa would necessarily have developed industrial capitalist societies; this we do not and cannot know.

For the Europeans and the Americans, the slave trade provided a significant part of the basis for the original accumulation of the early stages of capitalist development, and thus helped lay the foundation for nineteenth- and twentieth-century capitalism. In Africa, on the other hand, slavery actually helped prevent the accumulation of capital.

Capitalism in Western Europe required that the peasants be thrown off the land by such processes as the English enclosure acts, which turned farms into sheep runs. It required that the surplus population be deported or enticed to the New World and such other outposts of European colonization as Australia. Thousands of the poor, the landless, and the criminal were shipped to North America and Australia as indentured servants or convicts.

Capitalism, moreover, required the capital extracted from slave labor on the plantations and in the mines of the New World. It demanded that the stock of capital gained in the slave trade and through the labor in mines and on plantations be taken back into the mother country and that, at a later stage, the surplus labor force be kept at home, cheapening the cost of labor.

In West Africa, the slave trade led not to the freeing of the agricultural masses from the land but to their further bondage. In West Africa the slave trade created slavery both by transforming older institutions of clientage into slavery and creating new ways of enslaving people. Rodney summarizes this process:

> · . . . a large number of Africans on the Upper Guinea Coast at the end of the eighteenth century had been reduced to servile status through the agency of the Atlantic slave-trade. A few quickly emerged as trusted servants and lieutenants, but the majority signalled their oppression by rebelling or escaping when the opportunity presented itself . . . .[5]

Active involvement in the Atlantic slave-trade invariably meant the increase of such servile categories in the societies where they existed, and their creation where they had not previously existed. Thus it was that by the end of the eighteenth century a sizeable proportion of the inhabitants of West Africa found themselves under some sort of servitude.

With this background in West African history we can turn to a question which has plagued historians of slavery and which is crucial if we are to understand the nature of slave life in the New World. Why did Africans make better slaves than did the American Indians who were found in the New World? The usual assumption has been that as slavery had been present in West Africa, the West Africans were used to slavery, while American Indians were not. Also, it has been assumed that American Indians were more "noble" and "proud" and consequently braver in their opposition to being enslaved and that, romantically, they chose death rather than enslavement. The more craven Africans, this view holds, accepted slavery.

These formulations obscure the process of the adaptation of West Africans to New World plantation slavery. They are based on the erroneous assumption that the slavery that we are told existed in West Africa at the beginning of the Atlantic slave trade was chattel slavery, analogous to that which existed in the United States in the nineteenth century where slavery was an absolutely inherited status in which the master owned the work, the time, and the person of the slave. This false assumption is linked with a second, equally fallacious belief: that from the beginning of the slave trade African rulers and traders sold slaves to Europeans and American slavers because they had traditionally been in the slave trading business.

J. D. Fage indicates that there is something not altogether clear about the relationship between West African and New World slavery, but in language so equivocal that it gives the reader the impression that slavery in Africa and slavery in the New World were similar enough from the very beginning. Fage writes:

> The domestic slave was not, as the slave was only too apt to be on the American plantations, a mere beast of labour working in a gang of similar beasts. He was for the most part a member of his owner's household, an individual with recognized social rights. He might even on occasion inherit property, and, if a woman, might become the wife of a free man and bear free children.[6]

While such phrases as "for the most part" and "on occasion" seem to be examples of the exercise of scholarly care, they have no basis in fact, and they act only to confuse the issue.

By contrast, Rodney observes:

> Sometimes, what obtained was a quasi-feudal exploitation of labour by a ruling elite, who received the greater portion of the harvest. More often than not, however, the "domestic slaves," as they have been categorized, were members of their masters' household. They could not be sold, except for serious offences; they had their own plots of land and/or rights to a proportion of the fruits of their labour; they could marry; their children had rights of inheritance, and if born of one free parent often acquired a new status. Such individuals could rise to positions of great trust, including that of chief.[7]

Those whom Fage calls slaves and to whom Rodney refers with much greater accuracy as those who were subject to a "quasi-feudal exploitation of labour" did not lead lives of unremitting degradation and toil. "Slaves" were part of the total social fabric of West African societies. Slavery was a status within which much social mobility was possible. In Samuel Johnson's *History of the Yorubas* there is the story of Sango, a king of Oyo who had resolved to abdicate. One Biri, "his head slave and favourite," was assigned the task of asking him to reconsider this step. Biri was so chosen because he held the ceremonial and political role called "the king's best friend."[8] There are other accounts that indicate that slaves occupied high positions. For example, "slaves" often held the powerful position of Commander-in-Chief of the armies of Kamen-Bornu.

We must critically examine the assumption that from the beginning of the slave trade African rulers and traders sold the slaves to the European and American slavers and that without this business, there would have been no slave trade. Fage describes the process in the following words:

> When Europeans first began to ask for slaves in return for the goods they brought to West Africa, they were not repulsed. There was already an established demand for European goods among the Africans, and there was already an African merchant class on the coast accustomed to buying such goods and supplying the European traders in exchange with the commodities they wanted. If the Europeans wanted slaves as well as, or instead of, gold, ivory, pepper and gum, then the merchants were willing to provide slaves. The presence of a slave class among the coastal peoples meant that there was already a class of human beings who could be sold to Europeans

if there was an incentive to do so, and an economic incentive already existed in the form of the growing demand for European imports.[9]

Once again, Rodney offers a critique of Fage's analysis which places the matter in perspective and, consequently, liberates the discussion from the ancient framework which insists that the West Africans had a prior institution of slavery and a slave trade which fitted neatly into the needs of Europeans and Americans.

J. D. Fage is very careful in defining "domestic slavery" and circumscribing the numbers involved; but he feels that it "nevertheless" gave a fillip to the Atlantic slave-trade. This highlights a certain contradiction. The "domestic" slave was the member of a royal or noble household. What reason is there to suppose that the ruling class would first dispose of the affinal members of their own family? Perhaps the continued employment of the term "slave," however qualified, has some bearing on the conclusion. Rattray [the author of a major study of the Ashanti, published in 1923] himself ended by referring to the "so-called 'slaves,' " and though perhaps the label "domestic slave" is meant to express this idea, it carried with it the same associations with the Americas which the pro-slavery interests were at pains to evoke, especially since the literature on American slavery has already made familiar the distinction between the domestic or household slave and the field slave on the basis simply of their place of work; while it is well known what constituted the principal "domestic institution" of the Old South.[10]

While Rodney states that West African chieftains and merchants did engage in the slave trade, he specifies the time, place and nature of this relationship. Slavery, Rodney insists, was a *new* form of exploitation of the African people carried on through the interaction of African rulers and Europeans.

Though one can identify no African slavery, serfdom or the like on the Upper Guinea Coast during the first phase of European contact, that region was one of the first sections of the West African coast from which slaves were exported; and in the sixteenth century the transfer of Africans from the Upper Guinea Coast to the Spanish Indies was already a significant undertaking. No slave-class was necessary to make this possible, because there was in existence a fundamental class contradiction between the ruling nobility and the commoners;

and the ruling class joined hands with the Europeans in exploiting the African masses—a not unfamiliar situation on the African continent today.[11]

In response to European demands for slaves, the emergent West African ruling classes developed a highly complex system of raiding, punishment, and selling of political opponents in order to supply the slave trade.

Having abandoned explanations based on racial theories or upon the false belief that chattel slavery was an ancient West African practice, we must seek for an alternative understanding of why American Indians made poor slaves and West Africans adequate ones. The clue to the answer lies in the fact that whenever West Africans came to the New World from societies similar to those of most North American Indians—that is, from self-sufficient subsistence economies without elaborate social structures and state forms—they had an equally difficult time adjusting to slavery. There is a great deal of evidence to indicate that Africans from such societies as that of the Ibo had a tendency to die out or become despondent under slavery.

Melville Herskovits writes of the Ibo:

> Their tendency to despondency, noted in many parts of the New World, and a tradition of suicide as a way out of difficulties has often been remarked, as, for example, in Haiti, where the old saying *"Ibos pend' cor' a yo*—the Ibos hang themselves" is still current. . . . The same tendency was noticed among the "Calabar" Negroes— another generic name for Ibos among the slaves—in the United States, as indicated by the remark of the biographer Henry Laurens, that in South Carolina "the frequent suicides among Calabar slaves indicate the different degrees of sensitive and independent spirit among the various Negro tribes."[12]

Ulrich B. Phillips, the Southern historian of slavery, writes:

> The "kingdom of Gabon," which straddled the equator, was the worst reputed of all. From thence a good negro [sic!] was scarcely ever brought. They are purchased so cheaply on the coast as to tempt many captains to freight with them; but they generally die either on the passage or soon after their arrival in the islands. The debility of their constitution is astonishing.[13]

The slaves from Gabon came from societies generally similar to those of the Ibo.

Compare the reports on the Ibo and similar peoples with those about the "Coramantee," the general New World name for Akan-Ashanti slaves. Slaves from that highly complex empire, as well as those who were Yoruba, Hausa, Fanti, and Mandingo—that is, the people of the more complex empires and slave-trading states—were usually the leaders of the slave revolts and the most militant fighters. Speaking of the Maroon Wars in Jamaica, the student of Jamaican slavery Orlando Patterson writes: "It is remarkable that almost every one of the serious rebellions during the seventeenth and eighteenth centuries was instigated and carried out mainly by Akan slaves who came from a highly developed militaristic regime, skilled in jungle warfare."[14] It might be suggested that Patterson exaggerates the military explanation while largely ignoring the fact that these slaves had come from societies in which there had been complex agricultural economies. After all, we also know that these most militant fighters were also used in the West Indies as drivers, foremen, and trainers to "season" slaves who came from societies such as that of the Ibo. The West Indies were the staging point for the "seasoning" of newly arrived slaves, and many North American planters preferred slaves purchased from the islands, rather than directly from Africa, for this reason. Despite the fear that Coramantee slaves would be leaders of slave revolts, they were a part of the "mixture" thought necessary to build a work force for plantation economies.

More than the whip of the master is required to make a slave work regularly. There must be an integral social organization of work and the consequent internalization of values and attitudes conducive to work, an internalization that both comes from and reinforces traditions of daily, steady, regular work on a cooperative basis, but with a need and room for individual initiative. These skills were present among those West Africans from the more complex societies of the area.

People from folk societies have work discipline imposed through the mediation of the kinship system. One works because it is one's obligation to one's kinsmen. But work relations under chattel slavery in the New World could not be dependent upon kinship relations. More rationalized production was required for a market economy. Work had to be separated from other activities and the demands of production had to supersede at all times any other human demands. Production takes place in reference to a market, not simply to domestic consumption. A slave in that situation must be able to accept abstract authority or rebel against it.

Plantation labor requires that a large gang of men work cooperatively under general direction with a steady, regular rhythm. The individual must work from sunup to sundown, day in and day out, and not, as is true for subsistence agriculture, only from time to time, or under the whip of starvation. Moreover, plantation labor is monotonous and repetitive, as distinct from subsistence farming in which a small number of people perform a variety of tasks, going from one to another during the course of the day.

The Coramantees and those like them brought with them the social skills necessary for subordinates who must deal with superordination. Imitation and "putting-on the man," public performances of one's tasks and the ability to make it seem that tasks are either done or about to be done without actually doing them, bargaining and using such coercion as individual acts of aggression, strikes, sabotage, and even rebellion, were all part of the life of the slave. Coramantee slaves made good rebel leaders through that same ability to adjust which made them such valuable slaves. After all, *accommodation is not antithetical to rebellion; indeed, it is rebellion by other means.* One must remember that the greatest of all the leaders of slave rebellions, Toussaint L'Ouverture, was himself literate, the steward of his master's livestock, and did not join the rebellion for many months after it began. The great revolutionist had been the great accommodator.

The docile Sambo could and did become the revolutionary Nat Turner overnight. The slaves, under the leadership of those from the more complex African societies, fought and ran away, stole and feigned innocence, malingered on the job while seeming to work as hard as possible. And they lived to fight another day.

## Notes

1. Walter Rodney, *The Groundings with my Brothers,* p. 55.
2. See in particular the introduction of A. Norman Klein to a new paperback edition of W. E. B. Du Bois, *The Suppression of the African Slave-Trade to the United States of America 1638–1870,* pp. xxv–xxvii. We should not exaggerate this question of the relative weakness of state forms in West Africa. While there were stateless societies, that was not primarily the case. Walter Rodney in his *A History of the Upper Guinea Coast, 1545–1800,* pp. 28–29, points out that "the large majority of societies of the

Upper Guinea Coast could scarcely be termed 'stateless'." We are indebted to Rodney, ibid., for drawing our attention to the following definition of a society with a political state, taken from Jan Vansina, R. Mauny, and L. V. Thomas, *The Historian in Tropical Africa*, studies presented and discussed at the Fourth International African Seminar at the University of Dakar, Senegal, 1961 (London, 1964), p. 87:

> A state may be defined as a political structure in which there is a differentiated status between ruler and ruled. It is founded not only on relations of kinship but also on a territorial basis. The most important index is the presence of political offices, i.e. of persons invested with roles which include secular authority over others in given territorial aggregations for which there are effective sanctions for disobedience. Such political offices must furthermore be coordinated hierarchically.

See also Max Gluckman, *Politics, Law and Ritual in Tribal Society*.

The general discussion of West African history in this chapter depends primarily for its purely factual details upon Basil Davidson, *Africa in History*, and J. D. Fage, *An Introduction to the History of West Africa*. I do not, of course, necessarily agree with all of their often conflicting theoretical statements and analytical judgments.

3. Davidson, *Africa in History*, p. 186.

4. From a lecture given by Walter Rodney at the Black Writers Congress in Montreal in October 1968.

5. Walter Rodney, "African Slavery and Other Forms of Social Oppression in the Upper Guinea Coast in the Context of the Atlantic Slave Trade," *Journal of African History* 7 (1966):439.

6. Fage, *West Africa*, p. 78.

7. Rodney, "African Slavery," pp. 431–432.

8. Samuel Johnson, *The History of the Yorubas From the Earliest Times to the Beginning of the British Protectorate* (London, 1966), p. 151.

9. Fage, *West Africa*, p. 78.

10. Rodney, "African Slavery," p. 440.

11. Ibid., p. 434.

12. Melville J. Herskovits, *The Myth of the Negro Past*, p. 36.

13. Ulrich B. Phillips, *American Negro Slavery*, p. 43.

14. Orlando Patterson, *The Sociology of Slavery*, p. 276.

# 3

# THE RELIGION
# OF THE SLAVES

In many concrete ways the African past and the behavior of Afro-Americans under slavery were linked. The slaves used what they brought with them from Africa in their memories, nerve endings, and speech to help them adapt to the new environment and to build for themselves a new life.

We will not look for the simple retention of African traits, but rather seek out the processes whereby one set of cultural tools was used to build other, more adequate tools. A living people does not carry the past on its back if it is able to transcend it in order to meet the present and prepare for the future.

A living society is one that has not maintained rigid forms but has used the meanings of the past in order to create those new behavior patterns necessary for new circumstances. People change their behavior only as much as they are required to by the necessities of new realities, and they resist change whenever possible. In extreme circumstances people either change at a relatively rapid rate or they do not survive. In more moderate circumstances the basic conservatism of people can act to maintain as much as possible of the forms of past behavior.

William R. Bascom, a well-known anthropologist whose field work has been largely in West Africa, in an article on the acculturation of the so-called Gullah people, blacks living on the isolated Georgia sea islands, made a very clear and careful statement about the relationship between West Africa, Europe, and the United States. After asserting that "the differences in the general pattern of the cultures of Africa and Europe were not great; in fact their fundamental similarity justifies the concept of an Old World Area which includes both Europe and Africa," Bascom suggests a way of thinking about the relationship of American black life and Africa:

> The result of the contact of the Negroes with whites, both in slavery and in the period of freedom, seems to have been that in those cases where there was a difference or a conflict between African and European customs, the African customs have for the most part disappeared. But those institutions which were present in similar forms in both Africa and Europe, while manifesting a great many specifically European details, have retained an African stamp and have had a place in Gullah life the importance of which cannot be explained in terms of European forms alone. In these cases the two streams of tradition have reinforced one another.[1]

While Bascom here talks of Gullah life specifically, it is quite clear that the same method is applicable to all black American life.

Afro-American societies are not bundles of African traits but the products of the interactions of people whose ancestors had come from West Africa and who used West African forms in order to create new behaviors that enabled them to survive in the New World. Quite naturally, those Afro-American societies under the least amount of pressure to change look more like West African societies than those in which such pressures were at their greatest. If the ability of people to survive requires creative change adequate to the task at hand, then there is no more creative and innovative people in the New World than black Americans. The pressures upon North American blacks were much more extreme than upon blacks elsewhere in the New World. But despite the harsh atmosphere of the United States, African forms and meanings were not totally obliterated, and can be seen in all historical periods being used in creative ways.

Africans migrated involuntarily to North America in order to be worked as chattel slaves on plantations, in mines, in forests, on roads, on small farms of relatively diversified crops, and in towns and cities. They labored generally from sunup to sundown and often into the evening. Their work was usually difficult and tedious, they were driven to it by threats, fear, the lash, and the accustomed sense of work routines common to all settled agricultural and urban societies. While their life was dominated by the social relations of work, they did have a life outside of work in the time that was, or that they made, their own. That life was important in creating and recreating the slave personality and the slave communities.

Only if we understand this side of the slaves' lives can we understand how their personalities were kept from destruction, how they developed and built their communities. Out of the totality of the slaves' lives came the impetus, the tools, and the social relations necessary for their continual struggle against the condition of chattel slavery.

In the Afro-American community blacks were able to find a mooring which allowed them to survive as men and women. They created for others from sunup to sundown, but from sundown to sunup, on Sundays and holidays and at times on Saturday afternoon, and at all other times that they managed to get away from work (and frequently at work as well), they created and recreated themselves. They did this in a way that was consistent not only with the ability to work but with the ability to struggle against the social conditions and relations of that work. There is a complex interplay between the ability of any group of men and women to fight against their own oppression and the social "living space" they manage to carve out for themselves both at work and at home.

We shall here look at slave religion as a way of focusing upon a specific aspect of American slave thought and behavior. Close to the center of the slaves' lives from sundown to sunup was religion. The African slaves in the New World had come from societies in which there was no distinction between sacred and secular activities. The holy and the sacred were experienced as part of all activities. Divisions between this world and the next, between flesh and spirit, between the living body and the spirits of the dead were not conceived of as absolute. Men were thought to be able to slip across these boundaries with comparative ease.

For people from such a world, religious activities were areas of considerable potential creativity and social strength. The slaves in the New World used religion as the central area for the creation and recreation of community.

The masters' attitudes toward slave religion were complex. In North America before the second quarter of the eighteenth century, little pressure was put upon the slaves to become Christians. As long as the slaves worked well and were not unruly they were left alone. After that, for the remainder of the century, the efforts that were made to convert the slaves were sporadic, and while they resulted in getting most slaves to adopt the outward forms of Christianity, the relative neglect also allowed the slaves to develop Christianity's interior meanings and practices in their own way. Some slaves never became Christians in any sense. While we do not have very much direct evidence about the content of slave religion in North America before the nineteenth century, the fact that no efforts were made to Christianize the slaves for the first hundred years of slavery strongly suggests that there was sufficient time and opportunity for the establishment in North America of generalized West African religious forms.

In the nineteenth century there was a strong attempt by whites to use religion as a form of social control. If we read the thousands of interviews with ex-slaves taken in the 1920s and 1930s, as well as the accounts of slavery from contemporary sources of the nineteenth century, we can see an attempt on the part of the masters to superimpose a formal religion on the slaves. But that religion never seemed to gain the total adherence of the slaves who continued to carry on prayer meetings at night. What contemporaries referred to as the "African cult" not only did not disappear, it continued to flourish with great creativity and strength and was clearly the mainspring of black religion in the United States.

The slaves' emphasis upon religion has often been seen as simply a release from the daily world of work, a way of finding a refuge in the promise of salvation in the future. And this might indeed have been the case if the slaves had been generally secular and urban people and if the only religious expression they had was that dominated by the masters.

But that is a one-sided view of reality and ignores the independent basis of slave religion in the nighttime prayer meetings and sings. While religion certainly may at times be an opiate, the religion of the oppressed usually gives them the sustenance necessary for developing a resistance to their own oppression.

The religion of the slaves kept alive in them the desire and basis for a struggle for freedom. On a more immediate level, it made their daily lives bearable. If the community was not yet strong enough to overcome adversity, it could at least bear with it; the ability to survive adversity in the present is, of course, necessary to the ability to overcome it in the future.

In prayer meetings and night sings Africans became American slaves while American-born slaves renewed their contact with the

African experience through exchanges of ideas with newly arrived migrants from Africa. The slave narratives and slave autobiographies contain hundreds of references to such prayer meetings and night sings. Often they were held late at night in a cabin in the slave quarters. Sometimes they took place in an "arbor church," an outdoor meetingplace usually attached to a group of trees that were considered particularly sacred and as having magical properties. The evidence indicates that such meetings were usually held once a week on most plantations and that often slaves from several plantations would attend.

The slaves, men and women, would crowd into an earthen-floored hut to sing, to pray, to shout and get "happy." Often they would do a slow circle dance, each individual's hand on the next person's shoulder. Through these prayer meetings the bonds among people were tightened.

The slave narratives and other similar material indicate the richness of this religious life. Let us examine some of these accounts.

Carey Davenport, a retired black Methodist minister from Texas, had been born a slave in 1855. He had the following to say about slave religion:

> I don't 'member no culled preachers in slavery times. The white Methodist circuit riders come round on horseback and preach. There was a big box house for a church house and the culled folks sit off in one corner of the church.
>
> Sometimes the culled folks go down in dugouts and hollows and hold they own service and they used to sing songs what come a-gushing up from the heart.[2]

Note the two religious expressions: the official, Sunday service in the white church and the prayer meetings where the black Marannos sang the songs that came "a-gushing up from the heart."

Clara Brim, born in the 1830s in Louisiana, indicates the same bipartite religious system:

> When Sunday come Old Massa ask who want to go to church. Dem what wants could ride hoss-back or walk. Us go to de white folks church. Dey sot in front and us sot in back. Us had prayer meetin' too, regular every week. One old culled man a sort of preacher. He de leader in 'ligion.[3]

Cato Carter, born in 1836 or 1837 as a slave in Alabama, indicates how the slaves' own religion was often prohibited and practiced secretly:

> Course niggers had their ser'ous side too. They loved to go to church and had a li'l log chapel for worship. But I went to the white folks church. In the chapel some nigger mens preached from the Bible, but couldn't read a line no more than a sheep could. The Carters didn't mind their niggers prayin' and singin' hymns, but some places wouldn' 'low them to worship a-tall and they had to put their heads in pots to sing or pray.[4]

Carter's testimony that the slaves were sometimes prohibited from religious expression in the nineteenth century is verified by other slaves, who also indicate other nuances of slave religion. Adeline Cunningham was born a slave in Texas in 1852. She says of her master and his family and about slave religion:

> Dey was rough people and dey treat ev'rybody rough . . . . No suh, we never goes to church. Times we sneaks in de woods and prays de Lawd to make us free and times one of de slaves got happy and made a noise dat dey heerd at de big house and den de overseer come and whip us 'cause we prayed de Lawd to set us free.[5]

Ellen Butler, born a slave in Louisiana in 1859, had the following comment about slave religion:

> Massa never 'lowed us slaves go to church but they have big holes in the fields they gits down in and prays. They done that way 'cause the white folks didn't want them to pray. They used to pray for freedom.[6]

Adeline Hodges, born a slave in Alabama, indicates the importance of the independent slave religion to her:

> De slaves warn't 'lowed to go to church, but dey would whisper roun, and all meet in de woods and pray. De only time I 'members my pa was one time when I was a li'l chile, he set me on a log by him an' prayed . . . .[7]

Mingo White indicates the importance of mid-week prayer meetings in the total life of the slaves, and how they were related in the minds of the slaves to other aspects of autonomy such as having

their own gardens to work, Saturday night "frolics," and hostility
to going to Sunday church:

> After de day's wuk was done there warn't anything for de slaves
> to do but go to bed. Wednesday night they went to prayer meetin'.
> We had to be in de bed by nine o'clock. Ever' night de drivers
> come 'roun ter make sho' dat we was in de bed. I heard tell of
> folks goin' to bed an' den gittin' up and goin' to youther plantation.
> On Sat'day de hans' wukked 'twell noon. Dey had de res' of de
> time to wuk dey gardens. Ever' fambly had a garden of dere own.
> On Sat'day night the slave could frolic for a while. Dey would
> have parties sometimes an' whiskey and homebrew for de servants.
> On Sundays we didn't do anything but lay 'roun an' sleep, 'case
> we didn' lack to go to church.[8]

The slaves understood that the official religion was being used
as a method of social control and it is clear that for many slaves
it simply didn't work. Wes Beady, born about 1850 in Texas, told
it as he saw it:

> We went to church on the place and you ought to heard that
> preachin'. Obey your massa and missy, don't steal chickens and eggs
> and meat, but nary a word 'bout havin' a soul to save.[9]

Lewis Fabor, born a slave in Georgia in 1855, had this to say
about white preaching and black preaching under official auspices:

> On Sunday all were required to attend the white church in town.
> They sat in the back of the church as the white minister preached
> and directed the following text at them: "don't steal your master's
> chickens or his eggs and your backs won't be whipped." In the
> afternoon of this same day when the colored minister was allowed
> to preach the slaves heard this text: "Obey your masters and your
> mistresses and your backs won't be whipped."[10]

The slaves at times prayed in one way while the preacher
preached in another way. Minnie Davis, an ex-slave from Georgia,
about ten years old when the war ended, said:

> I recall that Dr. Hoyt used to pray that the Lord would drive
> the Yankees back. He said that "Niggers were born to be slaves."
> My mother said that all the time he was praying out loud like
> that, she was praying to herself: "Oh Lord, please send the Yankees
> on and let them set us free."[11]

One of the richest expressions of this counterposition of the slaves' reactions to the official religion and his practice of his own religion is in the following account of Richard Carruthers, born in Memphis, Tennessee, in the mid-1830s, and raised as a slave in Texas:

> When the white preacher come he preach and pick up his Bible and claim he gittin' the text right out from the Good Book and he preach: "The Lord say, don't you niggers steal chickens from your missus. Don't you steal your marster's hawgs." That would be all he preach . . . .

> Us niggers used to have a prayin' ground down in the hollow and sometimes we come out of the field, between eleven and twelve at night, scorchin' and burnin' up with nothin' to eat, and we wants to ask the good Lawd to have mercy. We put grease in a snuff pan or bottle and make a lamp. We takes a pine torch, too, and goes down to the hollow to pray. Some gits so joyous they starts to holler loud and we has to stop up they mouth. I see niggers git so full of the Lawd and so happy they draps unconscious.[12]

The slaves' religious ceremonies emphasized and tightened the social bonds among people. In the religious meetings the people of the slave quarters gathered together to discuss the events of the day, to gain new strength from the communal reality to face their individual realities, to celebrate the maintenance of life in the midst of adversity, and to determine the communal strategies and tactics. Out of these meetings came the modern black church and the many black lodges which play such an important role in the modern Afro-American community, and which continue to function as important social institutions both for accommodation and for struggle.

However, religious institutions among North American black slaves were not specifically African. If one looks for specifically African religious institutions among American slaves before the Civil War, one cannot find them. On the other hand, the African religious behavior was not completely obliterated. The slaves' churches were not the same as the European Christian churches. Their peculiarities are not accounted for by suggesting that such things as the intense emotionalism are part of the culture of deprivation and are irrational and regressive infantile expressions of people who were not allowed to become adults. There are indeed some resemblances between black religion and poor white religion in the South, some of which might just as well be traceable to black impact upon whites as to white upon blacks. But there were elements that were sharply different between the religious behavior of poor whites and that of black slaves, and the total tone of religious expression was certainly different.

The black slaves in North America utilized West African concepts in a new and totally different context. In so doing they transformed those West African forms into something which was neither African nor European-American but a syncretic blend of the two that produced a totality which must be looked at in its own terms. While it is true that all blends depend upon the elements being fused, it is also true that one cannot sift out "African" traits or "European-American" traits from the product which was qualitatively different from any of the influences that fed into its development. Several examples dealing with black religion ought to make clear the nature of this process.

The intense relationship in the black church between the preacher and the congregation is dependent upon the congregation being a community, a sacred family, in which the preacher is the leader and the head of the community. This relationship is similar to that of the elder in a West African village extended family compound. The elder is understood to have superior contact with the Unknown, but his relationshp to it is manifested through his relationship with his people.

If we look at the published autobiographies of black churchmen whose careers began before the Civil War, we find men who are seen by their communities as having special grace manifested by their deep knowledge of the people's needs. Such clergymen functioned as community leaders, political directors, healers and inspirers, physicians, and lawyers. The leaders of major slave revolts, such as Nat Turner, were usually such men.

The black minister functioned in a context controlled and limited by a shadowy but powerful group of elders or deacons and by older "sanctified" women. If these leaders failed to produce the results that were expected, the social cohesion and social solutions required, the congregation, or some segment of it, would look elsewhere. These roles have West African analogues.

In West Africa such elders could at moments of crisis do away with the king or the head priest in order to preserve the society, at least as they understood the needs of the society. Women in West Africa often played very significant independent roles in re-

ligious orders and similar activities. Such people were the real
residual representatives of the community.

Their power is not derived from some legal or constitutional
authority but from the traditional respect afforded elders because
they are believed to act not out of selfish self-seeking motives, but
out of their deep contact with the soul of the congregation and
the community. The cries of "Amen," "Halleluja," "Tell it to them,
Preacher," and the like that punctuate the sermon of the black
preacher are in effect affirmations that he is in tune with the soul
of the community.

While the roots of his behavior are African, the form is not, nor
are all of the meanings. Additional meanings have been added on
so that the affirmations of the preacher's sermons are also in part
a reflection of the urban, American black ghetto scene with its
rough democracy in which each man and woman is urged to "tell
it like it is." That is, there has been cultural reenforcement of certain
of the behavioral forms of West African religion, while at the same
time these forms have been reinterpreted so that their meanings
relate to life in contemporary America.

A graphic example of how West African meanings reemerged
in North America in totally different contexts with some of the
original behavior lost and new behavior added is the item, already
referred to, of the slaves using an iron kettle or pot in order "to
deaden" the sound during the nighttime prayer meetings and sings.
The stories of hundreds of ex-slaves not in contact with each other
tell similar stories about the iron pot.

A woman who was born a slave many years before the Civil
War has this account and explanation of the iron pot story:

> They used to have prayer meetings. In some places that they have
> prayer meetings they would turn pots down in the middle of the
> floor to keep the white folks from hearing them pray and testify,
> you know. Well, I don't know where they learned to do that. I
> kinda think the Lord put them things in their minds to do for
> themselves, just like he helps us Christians in other ways. Don't
> you think so?[13]

A Mrs. Sutton, another former slave, discussed the iron pot in
the following way:

> Lot of them would want to have meetings in the week, but the
> white people wouldn't let them have meetings, but they would get

a big ole wash kettle and put it right outside the door, and turn it bottom upwards to get the sound, then they would go in the house and sing and pray, and the kettle would ketch the sound. I s'pose they would kinda have it propped up so the sound would get under it.[14]

Another slave testified to the usefulness of the pot as a form of protection:

They'd have prayer meetings at times at home, but they had to get permission, and if they didn't I've know them to have to turn down a pot to keep the sound in. No'm, I have never known them to get caught while the pot was turned down at my home; but I have heard of them getting caught.[15]

Still another ex-slave explained why sometimes people got caught even though the pot was turned down:

When the niggers wanted prayer meeting they turned a pot down in the middle of the floor and sang and shouted and the white folks couldn't hear them. Of course, sometimes they might happen to slip up on them on suspicion.[16]

A woman who had been born in 1852 as a slave explained that the slaves would turn the pot up and pray and sing into it and that was why it deadened the sound.[17]

A retired black preacher who had been born a slave gave the following description of the use of the iron pot in an account which indicated how much shouting and noise the slaves made during their prayer meetings. Notice that he is describing an outdoor meeting in which the sound would be most likely to travel:

Meetings back there meant more than they do now. Then everybody's heart was in tune and when they called on God they made heaven ring. It was more than just Sunday meeting and then no more Godliness for a week. They would steal off to the fields and in the thickets and there, with heads together around a kettle to deaden the sound, they called on God out of heavy hearts.[18]

Siney Bonner, an ex-slave from Alabama, indicates how the idea of turning down the pot was well known to the masters.

Some of de niggers want to have dere own meetins, but Lawd chile, dem niggers get happy and get to shoutin' all over de meadow where dey built a bresh arbor. Massa John quick put a stop to dat. He say, "If you gwine to preach and sing you must turn de wash pot bottom up;" meanin' no shoutin'.[19]

These accounts of the pot being used in the weekday meetings and sings are typical of many hundreds of such references in the slave narratives taken from all of the Southern states.

It is clear that the iron pot could not have in fact been very effective in actually deadening the sound of the slaves' religious sings, particularly when we know that they were not quiet affairs. Only if the slaves could have actually put their heads in the kettles as some accounts suggest they did, could any impact upon the sound level have been created. After all, no iron pot placed face down on an earthen floor in a cabin in which more than a dozen people were probably singing, dancing, and shouting could possibly have deadened the sound. Moreover, the accounts of the use of the pots vary; the pot is sometimes turned up or placed outside of the door of the cabin, occasionally appearing even outdoors where it clearly could not significantly alter the sound level. Clearly, the iron pot or kettle is a symbolic element, the original associations of which have been lost.

B. A. Botkin draws our attention to a passage from an earlier work on black folksongs which discussed the entire pot–washpot syndrome in very general terms that indicated widespread knowledge of the practice, as well as the fact that those who had reflected upon it knew that it had nothing to do with muffling sound. Dorothy Scarbourough writes about one of her informants:

> Dr. Boyd told me incidents of the history of various songs. For example, he said of the familiar old spiritual, *Steal Away*, that it was sung in slavery times when the Negroes on a few plantations were forbidden to hold religious services. That was because the masters were afraid of gatherings which might lead to insurrections like some that had occurred. So the Negroes would gather in a cabin and hold their service by stealth. They would resort to a peculiar practice to prevent their singing from being heard at the big house. They would turn an iron washpot upside down on the dirt floor and put a stick under it, and would sing in such a way that they thought the sound would be muffled under the pot. Dr. Boyd says that he had often gone to such services with his mother in his childhood and seen this done. He said that, in fact, he believed the white people knew of the gatherings and allowed them, though the Negroes were fearful of being found out.[20]

The pot was believed to bring protection. With the pot one expected not to be caught engaged in what was clearly a prohibited activity. Why does the pot or kettle function in this way? There are several possible answers to this question, all of which are related.

In West Africa, pots are a regular part of the ceremonial paraphernalia. Herskovits tells us that in Dahomian funerals where all the ancestors, including those who died in America, are remembered, there is a little pot for each ancestor into which a young chick is placed as a sacrifice. The *loa* in Haitian vodun are also "kept" in pots.[21]

The pot is a ubiquitous item associated in West Africa with the gods, very often with those important river spirits who are seen as being the closest to men. Bascom gives us, for example, the following associations of pots with gods in Yoruba territory in West Africa:

(a) Each shrine of Yemoja, the goddess of the Ogun River,

> . . . contains a pot from which water is given to newborn children and to women who come to beg Yemoja for children. During her annual festival carved wooden figures which decorate her shrines and bowls to bring back fresh water for the shrine are carried on the head to a nearby river. The women who carry the bowls of water are possessed by Yemoja on their way back to the shrine, but they must not speak or spill a drop of water as they dance through town.[22]

(b) Erinle is a hunter who is the deity of a small river near Ibobu.

> River worn stones are his symbol; they are kept at this shrine along with a pot of water . . . . [H]is worshippers carry carved wooden shrine figures on their heads when they go to a nearby river to get water during his annual festival, at which time possession occurs.[23]

(c) In the shrines of Oshun, the goddess of the Oshun River, are pots of water from which worshippers may drink.[24]

(d) The shrine for Shopona [the god of Smallpox and the brother of the powerful god Shango, still worshipped today in Nigeria, Trinidad, Jamaica, and Cuba] contains an inverted pot with a broken hole at the top, beneath which are two iron standards to which the blood of sacrificial animals is fed.[25]

(The memory of this god is still very present in Cuba. Bascom writes: "If you remember the once very popular Cuban song which began 'Babalu, Babalu, Babaluaiye' you may be surprised to know that it was about the Yoruba God of Smallpox.")[26]

Bascom also tells us that among the Yoruba, "potters say that there is a special kind of pot for each of the hundreds of deities."[27] In some areas, water from rivers was brought in pots to the homes and turned over on the earthen floor, thus protecting the house and all in it.

The pots are special symbols of the gods who afford protection to men and women. The general meaning of the Yoruba river spirits, Bascom writes, is to "aid their worshippers by giving them good health and prosperity, and by helping them to achieve their destinies and live out their allotted spans of life on earth."[28] With such protection, men and women in Africa and in related ways, under slavery in the New World, had the courage to gather at night for prayer meetings to assert and develop their community, even though such meetings were prohibited.

The memory among Southern blacks that they had to pray in hidden places and ways, and the relationship of this reality to the use of an iron pot, did not die. In a recent book, the black Olympic runner Jesse Owens, talking about his father's illiteracy, wrote: "Yet if Henry Owens never was able to read the words of his religion, at least he didn't have to dig a hole in the ground or put a kitchen pot over his head to pray."[29] Owens has great admiration for those slaves who persevered in their own manner of worship, even though he does not understand what the iron pot symbolized. This admiration is well placed, for the slaves preserved the iron pot as part of their behavior in the New World, and the meanings of the iron pot, meanings of divine protection, permeated slave life. Indeed, not only did the slaves preserve the iron pot but the iron pot also played an important role in preserving them.

Sidney Mintz, commenting upon an earlier version of this discussion, offered another possible interpretation, from which the following are excerpts:

> I would like to call attention . . . to the significance of drums, drumming and other instrumentation in Afro-American religious expression . . . . The drum, like the pot, jar, or container, is hollow and resonant; Ortiz, in his study of Afro-Cuban musical instruments (1952:II), writes of one-membrane "open" drums, the general design

of which is analogous to a washtub or inverted basin. One is entitled to wonder whether a washtub that "catches" sound, rather than producing it, may not represent some kind of symbolic inversion on the part of a religious group—particularly since the suppression of drumming by the masters was a common feature of Afro-American history. Dennert (n.d.:22), in his very brief study of Curaçao musical instruments, pictures the drum-like *bastel,* which consists of a calabash partly submerged in water inside a washtub, and states specifically that this instrument was used when the slaves were forbidden to play drums. (Cf. also Hoetink 1969:66–67). Metraux (1959:177–178), in discussing the role of drums in Haitian *vodun,* remarks almost casually: "whenever the state has tried to suppress paganism it has begun by forbidding the use of the drum."[30]

It might be noted, also, that in the near-revolutionary rioting in Trinidad in 1938, the bamboo rods which had been used as percussion instruments were turned into staves to fight the police, and that the colonial government thereafter forbade their use. The populace, intent on having a popular percussion instrument, turned next to discarded oil drums and developed them into the steel band which has become such an important part of Trinidadian culture.

Mintz reminds us also of another, even more direct reference: Courlander's discussion of Haitian mosquito drums, portable mosquito drums, and earth bows. Courlander writes of the Haitian earth bow:

> This instrument has survived not only in Haiti but in the United States as well. The washtub device that is an important part of American Negro music is a clear development of the earth bow. The washtub is inverted and a cord is attached to the tin bottom. The other end of the cord is fastened to a stick which is braced against the lip of the bottom side of the tub. The stick and cord are manipulated precisely like the Haitian and African instruments. There is implicit evidence that the role of the washtub has been taken over in modern jazz orchestras by the double-bass fiddle.[31]

Mintz remarks that we might keep in mind that "the earth bow uses a hole in the ground as its resonance-chamber." The holes and dugouts that the ex-slaves refer to as a place for ceremonial activity may have some analogue in this use of the hole in the ground. Mintz finds one reference in Courlander which draws even more closely the possible linkage between pots and drums. Courlander points out that large clay urns are also used in Haitian vodun ritual: "they are sung into, tapped with sticks, and on some occasions are covered with goatskin heads and played like a drum."[32]

Mintz suggests that this entire matter of washtubs, jars, and drums represents "a case in which some original symbolic or instrumental commitment has outlived its original circumstantial significance. Rather than disappearing however, that commitment is somehow transmuted and preserved."[33] I am perfectly willing to accept this language and wish to note that, of course, it demonstrates how vibrant and remarkable was the adaptation of West African slaves and their descendants to their new environment.

Redoings of African meanings played an important role in other aspects of North American black religious life. A crucial example of this is the conversion experience. Experiences in which people faint and then undergo religious conversion are common to fundamentalist Christianity in the Southern United States. But in interviews taken in the late 1920s with black rural Southerners who had been slaves, there appear certain elements which are unique to blacks.

The conversion story follows a general pattern in which particular phrases are repeated. Before interpreting these stories, excerpts from a number of them must be offered.

(a) I left home and went into the thicket and fell down crying unto the Lord. There the power of God struck me and a little man appeared and said, "My little one, follow me."[34]

(b) I was killed dead by the power of God one evening about four o'clock . . . . Like a flash I saw my soul in the form of an angel, leap from my old body which was lying at the greedy jaws of hell. When I saw this, I prayed again to the Lord to have mercy. Then there appeared before me a little man dressed up in white linen and with golden locks hanging over his shoulders and parted in the middle. He said: "Follow me and I will lead you to the father."[35]

(c) First the informant tells of himself dying. Then, when he had regained consciousness:
I began to mourn and pray and as I did a little man appeared beside me standing in space. He spoke to me saying, "My little one, you must die for Jesus' sake."

The little man then led the informant to the east and to the everlasting gates of Glory.[36]

(d) When I was killed dead, I saw the devil and the fires of hell. The flames were blue and green. I left hell and came out pursued by the devil. God came to me as a little man. He came in my room and said, "Come and go with me." He was dressed in dark but later he came dressed in white and said: "Come and I will show you paradise and the various kinds of mansions there."[37]

(e) After talking of dying and being in hell, the informant says:
I became afraid and became faint again and there began crying on the inside, saying, "Mercy! mercy! mercy! Lord!" Then I began to cry and as I wept I looked and there by my side stood a little man, very small and with waxen hair. His eyes were like fire, his feet as burnished brass. On his shoulder he carried a spear and on the end of it was a star that outshone the morning sun. I saw the real sun go down and there was great darkness and I began to tremble with fear, but the little man spoke and said, "Be not afraid and follow Me for lo, I am a swift messenger and I will ever be thy guide. Keep thy feet on the straight and narrow path and follow Me and all the demons in hell shall not be able to cause thee to stumble or to fall."[38]

(f) I was afraid I was going to fall into the deep pit. It seemed that there was nothing to pity me. I was a little image and my body was standing beside me. While I stood there a little man came before me and said, "Don't you know that you will be devoured in here?" With this he took me in his arms and journeyed on a narrow white path that seemed no wider than a spider web. I saw three devils, one very large, one smaller, etc.

The informant then tells how he eventually is led to Heaven.[39]

(g) I got very faint and started to praying. Then I died and I saw my body lying on the edge of a deep gap. A little man came up and said, "Arise and go." I said, "Lord, I can't get up or move else I will fall." He reached out His hand, anointed my head and said, "Arise and follow me for I am the Way, the Truth, and the Light . . . . "[40]

(h) I died and saw a deep hole and a little man called to me saying, "Follow me." I journeyed on and came in sight of a beautiful green pasture and a beautiful mansion. There were sheep and they were all the same size. I don't know how I left but I do know how I went to heaven. I declare to you I saw myself in two bodies. Little me was standing looking down on the old dead me lying on a cooling board.

While I was in the mansion I saw a beautiful white bed and one man came and made it for me and turned and said to me, "That is yours."[41]

There are many other such accounts. One of them refers to a "little white man" in place of the usual "little man."[42] Sometimes no little man is seen, only his voice is heard.[43] There is some debate among the slaves as to the color of the little man: usually it is unspecified; occasionally it is white and on a few occasions, black. One respondent declared, "I don't believe in all that what the people say about having to see a little white man. That is all fogieism [sic!]. What was it for them to see? Always a little *white* man."[44]

There is nothing intrinsically African about this pattern of conversion experience stories. After living an unsaved life, the person dies spiritually; he goes to hell; a little man who is either an angel or some other emissary of the Lord or the Lord in some other form, appears and leads the repentant sinner to the Glory Seat, to God Himself. All seems in order, all could easily appear in European conversion stories. But there remains an unmistakeable African flavor to all of this, enough so that one can say that while it is not necessary that for people to go through these experiences they must be African, it is also clear that there is a way in which African belief would encourage this flow of events.

There is a similar figure to the "little man" in West African theology. The Yoruba god Elegba, or Legba, is an important deity throughout West Africa. He brings divinity down to earth, intervenes directly and often mischievously in the lives of men, acts as messenger of the other gods, and announces death. He delivers sacrifices to Olorun, the Sky God, he causes trouble for people who offend or neglect the gods, and he does good deeds for those whom the deities wish to aid. Not intrinsically an evil god, not the Devil that some Christians and Muslims have taken him to be, he is a sort of West African Hermes, a messenger of the gods who relates the gods to men.

This kind of personal relationship with the deities is something natural to the African slave in the New World. Thus, the "little man" in the conversion stories takes on an important role because in this way divinity can become immediate and at hand. The messenger of the gods who announces death' and is associated with tricks and mischief appears before the sinner as the symbol of his misdeeds, as the announcer of death and as the bringer of good fortune—the spiritual rebirth of conversion.

Legba and the Holy Spirit become mixed together, for both of them maintain the link between the world of man and the other world, both are announcers of the will of God. That the gods take many forms is no surprise to West Africans, and the belief that gods interpenetrate each other and appear to lack fully discrete identities is also not strange to West Africans. That God the Father, Christ the Son, and the Holy Spirit can be conceived of as separate but one is not a difficult concept for West Africans to accept.

Therefore, Legba and Jesus and the Holy Spirit and God, not to say elements of the Devil, all can become merged in this conversion experience. To all folk religion, including that of West Africa, such a seeming contradiction is commonplace. The West African in the New World had no difficulty in creating the necessary imagery which drew both upon West African and European sources, and produced something new.

The African ability to deal with mythology, to contemplate creatively a universe in which all things can be animate, is reflected in the following story told in the 1920s by a sophisticated old black preacher who had been a slave. The imagery, while not in conflict necessarily with Christianity, is certainly more pantheistic than is usual in Protestant Christianity:

> God looked down through the scope of time and saw every generation, even down to this day. Then God conceived the idea of making man. He stooped down and took a handful of clay. But the earth mourned and God made a contract with the earth saying, "Weep not for lo! I will repay every atom." Thus, when we die our bodies go back to mother earth and the soul to the God that giveth. Those who have been born of the spirit will be welcomed back into the house of God but those who have not been killed dead and made alive again in Jesus Christ, who have not been dug up, rooted and grounded and buried in the Lord, they will have their portion in outer darkness. This must be so, for not one iota of sin can enter that haven of rest.[45]

In a similar way, the black belief in folk and homeopathic remedies goes back to similar orientations in West Africa. It is not important that such beliefs are not uniquely African. What is meaningful is how the black slaves latched onto them and infused them with African tonal qualities. Harriet Collins, born in 1870 and thus too young to have been a slave, but out of the same culture, had the following to say about "doctoring":

Dere been some queer things white folks can't understand. Dere am folkses can see de spirits, but I can't. My mammy learned me a lots of doctorin', what she larnt from old folkses from Africy, and some de Indians larnt her. If you has rheumatism, ies' take white sassafrass root and bile it and drink de tea. You makes lin'ment by bilin' mullein flowers and poke roots and alum and salt. Put red pepper in you shoes and keep de chills off, or string briars round de neck. Make red or black snakeroot tea to cure fever and malaria, but git de roots in spring when de sap am high.[46]

What is important here is not the origins of the particular remedies, some of which are American Indian, some European, and some African; what is significant is that the belief in these kinds of remedies and methods persists among black people, reinforced by the circumstances of life, by the isolation of the black community, and by the fact that no doubt some of these remedies work. And besides, what were the alternatives?

Homeopathic remedies were mixed with charms and magical cures without the informant drawing any particular distinction between forms of doctoring. Notice in the following example how the informant invokes memories of Africa, not as some distant, unimaginable place, but as one that was close at hand:

If you kills de first snake you sees in spring, you enemies ain't gwine git de best of you dat year. For a sprain, git a dirt dauber's nest and put de clay with vinegar and bind round de sprain. De dime and de string round my ankle keeps cram[p]s out my leg, and tea from red coonroot good, too. All dese doctorin' things come clear from Africy, and dey allus worked for mammy and for me, too.[47]

Bascom summarized some of the American black religious beliefs, particularly those found on the isolated Georgia Sea Islands, that had African roots:

The belief in multiple souls, the very vivid belief in ghosts, the special burial rites for persons who die by drowning, lightning, smallpox, and suicide, all resemble African beliefs more closely than they do European. A baby that is taken to a funeral must be passed across the coffin so that its soul will not accompany that of the deceased. When a mother starts home after a visit she takes her baby in her arms, and then calls its name so that its soul will not be left behind. As in Africa, a distinction is made between ghosts and witches, who take off their skins and can be caught either by sprinkling pepper and salt about the room in good African tradition or by the distinctly European method of putting a Bible under the pillow.[48]

In 1934 Charles S. Johnson, in a classic work largely based on interviews with black plantation workers, wrote of the Southern black church:

> The church is the one outstanding institution of the community over which Negroes themselves exercise control, and because it stands so alone in administering to their own conception of their needs, its function is varied. The religious emotions of the people demand some channel of formal expression, and find it in the church. But more than this, the church is the most important center for face–to–face relations. It is in a very real sense a social institution. It provides a large measure of the recreation and relaxation from the physical stress of life. It is the agency looked to for aid when misfortune overtakes a person. It offers the medium for a community feeling, singing together, eating together, praying together, and indulging in the formal expression of the fellowship. Above this it holds out a world of escape from the hard experiences of life common to all. It is the agency which holds together the subcommunities and families physically scattered over a wide area. It exercises some influence over social relations, setting up certain regulations for behavior, passing judgments which represent community opinion, censuring and penalizing improper conduct by expulsion.[49]

All that Johnson says seems accurate and cogent. Yet by a strictly functional analysis he does not manage to focus on the deepest reasons for the power of the black church on the plantation and in the black communities.

The black church came out of three distinct experiences: the slaves' own religion, both in its pre-Christian and in its Christian form; the Christian churches of the freedmen in the cities; and the white church. We must remember that until the end of the eighteenth century, few slaves had been converted to Christianity. Yet they practiced some sort of religion, although we have virtually no description of it. It was, however, clearly out of this West African set of practices that the slaves' own religion—the one they practiced on weekdays and in the evenings, in the hollows and the holes in the fields, in the cabins protected by the iron pot, at the crossroads where a little man appeared before the sinner and announced salvation—came. It was this religion which fertilized the freedman's churches, although these were always Christian in doctrine. Upon the slaves' own religion was superimposed the official religion of the masters.

These two tendencies are clearly discernible in the contemporary black church. In a study done in the 1960s of a black church in St. Louis, a recent student of black religion noted the existence of two unfused expressions. One he called an "enabling religion," a religion of protest about this world; the other, which he called a "coping religion," was concerned with surviving this world in preparation for the next.[50] The first is clearly the heir to the slaves' own religion, while the second reflects more closely the impact of the masters' church.

Having a semi-independent origin, the black church was able to burrow deeper into the black community than Johnson understood, and in ways that he did not seem to imagine. Because the black religious expression contained the most significant forms of black culture in North America, the forms which most preserved the West African impulse and identity, it provided the basis for an independent struggle against slavery and racism. It was out of the religion of the slaves, the religion of the oppressed, the damned of this earth, that came the daily resistance to slavery, the significant slave strikes, and the Underground Railroad, all of which constantly wore away at the ability of the slave masters to establish their own preeminent society. Even the few but significant slave revolts, which panicked the South and ultimately made it impossible for the plantocracy to maintain its hegemony over Southern life, came out of black religion.

## Notes

1. William Bascom, "Acculturation Among the Gullah Negroes," *American Anthropologist* 43 (1941):44.
2. FWPSN, Texas, Part 1, p. 282.
3. Ibid., p. 118.
4. Ibid., pp. 206–207.
5. Ibid., pp. 266–267.
6. Ibid., p. 177.
7. FWPSN, Alabama, p. 184.
8. Ibid., pp. 416, 418.
9. FWPSN, Texas, Part 1, p. 135.
10. FWPSN, Georgia, Part 1, p. 323.

11. Ibid., p. 70.
12. FWPSN, Texas, Part 1, pp. 198–199.
13. Fisk University, "Unwritten History of Slavery," p. 24.
14. Ibid., p. 35.
15. Ibid., p. 53.
16. Ibid., p. 173.
17. Ibid., p. 282.
18. Fisk University, "God Struck Me Dead," p. 156.
19. FWPSN, Alabama, p. 40.
20. As quoted in B. A. Botkin, ed., *A Treasury of Southern Folklore,* p. 327.
21. See Melville J. Herskovits, *Dahomey: An Ancient West African Kingdom,* I:194–208, and Harold Courlander, *The Drum and the Hoe: Life and Lore of the Haitian People,* p. 33 passim.
22. William Bascom, *The Yoruba of Southwestern Nigeria,* p. 88.
23. Ibid.
24. Ibid., p. 90.
25. Ibid., p. 92.
26. Ibid.
27. Ibid., pp. 101–102.
28. Ibid., p. 97.
29. Jesse Owens and Paul G. Neimark, *Blackthink,* p. 40.
30. These extensions of my argument are from a revised version of remarks made by Professor Mintz as commentator upon my paper, "West African Culture and North American Slavery: A Study of Culture Among American Slaves in the Ante-Bellum South with Focus upon Slave Religion," given at the 1970 meetings of the American Ethnological Society. Both my paper and a version of Professor Mintz's comments appear in *Migration and Anthropology: Proceedings of the 1970 Annual Spring Meeting of the American Ethnological Society,* pp. 149ff. This chapter is an expanded version of that paper.
31. Courlander, *The Drum and the Hoe,* p. 201.
32. Ibid.
33. From the revised version of Professor Mintz's remarks on my paper given at the 1970 meetings of the American Ethnological Society.
34. Fisk University, "God Struck Me Dead," p. 22.
35. Ibid., pp. 30–31.
36. Ibid., pp. 32–33.
37. Ibid., p. 39.
38. Ibid., p. 5.
39. Ibid., p. 61.
40. Ibid., p. 63.
41. Ibid., p. 84.
42. Ibid., p. 86.
43. Ibid., p. 87.
44. Fisk University, "Unwritten History of Slavery," p. 50.
45. Fisk University, "God Struck Me Dead," p. 2.
46. FWPSN, Texas, Part 1, p. 243.
47. Ibid., p. 245.
48. Bascom, "The Gullah Negroes," p. 49.
49. Charles Johnson, *Shadow of the Plantation,* p. 150.
50. Robert Bruce Simpson, "A Black Church: Ecstasy in a World of Trouble," pp. 175–211.

# 4

# MASTER
# AND SLAVE:
# TREATMENT

While there has been a great deal of discussion about the life of the American slave at work, there has been relatively little focus and even less consensus about the quality of slave life "from sundown to sunup." How common was whipping? Were slaves decently fed, housed, and clothed? What was the structure and strength of the slave family? Did slaves rebel? Were there other kinds of resistance? Why was there a much lower incidence of slave revolts in North America than elsewhere in the New World?

Partially as a result of the lack of direct evidence, the debate over these questions has usually revolved about several extreme theses which clearly serve ideological needs. The first of these ought to be immediately dismissed: the jasmine and magnolia tale about happy, well-fed, pampered, banjo-plucking "darkies," wearing simple but clean going-to-meeting-clothes, eating chickens stolen from "massa," smiling watermelon-slice-sized grins, cared for by the loving hands of beautiful and noble white women when sick, singing spirituals and children's songs as they worked, telling animal stories with the wisdom of old primitives, and only requiring occasional physical punishment, as do children and house pets. But unfortunately we cannot thoroughly ignore this racist fantasy because parts of it permeate even the serious discussion of slavery in North America.

If this were accurate, then the average black slave in the American South was treated much better than the average poor white, indentured servant, or factory worker of the period. Take one item: food. The standard diet of most of the world's people in preindustrial societies has been one low in proteins and high in fats and starches. If hundreds of millions of the world's population at present go to bed hungry, what possible reason is there to assume that the chattel slave was well fed? Was he better fed than Southern rural poor whites, who have suffered for generations from such nutritional diseases as pellagra?

Two opposite views of slavery, derived from the view that the slaves in North America were indeed poorly treated, are deserving of more serious attention. One of these argues that the treatment of the slaves was so bad in North America that their condition was analogous to that of the inmates of German concentration camps in the Hitler era. Slavery, like the concentration camp, was a total institution which completely dominated the lives of the slaves. No sustained, serious resistance was possible because American black slaves did not have enough psychic autonomy to be able to conceive of meaningful rebellion. All that was possible were childish acts which did not alter the situation. The very severity of North American slavery made the slave into Sambo—the shuffling man-child, the absolute victim.[1] In this vein, a lecturer at the University of Chicago once began a lecture on slavery by announcing that "the worst thing about slavery was that it produced slavish personalities."[2]

Others who have believed that the treatment of the slaves in North America was very bad have reached an opposite conclusion. Slavery was so bad that the slaves were almost always either plotting insurrection or actually at the barricades. There were hundreds of slave revolts and rebellions. American black slaves had a heroic record of rebellion against overwhelming odds.[3] While we shall return in Chapter 6 to a concrete discussion of revolt and rebellion among North American slaves, at this point one can only wonder both why these rebellions were so universally unsuccessful if they were so ubiquitous, and why the slaves were so foolish as to revolt so often without a chance of victory?

Both of these theories are weighed down by heavy ideological concerns. The first has become the historical justification for the theory that blacks in America are psychological victims, incapable of helping themselves and requiring virtual clinical help from those more fortunate to break out of poverty and become fully functioning adult human beings.[4] The second is the grounding for all sorts of views which transform blacks into instant revolutionaries instinctively spilling their blood and that of their enemies in behalf of "the revolution."[5]

The picture of slave treatment and of slave response which we get from the slave narratives and interviews provides a much more balanced and concretely realistic view. The interviews enable us to see maltreatment of the slaves within the context of the total life of the slaves who, while oppressed and exploited, were not turned into brutalized victims, but found enough social living space to allow them to survive as whole human beings. The interviews enable us to see that there were certain areas of autonomy carved out by the slaves in a situation which usually produced neither absolute victims nor instant revolutionaries. Thus they enable us to see in specific form the very significant ways in which slaves did resist their condition. They enable us to take the questions of slave treatment and slave opposition to slavery out of the realm of pure ideology and fantasy.

The views of their history presented by the ex-slaves in the narratives and interviews enable us to see the conflicts between master and slave that took place day by day, and how these developed over time. They enable us to see that slave society was a harsh, brutal, but in some senses, viable way of arranging social relations; that whites and blacks were constantly interacting; and that blacks had their own community and culture. Resistance flowed from the network of informal organization of that community and assumed forms that took their meanings from that community.

The ex-slaves' accounts of their treatment make clear that most slaves suffered beatings and whippings; that they were often poorly fed, clothed, and housed; that they were often overworked; and that slave women were regularly used as sexual objects by whites, while slave men were often used as breeding bulls and slave children were frequently abused. They also indicate that the slaves had many ways of adding to the food and clothing supplied them by their masters; that they were given and found ways of having nonregimented social relations with their fellow slaves; that they were often able to break through the legal boundaries of slavery in such matters as learning to read despite prohibitions against teaching them this skill; and that the social structure of the slave community with its divisions of house slaves, field slaves, slaves who hired out their own time, and freedmen provided a circulation of needed news and information in that community. In the slave narratives and interviews we find a great deal of evidence about the nature of daily resistance to slavery and how it flowed from the semi-independent slave community.

Physical coercion was necessary to slave society, particularly when the slaves often greatly outnumbered the masters and nonslaveholding whites. George Fitzhugh, one of the ideologists of Southern slavery, wrote, "Physical force, not moral suasion, governs the world. The negro sees the driver's lash, becomes accustomed to obedient cheerful industry, and is not aware that the lash is the force that impels him."[6] Fitzhugh was quite right that physical force governed the slave world, but it is also clear from the narratives and interviews that the slaves well understood that it was the lash that drove them to work. A Swiss traveler in the West Indies, writing at the beginning of the nineteenth century, noted that a "mournful silence" pervaded slave communities.[7] While no doubt slaves sang and talked, it becomes quite clear from the narratives and interviews that the traveler had properly judged the quality of slave response, including understanding that this "silence" bred rebellion.

The overwhelming majority of the several thousand interviews with ex-slaves recorded in the 1920s and 1930s, and all of the slave narratives published before the Civil War, talk of physical force being used to keep the slaves in line. Not only are whippings described, but they appear central to slave life. The following excerpts are chosen because they are representative, not because they are unique, of the description of slavery in the thirty years before the Civil War.

Almost all accounts of punishment indicate that whippings very often were the consequence of individual acts of resistance. Indeed, this sequence of events was so prevalent that one might better present the description of rebellion first and of treatment last. However, it is not that either rebelliousness "caused" mistreatment or that mistreatment "caused" rebelliousness. As becomes clear from the interviews and narratives, they both were part of the same total set of social relations between masters and slaves.

The slave not only had to see the lash in order to become pliant to the work routines; he very often had to feel it. The slaves' accounts of the feel of the lash and the paddle on the back are more convincing than Fitzhugh's assertion that it was seeing the lash that caused the slaves' industry and that that industry was often "cheerful."

Eli Coleman, born a slave in Kentucky in 1846, recalled:

Massa whooped a slave if he got stubborn or lazy. He whopped one so hard that the slave said he'd kill him. So Massa done put a chain round his legs, so he jes' hardly walk, and he has to work in the field that way. At night he put 'nother chain round his neck and fastened it to a tree. After three weeks massa turn him loose and he the prodes' nigger in the world, and the hardes' workin' nigger massa had after that.[8]

There are many other similar accounts of slaves working with chains. The chain-gang as a method of dealing with the most rebellious blacks was not, it would seem, an invention of Southern penologists after the Civil War. Are the wearers of chains submissive, docile, cowed people or are they people so defiant that there is no other way to keep them "in line"? The chains may work, as in the case described above, but there is the ever-present danger of other incorrigibles threatening to kill "massa."

The slave narratives contain many stories of complicated and indeed gruesome methods of punishment. Wes Beady, born in 1849 in Texas, had this account of one particular overseer's practice:

He'd drive four stakes in the ground and tie a nigger down and beat him till he's raw. Then he'd take a brick and grind it up in a powder and mix it with lard and put it all over him and roll him in a sheet. It'd be two days or more 'fore that nigger could work 'gain. I seed one nigger done that way for stealin' a meat bone from the meathouse.[9]

Richard Carruthers, born in 1829 in Memphis, Tennessee, said of his master who he called "Old Debbill":

. . . he used to whup me and the other niggers if we don't jump quick enough when he holler and he stake us out like you stake out a hide and whup till we bleed. Many the time I set down and make a eight-plait whip, so he could whup from the heels to the back of the head 'til he figger he get the proper re'ibution. Sometimes he take salt and rub on the nigger so he smart and burn proper and suffer mis'ry. They was a caliboose right on the plantation, what look like a ice-house, and it was sho' bad to sit locked up in it.[10]

Thomas Cole, born in 1845 in Alabama, was on a plantation where the slaves were not beaten, but he knew many details of beatings "on other plantations":

> . . . us lucky, 'cause Massa Cole don't whip us. De man that have a place next ours, he sho' whip he slaves. He have de cat-o-nine-tails of rawhide leather platted round a piece of wood for a handle. De wood 'bout ten inches long and de leather braided on past de stock quite a piece, and 'bout a foot from dat all de strips tied in a knot and sprangle out, and makes de tassle. Dis am call de cracker and it am what split de hide. Some folks call dem bullwhips, 'sted of cat-o-nine-tails. De first thing dat man do when he buy a slave, am give him de whippin'. He call it puttin' de fear of Gawd in him.[11]

Anne Clark, aged 112 in 1937, was a repository of horror stories, tales that unfortunately had their counterparts in the reminiscences of many other former slaves:

> They'd whop us with a bullwhip. We got up at 3 o'clock, at 4 we done et and hitched up the mules and went to the fields. We worked all day pullin' fodder and choppin' cotton. Master'd say, "I wan' you to lead dat field today, and if you don't do it I'll put you in de stocks." Then he'd whop me iffen I didn't know he was talkin' to me.

> My poppa was strong. He never had a lick in his life. He helped the marster, but one day the marster says, "Si, you got to have a whoppin'," and my poppa says, "I never had a whoppin' and you cain't whop me." An' the marster says, "But I kin kill you," an' he shot my poppa down. My mama tuk him in the cabin and put him on a pallet. He died.

> When women was with child they'd dig a hole in the groun' and put their stomach in the 'ole, and then beat 'em. They'd allus whop us.[12]

Punishments often became complex and ingenious. Louis Cain, born in North Carolina in 1849, told the following story:

> One nigger run to the woods to be a jungle nigger, but massa cotched him with the dog and took a hot iron and brands him. Then he put a bell on him, in a wooden frame what slip over the shoulders and under the arms. He made that nigger wear the bell a year and took it off on Christmas for a present to him. It sho' did make a good nigger out of him.[13]

There were many stories about making the captured runaways wear chains and bells. Carey Davenport, born in slavery in the early 1850s, said:

> Old man Jim, he run away lots and sometimes they git the dogs after him. He run away one time and it was so cold his legs git frozen and they have to cut his legs off. Sometimes they put chains on runaway slaves and chained 'em to the house. I never knowed of 'em puttin' bells on the slaves on our place, but over next to us they did. They had a piece what go round they shoulders and round they necks with pieces up over they heads and hung up the bell on the piece over they head.[14]

Ida Henry, born in Marshall, Texas, in 1854, also referred to the use of the ball and chain. She said, "When a slave was hard to catch for punishment dey would make 'em wear ball and chains. De ball was 'bout de size of de head and made of lead."[15]

Whipping was not only a method of punishment. It was a conscious device to impress upon the slaves that they were slaves; it was a crucial form of social control, particularly if we remember that it was very difficult for slaves to run away successfully. Katie Darling, born in 1849 in Texas, indicated that slaves were whipped whether they had broken the master's rules or not:

> When the niggers done anything massa bullwhip them, but didn't skin them up very often. He'd whip the men for half doin' the plowin' or hoein', but if they done it right he'd find something else to whip them for.[16]

Slaves were whipped as a lesson for other slaves. Whipping was part of the entire social structure of slavery; slaves who were foremen or drivers were often the instruments of super-brutality toward the slaves under them. At times slaves would be killed by masters in order to educate other slaves that captured runaways would not be let off with light punishments. Cato Carter, born in 1836 or 1837 in Alabama, summarized this set of relationships between punishment and social control:

> They whupped the women and they whupped the mens. I used to work some in the tan'ry and we made the whups. They'd tie them down to a stob, and give 'em the whuppin'. Some niggers, it takes four men to whup 'em, but they got it. The nigger driver was meaner than the white folks. They'd better not leave a blade

of grass in the rows. I seed 'em beat a nigger half a day to make him 'fess up to stealin' a sheep or a shoat. Or they'd whup 'em for runnin' away, but not so hard if they come back of their own 'cordance when they got hungry and sick in the swamps. But when they had to run 'em down with the nigger dogs, they'd git in bad trouble.

The Carters never did have any real 'corrigible niggers, but I heard of 'em plenty on other places. When they was real 'corrigible, the white folks said they was like mad dogs and din't mind to kill them so much as killin' a sheep. They'd take 'em to the graveyard and shot 'em down and bury 'em face downward, with their shoes on. I never seed it done, but they made some the niggers go for a lesson to them that they could git the same."[17]

Mingo White, an adolescent when the Civil War began, told the story of Ned White:

I 'members once ol' Ned White was caught prayin'. De drivers took him de nex' day an' carried him to de pegs, what was fo' stakes drofe in de groun'. Ned was made to pull off ever'thang but his pants an' lay on his stomach 'tween de pegs whilst somebody stropped his legs an' arms to de pegs. Den day whupped him 'twell de blood run from him lack he was a hog. Dey made all of de han's come an' see it, an' dey said us'd git de same thang if us was cotched. Dey don't 'low a man to whip a horse lack dey whupped us in dem days.[18]

We shall return to Ned White when talking of slave resistance, because this whipping did not make him docile; it led him to run away and join the Union Army when the war came. And other slaves on the same plantation followed his example.

Black slave-drivers often were the meanest blacks that the master or overseer could find. Walter Calloway, born in Virginia in 1848, testified:

Marse John good 'nough to us an' we git plenty to eat, but he had a oberseer name Green Bush what sho' whup us iffen we don't do to suit him. Yassuh, he mighty rough wid us but he didn't do de whuppin' hisself. He had a big black boy name Mose, mean as de debil an' strong as a ox, and de oberseer let him do all de whuppin'. An', man, he could sho' lay on dat rawhide lash. He whupped a nigger gal 'bout thirteen years ole so hard she nearly

die, an' allus attera' she hab spells of fits or somp'in. Dat make
Marse John pow'ful mad, so he run dat oberseer off de place an'
Mose didn' do no mo' whuppin.[19]

The patrol system was a very important part of the system of
social control over the slaves. Poor whites were used to chase runaway slaves, to punish them, and generally to frighten and intimi-
date the slave population. They acted in a very brutal fashion;
they would often simply go into the slave quarters at night and
with the slightest provocation whip slaves and generally torment
them. Elige Davison, born a slave in Virginia, graphically and perceptively described the patrol system:

> Us couldn't go nowhere without a pass. The patterrollers would
> git us and they do plenty for nigger slave. I's went to my quarters
> and be so tired I jus' fall in the door, on the ground, and a patterroller
> come by and hit me several licks with a cat-o-nine-tails, to see if
> I's tired 'nough to not run 'way. Sometimes them patterrollers hit
> us jus' to hear us holler.[20]

While many slaves would try to run away after being whipped,
the patrollers "caught a lot of 'em and den dey'd get it harder
dan ever befo' and have shackles put on dere feet wid jes' enough
slack for 'em to walk so dey could work."[21]

Sylvester Brooks, born a slave in 1850 in Alabama, told of the
success of the patrol system in controlling the slaves:

> Next thing I 'members is de patterrollers, 'cause dey whip me every
> time dey catches me without my pass. Dat de way dey make us
> stay home at night, and it made good niggers out of us, 'cause
> we couldn't chase round and git in no meanness.[22]

At all times the slaves were subject to the intrusion of the patrollers. Sallie Carder, born in Tennessee in 1849, described the activities
of the patrollers:

> De patrollers would go about in de quarters at night to see if any
> of de slaves was out or slipped off. As we sleep on de dirt floors
> on pallets, de patrollers would walk all over and on us and if we
> even grunt dey would whip us. De only trouble between de whites
> and blacks on our plantation was when de overseer tied my mother
> to whip her and my father untied her and de overseer shot and
> killed him.[23]

The matter-of-fact way that the last sentence above was tossed off by Mrs. Carder is worth noting if one is to understand the quality of life for black people under slavery.

The patrol system was summed up in a song recited by Anthony Dawson, born a slave in 1832 in North Carolina, and in Mr. Dawson's perceptive comment about the song. The song went:

> Run, nigger, run,
> De Patteroll git you!
> Run, nigger, run,
> De Patteroll come!
>
> Watch, nigger, watch,
> De Patteroll trick you!
> Watch, nigger, watch,
> He got a big gun!

Dawson commented that this was a song that all the slaves knew and that "Sometimes I wonder iffen de white folks didn't make dat song up so us niggers would keep in line."[24]

The patrollers intervened in every aspect of slave life. Moreover, as they were not the owners, they often had less concern that slaves would be unable to work as a result of brutal treatment. Ida Henry of Oklahoma City described the patrollers:

> De patrollers wouldn't allow de slaves to hold night services, and one night dey caught me mother out praying. Dey stripped her naked and tied her hands together and wid a rope tied to de handcuffs and threw one end of de rope over a limb and tied de other end to de pommel of a saddle on a horse. As me mother weighted 'bout 200, dey pulled her up so dat her toes could barely touch de ground and whipped her. Dat same night she ran away and stayed over a day and returned.[25]

Slavery, as is the case with any social system, created reciprocity between slaves and masters. Since they did not live in worlds hermetically sealed off from each other but had intimate, face-to-face contact, such matters as status, rank, and masculine prowess became involved in the relationship. The whites and the blacks were part of the same social system, and therefore had to keep jockeying for position with each other. The relationship was a highly problematic one and required the constant creation and recreation of a day-to-day etiquette in order to help humanize social relationships that were hierarchical and based on naked power.

Morris Hillyer of Rome, Georgia, born a slave in the early 1850s, told the story of one such relationship between patroller and slave:

> Jim Williams was a patroller, and how he did like to catch a nigger off de farm without a permit so he could whip him. Jim thought he was de best man in de country and could whip de best of 'em. One night John Hardin, a big husky feller, was out late. He met Jim and knowed he was in for it. Jim said, "John, I'm gonna give you a white man's chance. I'm gonna let you fight me and if you are de best man, well and good."
>
> John say, "Master Jim, I can't fight wid you. Come on and give me my licking, and let me go home."
>
> But Jim wouldn't do it, and he slapped John and called him some names and told him he is a coward to fight him. All dis made John awful mad and he flew into him and give him the terriblest licking a man ever toted. He went on home but knew he would git into trouble over it.
>
> Jim talked around over the country about what he was going to do to John but everybody told him dat he brought it all on hisself. He never did try to git another nigger to fight with him.[26]

One former slave, Tom Woods of Alderson, Oklahoma, born in the early 1850s, understood how important was the relationship of slaves to poor whites:

> Lady, if de nigger hadn't been set free dis country wouldn't ever been what it is now! Poor white folks wouldn't never had a chance. De slave holders had most of de money and de land and dey wouldn't let de poor white folks have a chance to own any land or anything else to speak of. Dese white folks wasn't much better off dan we was. Dey had to work hard and dey had to worry 'bout food, clothes and shelter, and we didn't. Lots of slave owners wouldn't allow dem on deir farms among deir slaves without orders from de overseer. I don't know why unless he was afraid dey would stir up discontent.[27]

Fred Brown, born in the early 1850s in Baton Rouge Parish, Louisiana, gave a full description of runaways, the patrol system, and punishments:

> De overseer give all de whippin's. Sometimes when de nigger gits late, 'stead of comin' home and takin' de whippin' him goes to de

caves of de river and stays and jus' comes in night time for food. When dey do dat, de dawgs is put after dem and den it am de fight 'tween de nigger and de dawg. Jus' once a nigger kills de dawg with de knife, dat was close to freedom and it come 'fore dey ketches him. When dey whips for runnin' off, de nigger am tied down over a barrel and whipped ha'd, till dey draws blood, sometimes.

Dem fool niggers what sneak off without de pass, have two things for to watch, one is not to be ketched by de overseer and de other am de patter-rollers. De nigger sho' am skeart of de patters. One time my pappy and mammy goes out without de pass and de patters takes after dem. I'se home 'cazuse I'se too young to be pesterin' roun'. I sees dem comin', and you couldn' catched dem with a jackrabbit. One time anoudder nigger am runnin' from de patters and hides under de house. Dey fin' him and make him come out. You's seen de dawg quaver when him's cold? Well dat nigger have quaverment just like dat. De patters hits him five or six licks and lets him go. Dat nigger have lots of power—him gits to de quarters ahead of his shadow.[28]

Sallie Carder of Burwin, Oklahoma, matter-of-factly describes some of the needed equipment for punishing slaves:

Dere was a white post in front of my door with ropes to tie the slaves to whip dem. Dey used a plain strap, another one wid holes in it, and one dey call de cat wid nine tails which was a number of straps plated and de ends unplated. Dey would whip de slaves wid a wide strap wid holes in it and de holes would make blisters. Den dey would take de cat wid nine tails and burst de blisters and den rub de sores wid turpentine and red pepper.[29]

Slavery released normal people from the usual human restraints. Amy Chapman, born in 1843 in Alabama, told about "Uncle Tip Toe" in a story more graphic and, if the slave narratives and interviews are in any way valuable for documentation of the life of the slave, more accurate than the Uncle Remus tales of Joel Chandler Harris:

One day I seed ole Unker Tip Toe all bent over a-comin' down de road an' I ax him whut ail him an' he say: "I's been in de stocks an' been beat till de blood come. Den ole Massa 'ninted my flesh wid red pepper an' turpentine an' I's been most dead but I is somewhat better now." Unker Tiptoe belonged to de meanes' ol' marster around here.[30]

There are many other examples of such treatment of the real Uncle Remuses.

Henry Butler, a former slave and then a schoolteacher, born in Virginia in 1850, said that "on the Sullivan place there existed consideration for human feelings, but on the Rector place neither the master nor the overseer seemed to understand that slaves were human beings." One old slave, Uncle Jim,

> . . . disobeyed some rule and early one morning they ordered him to strip. They tied him to the whipping post and from morning until noon, at intervals, the lash was applied to his back. I, myself, saw and heard many of the lashes and his cries for mercy.[31]

Not all masters used "excessive" punishment, but very few used none. And if the master did not use any whipping, his slaves knew that they were particularly privileged. Most slaves who reported that they were not whipped said that they consequently called "free niggers." The essence of freedom, for the slave, apparently meant immunity from physical punishment. Jack Cauthers, born in the early 1850s near Austin, Texas, described one such situation:

> My master was Dick Townes and my folks come with him from Alabama. He owned a big plantation fifteen miles from Austin and worked lots of slaves. We had the best master in the whole county, and everybody called us "Townes' free niggers," he was so good to us, and we worked hard for him, raisin' cotton and corn and wheat and oats.[32]

Behavioral norms for masters under slavery were not purely voluntary. Thus, it was very difficult for a master to be particularly good to his slaves. The patrol of poor whites would see to it that slaves were not given special privileges even though individual masters tried to protect the slaves on their own plantations. One elderly black preacher told the following story to an interviewer:

> We were called Dr. Gale's free niggers. He never did allow the padderollers on our place. My old marster had some relatives here named McNairy and he always looked after it if they bothered us. We had to get a pass to go off the place but McNairy's place was right joining ours and right across the road was Mrs. Cantrell's place and we could go to their places without a pass. Some of the

others [owners] would shut down on them [slaves]. Many a time
they'd have church there and there was a thicket near and the pad-
derollers would get in there and wait and whip them as they were
leaving church. Old Alfred Williams was the preacher, and he would
send somebody after his marster Andrew and he would sit there
with his gun on his lap to keep them from whippin' him 'til his
marster would come and take him home. Yes, he was colored and
a slave too, but they used to have good meetings there 'til old Mr.
Cantrell said they would have to stop that. He was a Presbyterian
minister and he said that they had God troubled on the throne,
and they didn't 'low no two or three men to be standing about
talking either. They feared they was talking about being free. They
didn't bother the women that way, but no man better not try it;
they would search the slave houses for books too.[33]

There is little doubt that there were many masters who were
decent, some even with abolitionist sentiments. But individual sentiments only slightly alter social behavior because the pressures of
the social system on any individual, even though he is part of the
dominant class, are very great. Not only was it impossible for individual slaveowners with abolitionist sentiments to abolish slavery;
despite their ideology, all they could be was particularly paternalistic and kindly masters, good patrons. Even those who treated their
slaves well perpetuated the basic social relations of slavery. One
former slave, Laura Cornish, told about an abolitionist master who
nevertheless owned slaves. He would not allow the slaves to call
him master—*they had to call him Papa Day!* Even under slavery
it was possible for some masters to act out the most egotistical
fantasies:

One time us chillen playin' out in de woods and seed two old men
what look like wild men, sho' 'nough. Dey has long hair all over
de face and dere shirts all bloody. Us run and tell Papa Day and
he makes us take him dere and he goes in de briar patch where
dem men are hidin'. Dey takes him round de knees and begs him
do he not tell dere mas[s]a where dey at, 'cause dey maybe git
kilt. Day say dey am old Lodge and Baldo and dey run 'way 'cause
dere massa whip dem, 'cause dey so old dey can't work good no
more. Poppa Day has tears comin' in he eyes. Dey can't hardly
walk, so he sends dem to de house and has Aunt Mandy, de cook,
fix up somethin' to eat quick. I never seed sech eatin', dey so hongry.
He puts dem in a house and tells us not to say nothin'. Den he

rides off on he hoss, and goes to dere massa and tells him 'bout it, and jes' dares him to come git dem. He pays de man some money and Lodge and Baldo stays with Poppa Day and I guess dey thunk dey in Heaven.[34]

Usually, however, the master did not act out such sanctimonious fantasies. His slaves thought of him in an accurate way, as a slave-owner who managed a successful plantation and treated his slaves well, but they had no illusions that they were not slaves. Most slaveowners were not villains out of an old-fashioned melodrama but simply men of their times getting along while treating the slaves as well as could be expected. One ex-slave, John Day, told of one such master:

He was a preacher and good to us, never beat none of us. He didn't have no overseer, but saw to all de work heself. He had twenty-five slaves and raised wheat and corn and oats and vegetables and fruit.[35]

This master was an example of that contradictory social type who appeared under slavery: the democratic plantation owner who had nothing of the aristocrat about him, the planter with the manners and behavior patterns of the plebeian, egalitarian freeholder.

Some slaves were freed by masters who believed slavery to be wrong, but they stayed on the plantation because there really was nowhere else to go. In the following account of James Southall, born in Clarksville, Tennessee, in the early 1850s, we have an example of this kind of relationship:

We was known as "Free Niggers." Master said he didn't believe it was right to own human beings just because dey was black, and he freed all his slaves long before de War. He give 'em all freedom papers and told dem dat dey was as free as he was and could go anywhere dey wanted. Dey didn't have nowhere to go so we all stayed on wid him. It was nice though to know we could go where we pleased 'thout having to get a pass and could come back when we pleased even if we didn't take advantage of it.

He told his slaves dat dey could stay on at his farm but dey would have to work and make a living for deyselves and families. Old Master managed de farm and bought all de food and clothes for us all. Everybody had to work, but dey had a good time.[36]

While the average slave did not starve, he was not fed lavishly by the master. The usual diet provided by the masters consisted of cornmeal, sidebacon, and molasses. One slave described the official ration in terms that were virtually identical with those of hundreds of other ex-slaves interviewed. Campbell Armstrong from Arkansas, who was about ten years old when the Civil War began, recalled:

> They'd give you three pounds of meat and a quart of meal and molasses when they'd make it. Sometimes they would take a notion to give you something like flour. But you had to take what they give you. They give out the rations every Saturday. That was to last you a week.[37]

George Kye, born in Virginia in the 1820s, described the typical diet: "We had stew made out of pork and potatoes, and sometimes greens and pot liquor, and we had ash cake mostly, but biscuits about once a month."[38]

Salomon Oliver, born in Mississippi in 1859, described the food given out by the master:

> Ration day was Saturday. Each person was given a peck of corn meal, four pounds of wheat flour, four pounds of pork meat, quart of molasses, one pound of sugar, the same of coffee and a plug of tobacco. Potatoes and vegetables came from the family garden and each slave family was required to cultivate a separate garden.[39]

The figures cited in this account seem much too large and on the basis of all other evidence, either this was a very privileged plantation or Oliver was exaggerating.

Tom Woods of Alderson, Oklahoma, said that children were sometimes fed better than adults:

> Our food was placed on a long table in a trough. Each child had a spoon and four of us eat out of one trough. Our food at night was mostly milk and bread. At noon we had vegetables, bread, meat and milk. He gave us more and better food than he did his field hands. He said he didn't want none of us to be stunted in our growing.[40]

Sallie Crane, born about 1845 in Arkansas, told about the food of children and let us glimpse some of the games white children played with their slave friends:

> We et out of a trough with a wooden spoon. Mush and milk. Cedar trough and long handled cedar spoons. Did'nt know what meat was.

Never got a taste of egg. Oo-ee! Weren't allowed to look at a biscuit. They used to make citrons. They were good too. When the little white chilen would be comin' home from school, we'd run to meet them. They would say, "Whose nigger are you?" And we would say, "Yor'm!" And they would say, "No, you ain't." They would open those lunch baskets and show us all that good stuff they'd brought back. Hold it out and snatch it back! Finally, they'd give it to us, after they got tired of playing.[41]

→ House slaves were often better fed than field slaves and they often would take food to give to those, particularly children, who were not allowed in the "Big House." The slave economy was a make-do one in which "taking" (which was different from "stealing"—one *took* from the master, but *stole* from a fellow slave) was a crucial part. Mary Raines, born a slave in South Carolina in 1836 or 1837, tells it this way:

I was a strong gal, went to de field when I's twelve years old, hoe my acre of cotton, 'long wid de grown ones, and pick my 150 pounds of cotton. As I wasn't scared of de cows, they set me to milkin' and churnin'. Bless God! Dat took me out of de field. House servants 'bove de field servants, them days. If you didn't git better rations and things to eat in de house, it was your own fault, I tells you! You just have to help de chillun to take things and while you doin' dat for them, you take things for yourself. I never call it stealin'. I just call it takin' de jams, de jellies, de biscuits, de butter and de 'lasses dat I have to reach up and steal for chillun to hide 'way in deir little stomachs and me, in my big belly.[42]

Many slaves were allowed to keep gardens of their own or use the crops from the master's garden. They raised such vegetables as potatoes, turnips, collards, and peas, which supplemented their regular diet.[43]

On occasion slaves were allowed to raise vegetables and chickens and sell the produce on the open market. Octavia George, born in Louisiana in the early 1850s, reported:

We were never given any money, but were able to get a little money this way: our Master would let us have two or three acres of land each year to plant for ourselves, and we could have what we raised on it. We could not allow our work on these two or three acres to interfere with Master's work, but we had to work our little crops on Sundays. Now remind you, all the Negroes didn't get these two or three acres, only good masters allowed their slaves to have a little crop of their own. We would take the money from our little crops and buy a few clothes and something for Christmas. The men would save enough money out of the crops to buy their Christmas whiskey. It was all right for the slaves to get drunk on Christmas and New Year's Day; no one was whipped for getting drunk on those days. We were allowed to have a garden and from this we gathered vegetables to eat; on Sundays we could have duck, fish and pork.[44]

Bert Luster was a slave in Texas. He told the interviewer that "we raised gardens, truck patches and such for spending change."[45] On the other hand, Mrs. Mattie Logan, who had been a slave in Mississippi, said: "The slaves got small amounts of vegetables from the plantation garden, but they didn't have any gardens of their own. Everybody took what old Master rationed out!"[46] Stephen McCray from Huntsville County, Alabama, which, he told the interviewer, was "right where the Scottsboro boys was in jail" said: "Slaves had their own gardens. All got Friday and Sadday to work in garden during garden time."[47] While our evidence is scanty, it seems very likely that in some areas some slaves at certain seasons of the year did get as much as two-and-a-half days a week, including Sundays, to take care of their own chores. They made up for this at other times of the year when they worked by moonlight. The rhythms of agricultural work made it possible for slaves to have, at various seasons of the year, relatively long periods of time to themselves or at least with minimal chores. This comparatively loose discipline of agricultural life under such conditions helped create the slave community by giving slaves time to pay attention to and develop their own lives and needs, even though it often demanded the utmost ingenuity to do so.

Slave houses in the nineteenth century were generally rude, one-room boxlike affairs. One ex-slave said that he lived in a "little one room log cabin, chinked and daubed."[48] Salomon Oliver described the physical layout of the buildings on the large Mississippi plantation where he was born, one that had some 300 slave families:

About three hundred negro families living in box-type cabins made it seem like a small town. Built in rows, the cabins were kept white-washed, neat and orderly, for the Master was strict about such things.

Several large barns and storage buildings were scattered around the plantation. Also, two cotton gins and two old fashioned presses, operated by horses and mules, made Miller's plantation one of the best equipped in Mississippi.[49]

A large plantation was a very sizeable, heavily capitalized operation.

Hal Hutson, born in Tennessee in 1847 as a slave, compared his master's living arrangements with his own:

> Master Brown had a good weather-board house, two story, with five or six rooms. They lived pretty well. He had eight children. We lived in one-room log huts. There was a long string of them huts. We slept on the floor like hogs. Girls and boys slept together— jest everybody slept every whar.[50]

Daniel Dowdy, born in 1856 in Georgia as a slave, described how they lived. His mother was the cook in the Big House:

> We lived in weatherboard houses. Our parents had corded-up beds with ropes and we chillun slept on the floor for the most part or in a hole bored in a log. Our house had one window jest big enough to stick your head out of, and one door, and this one door faced the Big House which was your master's house. This was so that you couldn't git out 'less somebody seen you.[51]

Most slaves supplemented their diets by hunting and fishing. On some plantations trusted slaves could obtain shotguns for the purpose of hunting, although most slaves had to use homemade snares to catch small game. On many plantations the fishing and small game catch made up a significant portion of the slaves' diet.

Cooking methods were simple but involved communal activity and were social events. On some large plantations food was prepared for everyone by a crew of slaves who were specially designated. On most plantations, however, food was taken in smaller family units, with the women preparing the food before going to the fields or placing it on the fire while at work and letting it simmer or slowly bake, or cooking it quickly at the end of the day's work. Older men and women who were released from field work also would take over much of the cooking. Polly Colbert described cooking as she knew it under slavery:

> We cooked on de fire place wid de pots hanging over de fire on racks and den we baked bread and cakes in a oven-skillet. We didn't use soda and baking powder. We'd put salt in de meal and scald

it wid boiling water and make it into pones and bake it. We'd roll de ash cakes in wet cabbage leaves and put 'em in de hot ashes and bake 'em. We cooked potatoes, and roasting ears dat way also. We sweetened our cakes wid molasses, and dey was plenty sweet too.

Dey was lots of possums and coons and squirrels and we nearly always had some one of these to eat. We'd parboil de possum or coon and put it in a pan and bake him wid potatoes 'round him. We used de broth to baste him and for gravy.[52]

Mrs. Mattie Logan, born a slave, gives us other details about cooking:

Each slave cabin had a stone fireplace in the end, just like ours, and over the flames at daybreak was prepared the morning meal. That was the only meal the field negroes had to cook.

All the other meals was fixed up by an old man and woman who was too old for field trucking. The peas, the beans, the turnips, the potatoes, all seasoned up with fat meats and sometimes a ham bone, was cooked in a big iron kettle and when meal time come they all gathered around the pot for a-plenty of helpings! Corn bread and buttermilk made up the rest of the meal.

Ten or fifteen hogs was butchered every fall and the slaves would get the skins and maybe a ham bone. That was all, except what was mixed in with the stews. Flour was given out every Sunday morning and if a family run out of that before the next week, well, they was just out, that's all!

The slaves got small amounts of vegetables from the plantation garden, but they didn't have any gardens of their own. Everybody took what old Master rationed out.

Once in a while we had rabbits and fish, but the best dish of all was the 'possum and sweet potatoes—baked together over red-hot coals in the fireplace. Now, that was something to eat.[53]

A slave from a better-than-average plantation, one where the slaves were taught (illegally) to read, indicates that in such situations, slaves were decently fed and clothed. Benjamin Russel, born a slave about 1854 in South Carolina, said:

Money? Yes, sometimes white folks and visitors would give me coppers, 3 cent pieces, and once or twice dimes. Used them to buy extra clothing for Sundays and fire crackers and candy at Christmas. We had good food. In the busy seasons on the farm the mistress saw to it that the slaves were properly fed, the food cooked right and served from the big kitchen. We were given plenty of milk and sometimes butter. We were permitted to have a fowl-house for chickens, separate from the white folks. We wore warm clothes and stout brogan shoes in winter, went barefooted from April until November and wore cotton clothes in summer.[54]

As a rule, however, clothing was barely adequate by minimal standards for all but privileged house servants. Children wore home-spun shirts and little slips and nobody but the big boys wore britches, George Kye and many other ex-slaves reported.[55]

Sarah Wilson, who was a slave in Oklahoma Cherokee Indian country under a Cherokee master, described her clothing:

For clothes we had homespun cotton all year round, but in winter we had a sheep skin jacket with the wool left on the inside. Sometimes sheep skin shoes with the wool on the inside and sometimes real cow leather shoes with wood peggings for winter, but always bare-footed in summer, all the men and women too.[56]

Sylvia Cannon of Florence, South Carolina, who was born a slave in 1855, gave the following description of slave clothing:

Didn' get much clothes to wear in dat day en time neither. Man never wear no breeches in de summer. Go in his shirt tail dat come down to de knees en a 'oman been glad enough to get one piece homespun frock what was made wid dey hand. Make petticoat out of old dress en patch en patch till couldn't tell which place weave. Always put wash out on a Saturday night en dry it en put it back on Sunday. Den get oak leaves en make a hat what to wear to church. We didn' never have but one pair of shoes a year en dey was dese here brogans wid thick soles en brass toes. Had shop dere on de plantation whe' white man made all de shoes en plows. Dey would save all de cowhide en soak it in salt two or three weeks to get de hair off it en dey have big trough hewed out whe' dey clean it after dey get de hair off it. After dat, it was turn to de man at de shop.[57]

Privileged house slaves and many urban slaves dressed elegantly both while at work and on Sundays. Their clothes, of course, represented the honor and prestige of their masters. Even ordinary slaves had a few items of good clothing, often for holidays. A woman might have a printed calico dress and perhaps some cheap jewelry; a man might have a hat, a good shirt, and a decent pair of pants. But this was not common to all slaves.

Kenneth Stampp, an outstanding historian of American slavery, described the situation with a tendency to make it appear worse than it generally was.

> Carelessness, indifference, and economy—a desire to reduce annual expenditures for clothing which, unlike food, usually involved cash outlays—these were the chief reasons why a large proportion of the slaves wore shabby and insufficient apparel made from some variety of cheap "Negro cloth." During the long summers, ragged and meager clothing merely added to the drabness of slave life; but during the winters it caused real discomfort and posed a serious threat to health.[58]

Stampp tends to overdo the case with such phrases as "serious threat to health." It was certainly bad enough, but Stampp's hyperbole makes it difficult to trust his argument even when it is, as here, relatively accurate. Slavery need not have been universally harmful to the slave in order to have been far less than a minimally satisfactory form of human existence.

## Notes

1. Stanley Elkins, *Slavery* (Chicago, 1958), pp. 81-139.
2. The lecturer was myself, then active in the early civil-rights movement of the late 1950s, and eager to offer direction and leadership to black people whose "consciousness" I thought had to be raised. The entire discussion of slavery and Sambo was, for me, an explanation of why black people had not become "revolutionaries." Like most of the left in America, then and now, I felt that I was the product of a superior consciousness because of my superior education. This disguised and implicit racism and elitism permeated my lecture on slavery and led me at the time to agree thoroughly with Stanley Elkins's volume, which he asked me to read in its manuscript form after he heard of my lecture. While I was bothered by his negative assessment of the abolitionists, I had at the time nothing to replace it. (See my introduction to the forthcoming publication of *The Civil War Diary of Rufus Kinsley*, ed. Paul Kinsley, George P. Rawick, and Tom Waters, to be published by Greenwood Publishing Company in 1972, for an assessment of abolitionism.)
3. See Herbert Aptheker, *American Negro Slave Revolts*. This volume should be used cautiously because it needlessly exaggerates the incidence of slave revolts, relies heavily on rumor, and seems to suggest that resistance to slavery could be best demonstrated by portraying black slaves as virtually

always on the barricades. If black slaves in North America, faced with a huge expanse of territory, controlled by a white majority, faced with overwhelming odds, had engaged in the large number of extensive slave revolts that Aptheker suggests they did, they would have not been brave, but foolhardy and absurd. Indeed, it would have been childlike behavior.

4. This is the thesis of the report which was written by Daniel Moynihan for top government circles in the Lyndon Johnson administration as a guide to policy making. See Daniel P. Moynihan, *The Negro Family: The Case for National Action*. The discussion of this work is contained in many places. The reader edited by Lee Rainwater and William Yancey, *The Moynihan Report and the Politics of Controversy*, is useful. Excellent presentations of the counter argument are contained in Charles A. Valentine, *Culture and Poverty*, and Norman E. Whitten, Jr., and John F. Szwed, eds., *Afro-American Anthropology Contemporary Perspectives*. Foreword by Sidney W. Mintz.

5. While it is currently fashionable in some circles to attack Aptheker's *American Negro Slave Revolts*, which clearly is often very wrong, nevertheless I must insist that its bias is preferable and has been more fruitful for serious scholarship than that of those scholars who have emphasized the "docility" of black slaves in North America.

6. George Fitzhugh, *Cannibals All Or Slaves Without Masters* (1857; reprinted, Cambridge, Mass.: 1960), pp. 248–249, as quoted in Eugene Genovese, *The World the Slaveholders Made*, p. 162.

7. As quoted in George Lamming, *The Pleasures of Exile*, p. 120.

8. FWPSN, Texas, Vol. 1, p. 237.

9. Ibid., p. 134.

10. Ibid., p. 205.

11. Ibid., p. 227.

12. Ibid., pp. 223–224.

13. Ibid., p. 186.

14. Ibid., p. 282.

15. FWPSN, Oklahoma, p. 135.

16. FWPSN, Texas, Vol. 1, p. 279.

17. Ibid., p. 205.

18. FWPSN, Alabama, p. 416.

19. Ibid., p. 52.

20. FWPSN, Texas, Vol. 1, p. 299.

21. FWPSN, Alabama, p. 426.

22. FWPSN, Texas, Vol. 1, p. 149.

23. FWPSN, Oklahoma, p. 28.

24. Ibid., p. 65.

25. Ibid., p. 136.

26. Ibid., pp. 142–143.

27. Ibid., p. 354.

28. FWPSN, Texas, Vol. 1, pp. 157–158.

29. FWPSN, Oklahoma, p. 28.

30 FWPSN, Alabama, p. 60.

31. FWPSN, Texas, Vol. 1, p. 180.

32. Ibid., p. 212.

33. Fisk University, "Unwritten History of Slavery," p. 4.

34. FWPSN, Texas, Vol. 1, p. 255.

35. Ibid., p. 302.

36. FWPSN, Oklahoma, p. 306.

37. FWPSN, Arkansas, Part 1, p. 69.

38. FWPSN, Oklahoma, p. 172.
39. Ibid., p. 234.
40. Ibid., p. 356.
41. FWPSN, Arkansas, Part 2, p. 54.
42. FWPSN, South Carolina, Part 4, p. 2
43. Ibid., p. 6.
44. FWPSN, Oklahoma, pp. 111–112.
45. Ibid., p. 205.
46. Ibid., p. 189.
47. Ibid., p. 207.
48. Ibid., p. 172.
49. Ibid., p. 233.
50. Ibid., p. 145.
51. Ibid., p. 76.
52. Ibid., p. 35.
53. Ibid., pp. 188–189.
54. FWPSN, South Carolina, Part 4, pp. 51–52.
55. FWPSN, Oklahoma, p. 172.
56. Ibid., p. 349.
57. FWPSN, South Carolina, Part 1, pp. 189–190.
58. Kenneth Stampp, *The Peculiar Institution: Slavery in the Ante-Bellum South*, p. 289.

# 5

# THE BLACK
# FAMILY UNDER
# SLAVERY

In his history of slavery, Kenneth Stampp describes the slave houses as having been in the majority rude, one-room huts, but with a substantial minority of slaves having "snug dwellings of logs covered with weather boarding, or frame houses of bricks, clapboards, or shingles." Turning to the social consequences of these arrangements, he writes:

> Since slave mothers and fathers both customarily labored full-time for the master, while their children were supervised by the mistress or by an old slave woman, their cabins merely served as places to sleep and as shelters during the inclement weather. Most of their dwellings were obviously designed for these simple purposes, not as centers of an active family life.[1]

One is struck by the implications of the last phrase "not as centers of an active family life." Literally, of course, that was true. The slaves spent a good deal of time when awake outside of the cabins when the weather permitted. Cooking was usually done outdoors or in a cooking shed; people sat out in front of the cabins and talked and smoked; children played in front of the huts; young men and women courted wherever they could find privacy; gossip was exchanged while engaging in common chores outdoors. But this is hardly unusual. Most people, at most times and places, have lived that way. Urban and suburban American complexes where most of life is lived behind the door of one's "fortress" are fairly unique arrangements, duplicated only by such people as the Eskimo

during the long Arctic winter. But the further implications that
Stampp draws are not true. When Stampp declares in specific reference to the slave family arrangements, "Here as at so many other
points, the slaves had lost their native culture without being able
to find a workable substitute and therefore lived in a kind of cultural
chaos,"[2] he is on very weak grounds. This misinterpretation is
dictated by two facts: Stampp's sources were almost exclusively
white, and Stampp himself cannot overcome the ideological obses-
sion that "innately Negroes *are*, after all, only white men with
black skins, nothing more, nothing less,"[3] and could be just like
white men if given the chance. But unfortunately, according to
Stampp, the slaves were deprived of this chance and therefore had
to live "in a kind of cultural chaos." For Stampp, white behavior
is normal and everyone would "act white" if permitted.

The myth that the slaves had no normal, significant family life,
that for the most part, they lived promiscuously, jumbled all together, with no male having a regular relationship with his children
dies hard. It was a commonplace of white abolitionist thought, although usually placed in a somewhat contradictory framework in
which on the one hand slaves struggled for some inexplicable (inexplicable, that is, if one believes that slave children never knew
family life) reason to maintain the "purity" of the family, but on
the other hand were denied it. The historian John Hope Franklin
emphasized all tendencies that operated to destroy the black family;
he asserted that "courtship and the normal relationships preliminary
to marriage seldom existed"; that the slave woman "may have
learned to care for her husband who had been forced upon her,
but the likelihood was not very great"; and that the slave woman
did not have "much opportunity to develop any real attachment
for her children."[4]

The sociologist E. Franklin Frazier avoided any language that
implied the destruction of the black family and emphasized, correctly enough, that

> in the absence of institutional controls, the relationship between
> mother and child has become the essential social bond in the family
> and the woman's economic position has developed in her those quali-
> ties which are associated with a "matriarchal" organization.[5]

Frazier believed, again correctly, that "there is also plenty evidence
of the devotion of the slave mother to her own offspring."[6] On
the other hand, the role of the father was much less significant,

because black fathers were often sold away from their children while mothers were usually not, and because "the father was often a visitor to the cabin two or three times a week, while his interests in his children might only be adventitious."[7] Frazier concluded that "Thus there developed among the slaves a type of family that was held together principally by the bonds of blood and feeling existing between the children in the same household."[8] The picture of the slave family that emerges from a study of the slave narratives and interviews indicates that Franklin's view is not consistent with the facts and that Frazier was generally correct, although often the bond between the slave father and his children appears stronger than Frazier indicated. In any case, one is struck by the fact that most of the historical and sociological discussions of the subject which attempt to root the slave family in the polygamous African past or to see it as an imperfect and loosely defined variant of the European-American family are misleading. The Afro-American family under slavery was part of a distinct, viable black culture, adapted to slavery and deprivation.

While it is true that slaves were not allowed to make legal marriage contracts, it is also true that men and women under slavery did not simply breed promiscuously. There were a variety of socially approved and culturally sanctioned relationships between men and women as well as less structured sexual contacts which led to the birth of progeny.

In certain of these relationships, men had acknowledged kinship relationships with specific slave women, but did not live with them. There were also socially recognized marriages in which the father and mother lived together under the same roof with their children. The entire living unit functioned socially and economically as a single family unit, not dissimilar to the European-American kinship pattern, although sometimes broken up by the sale of members of the family to different masters, a situation which often happened upon the death of a master.

In some situations, certain male slaves were encouraged to have sexual relationships with more than one slave woman, without any permanent alliance being required. Masters, their male offspring, white overseers, and other non-slaveowning whites were usually permitted to make sexual alliances on either a casual or more formal basis with one or more slave women.

Selections taken at random from the interviews from one state with ex-slaves give us a picture of the range of possible family arrangements and marriage customs under slavery. Much the same picture could be derived from the interviews taken in any of the other states in which interviews were taken.

Sallie Carder, born in Jackson, Tennessee, in the early 1850s, reported that her mother was Harriet Neel and her father Jeff Bills, that she had one brother, J. B. Bills, and some unnamed sisters. She remembers her own wedding shortly after the end of slavery and reports that she wore at the wedding a blue calico dress, a man's shirt tail as a head rag, and a pair of brogan shoes. Mrs. Carder is the ex-slave previously quoted who reported that the overseer killed her father when he had tried to save her mother from being beaten.[9]

Betty Foreman Chessier, born a slave in Raleigh, North Carolina, in 1843, reported:

> My mother was named Melinda Manley, the slave of Governor Manley of North Carolina, and my father was named Arnold Foreman, slave of Bob and John Foreman, two young masters. They come over from Arkansas to visit my master and my pappy and mammy met and get married, 'though my pappy only seen my mammy in the summer when his masters come to visit our master and dey took him right back. I had three sisters and two brothers and none of dem was my whole brothers and sisters. I stayed in the Big House all the time, but my sisters and brothers were given to the master's sons and daughters when dey got married and dey was told to send back for some more when dem died. I didn't never stay with my mammy doing of slavery. I stayed in the Big House. I slept under the dining room table with three other darkies.
>
> After the War, I went to mammy and my step-daddy. She done married again, so I left and went to Warrington and Halifax, North Carolina, jest for a little while nursing some white chillun. I stayed in Raleigh, where I was born till 7 years ago, when I come to Oklahoma to live with my only living child. I am the mother of 4 chillun and 11 grandchillun.
>
> When I got married I jumped a broomstick. To git unmarried, all you had to do was to jump backwards over the same broomstick.[10]

Polly Colbert, age eighty-three in 1935, was born in Oklahoma. She said:

> My mother, Liza, was owned by de Colbert family and my father, Tony, was owned by de Love family. When Master Holmes and

Miss Betty Love was married dey fathers give my father and mother to dem for a wedding gift. I was born at Tishomingo and we moved to de farm on Red River soon after dat and I been here ever since. I had a sister and a brother, but I ain't seen dem since den.

My mother dies when I was real small, and about a year after dat my father dies. Master Holmes told us children not to cry, dat he and Miss Betty would take good care or us. Dey did, too.[11]

Mrs. Colbert reported that she was married shortly after the war, that she had a big wedding to which her former mistress came, that they had a dance and a wedding supper and a frolic that lasted for almost two days. "My husband and I had nine children and now I've got seven grandchildren." She lived with her son at the time she was interviewed.[12]

Anthony Dawson, born in 1832, said:

My pappy's name was Anthony, and mammy's name was Chanie. He was the blacksmith and fixed the wagons, but he couldn't read and figger like Uncle John. Mammy was the head house woman but didn't know any letters either.

They was both black like me. Old man Isley, where they come from, had lots of niggers, but I don't think they was off the boat.[13]

He reported that he had seven boys and seven girls of his own.

Daniel Dowdy, born in 1856 in Georgia, said:

Father was named Joe Dowdy and mother was named Mary Dowdy. There were 9 of us boys, George, Smith, Lewis, Henry, William, myself, Newt, James and Jeff. There was one girl and she was my twin, and her name was Sarah. My mother and father come from Richmond, Va., to Georgia. Father lived on one side of the river and my mother on the other side. My father would come over ever' week to visit us. Noah Meadows bought my father and Elizabeth Davis, daughter of the old master took my mother. They married in Noah Meadow's house .... My mother couldn't be bought 'cause she done had 9 boys for one farm and neither my father, 'cause he was the father of 'em.[14]

Dowdy reported that his cousin Eliza was the daughter of her master and that she was sold to a man from New York because she was too pretty. His father, he said, was a preacher and an educated man, whose advice was sought by his master.

Octavia George said:

I was born in Mansieur, Louisiana, 1852, Avoir Parish. I am the daughter of Alfred and Clementine Joseph. I don't know much about my grandparents other than my mother told me my grandfather's name was Fransuai, and was one time a king in Africa.[15]

Robert R. Grinstead told the interviewer:

I was born in Lawrence County, Mississippi, February 17, 1857. My father's name is Elias Grinstead, a German, and my mother's name is Ann Grinstead after that of her master. I am a son by mother and her master. I have four other half brothers: William (Bill) oldest, Albert, Silas, and John . . . . On account of being the son of my master's I received no hard treatment and did little or no work . . . . I was the only child of my Master as he had no wife. When the War broke out he went to the war and left the plantation in charge of his overseer and his two sisters. As the overseers were hard for them to get along with they were oftener without an overseer as with one, and therefore they used one of the Negroes as overseer for the most of the time.[16]

He reported later in the interview that as a boy he did not know that he was the son of his master. He said that he himself had an ordinary marriage ceremony and that he had eleven children, fifteen or twenty grandchildren, and three great-grandchildren.[17]

Annie Hawkins was about ninety in 1935. She reported that her master was a mean man named Dave Giles, that he didn't have many slaves, only "my mammy, and me, and my sister, Uncle Bill, and Truman. He had owned my grandma but he give her a good whupping and she never did git over it and died."[18]

Hal Hutson said:

I was born at Galveston, Tennessee, October 12, 1847. There were 11 children; 7 brothers: Andrew, George, Clent, Gilbert, Frank, Mack and Horace; and 3 girls; Rosie, Marie, and Nancy. We were all Hutsons. Together with my mother and father we worked for the same man whose name was Mr. Barton Brown . . . .[19]

After the war he married without a ceremony:

Married at my mother's house 'cause my wife's mother didn't let us marry at her house, so I sent Jack Perry after her on a hoss and we had a big dinner—and jest got married.[20]

Nellie Johnson had been the slave of the Creek Indian chief Rolley McIntosh and her "mammy and pappy have a big, nice, clean log house to live . . . . My pappy's name was Jackson McIntosh, and my mammy name was Hager. I think old Chief bring them out to the Territory when he come out with his brother Chili and the rest of the Creek people."[21] She had eight brothers and sisters. She said: "I was one of the youngest children in my family; only Sammy and Millie was younger than I was. My big brothers was Adam, August, and Nero, and my big sisters was Flora, Nancy, and Rhoada."[22]

Martha King reported:

My mother was Harriet Davis and she was born in Virginia. I don't know who my father was. My grandmother was captured in Africa when she was a little girl. A big boat was down at the edge of a bay an' the people were all excited about it an' some of the bravest went up purty close to look at it. The men on the boat told them to come on board and they could have the pretty red handkerchiefs, red and blue beads and big rings. A lot of them went on board and the ship sailed away with them. My grandmother never saw any of her folks again.[23]

When Mrs. King was five, she was sold along with her grandmother, mother, two aunts, and two uncles. She was sold with her grandmother, an aunt and an uncle, while her mother went elsewhere. She said: "Uncle Henry looked after me when he could. I could see my mother once in a while but not often." She lived in the slave quarters with the few slaves owned by her master, nearly all of whom were her kinfolk. After the war she heard that her mother was in Walker County, Alabama, and went to live with her.[24]

Kiziah Love reported that her owner was a fullblooded Choctaw Indian who owned her mother but that she didn't remember much about her father, who died when she was young. She married under slavery "Isom Love, a slave of Sam Love, another fullblood Indian that lived in a'jining farm. We lived on Master Frank's farm and Isom went back and forth to work fer his master and I worked every day fer mine. I don't 'spect we could of done that way iffen we hadn't of had Indian masters. They let us do a lot like we pleased jest so we got our work done and didn't run off."[25] She and her husband built a log cabin halfway between their two master's farms: "I would go to work at Master Frank's and Isom would go to work at Master Sam's."[26]

Bert Luster reported that he was born in 1853 in Tennessee, and that his father and mother were owned by different masters, and that he and his mother were taken by their master to Texas without the father.[27] After the war he went with his mother and stepfather to Greenville, Texas. He described his wedding after slavery:

> I married my woman, Nannie Wilkerson, 58 years ago. Dat was slavery, and I love her, honest to God I does. Course in dem days we didn't buy no license, we jest got permission from old Master and jumped over a broomstick and jest got married.[28]

Stephen McCray, born in Alabama in 1850, discussed his family:

> My parents was Wash and Winnie McCray. They was the mother and father of 22 chillun. Jest five lived to be grown and the rest died at baby age. My father's mother and father was named Mandy and Peter McCray, and my mother's mother and father was Ruthi and Charlie McCray. They all had the same Master, Mister McCray, all the way thru. We live in log huts and when I left home grown, I left my folks living in the same log huts.[29]

He offered the following description of marriage:

> Marriage was performed by getting permission from Master and go where the woman of your choice had prepared the bed, undress and flat-footed jump a broomstick together into the bed.[30]

Marshall Mack, born in 1854, reported that his mother was Sylvestus Mack and his father Booker Huddleston. His father was owned by his own half-brother, who beat him often. His "father had to slip off a night to come and visit . . . . He lived a mile and a half from our house . . . . He'd oversleep hisself and git up running. We would stand in our door and hear him running over them rocks till he got home. He was trying to git dere before his master called him."[31]

Allen Manning, who was born in 1849, came from a family of nine children, six of them born during slavery and three born free. His family stayed together during the entire period.[32]

Salomon Oliver's mother was the daughter of her own master. She was married to Salomon Oliver, Sr. under slavery. He was the preacher. His son reported: "Father use to preach to the slaves when a crowd of them could slip off into the woods . . . . He was caught several times slipping off to the woods and because he was the preacher I guess they layed on the lash a little harder trying to make him give up preaching."[33]

Andrew Simms was born in Florida about 1856 of parents who came from Africa twenty years before he was born. (This would mean that his parents were brought in illegally after the slave trade was ended.) His parents, he said, did not know each other in Africa; both came over quite young, and met in Florida. The parents were owned by different masters. When he was four, his master moved to Texas and they left his father behind. Commenting on this, Simms said: "They didn't get married. The Master's say it is alright for them to have a baby. They never gets married, even after the War. Just jumped the broomstick and goes to living with somebody else I reckon." When he was married himself the "wedding was a sure enough affair with the preacher saying the words just like the white folks marriage. We is sure married."[34]

James Southall, born in Tennessee in the 1850s, came from a plantation where the master did not believe in slavery. His father had been born on the plantation and his mother had been bought by the master when she was young. His father's mother lived with them and the family continued to live there after slavery was abolished.[35]

John White claimed to have been born in 1816, which would have made him 121 years old when interviewed. He told an interesting story about his parents:

Of all my mammy's children I am the first born and the longest living. The others all gone to join Mammy. She was named Mary White, the same name as her Mistress, the wife of my first master, James White.

About my pappy. I never hear his name and I never see him, not even when I was the least child around the old Master's place 'way back there in Georgia more'n one-hundred-twenty years ago!

Mammy try to make it clear to me about my daddy. She married like the most of the slaves in them days.

He was a slave on another plantation. One day he come for to borrow something from Master White. He sees a likely looking gal, and the way it work out that gal was to be my Mammy. After that he got a paper saying it was all right for him to be off his own plantation. He come a'courting over to Master White's. After a while he talks with the Master. Says he wants to marry the gal, Mary. The Master says it's all right with Mary and the other white folks. He finds out it is and they makes ready for the wedding. Mary says a preacher wedding is the best but Master say he can marry them just as good. There wasn't no Bible, just an old Almanac. Master White read something out of that. That's all and they was married. The wedding was over!

Every night he gets a leave paper from his Master and come over to be with his wife, Mary. The next morning he leaves her to work in the fields. Then one night Mammy says he don't come home. The next night is the same, and the next. From then on Mammy don't see him no more—never find out what happen to my pappy.

When I was born Mammy named me John, John White. She tells me I was the blackest "white" boy she ever see! I stays with her till I was eleven year old. The Master wrote down in the book when I was born, April 10, 1816, and I know it's right. Mammy told me so, and Master told me when I was eleven and he sold me to Sarah Davenport.

White commented on the sexual relations between whites and slave women:

Sometimes the white folks go around the slave quarters for the night. Not on the Davenport plantation, but some others close around. The slaves talked about it amongst themselves.

After a while they'd be a new baby. Yellow. When the child got old enough for chore work the master would sell him (or her). No difference was it his own flesh and blood—if the price was right![36]

Tom Woods lived in Alabama. His parents belonged to two different masters on adjoining plantations. His father "worked for his Master ever' day but spent each night wid us. He walked 'bout a mile to his work ever' day."[37]

The practice of "jumping the broom" as a form of marriage ceremony was common under slavery and continued after slavery. I have not been able to ascertain the origins of this custom, but its widespread use is established, as we have already indicated above. Here are some descriptions of it. Fred Brown, born in 1853 in

Baton Rouge, Louisiana, said:

> Den sometimes a couple am 'lowed to git married and dere am
> extry fixed for supper. De couple steps over de broom laid on de
> floor, dey's married den.[38]

Jeff Calhoun, who was born in Alabama in about 1838, gives
some specific details about marrying by jumping the broom:

> De way dey done at weddings dem days, you picks out a girl and
> tells your boss. If she was from another plantation you had to git
> her bosses 'mission and den dey tells you to come up at night and
> get hitched up. They says to de girl, "You's love dis man?" Dey
> say to de man, "You loves dis girl?" If you say you don't know,
> it's all off, but if you say yes, dey brings in de broom and holds
> it 'bout a foot off de floor and say to you to jump over. Dene
> he says you's married. If either of you stumps yor toe on de broom,
> dat mean you got trouble comin' 'tween you, so you sho' jumps
> high.[39]

Will Daily, born in 1858 near St. Louis, tells of getting married
by jumping the broom twice after slavery was ended:

> De first time I was married was to Phillis Reed in Missouri and
> we jes' jumps over de broom, and after Phillis die and I comes
> to Texas I's gits married again to Susie, here in San Angelo; we
> jes' jumps ov'r de broom too."[40]

George Eason, a former slave, who had been almost grown when
the war ended, told an interviewer:

> A preacher was never used to perform a wedding ceremony on
> the Ormond plantation. After the man told the master about the
> woman of his choice and she had been called and had agreed to
> the plan, all that was necessary was for the couple to join hands
> and jump over a broom which had been placed on the ground.[41]

There were other forms of informal wedding arrangements. Eli
Davidson, born in West Virginia in 1844, told the following story:

> I married Sarah Keys. We had a home weddin' and 'greed to live
> together as man and wife. I jus' goes by her home one day and
> captures her like. I puts her on my saddle behind me and tells her
> she's my wife then. That's all they was to my weddin'. We had
> six chillun and they's all farmin' round here. Sarah, she dies seventeen

years ago and I jus' lives round with my chillun, 'cause I's too old to do any work.[42]

Marriage is any formally sanctioned arrangement whereby people live together and have children, and there is every indication here of a sociologically stable relationship.

Eli Coleman, born in 1846 in Kentucky, also told of a "home wedding":

'Bout a year after the war I marries Nora Brady, jus' a home weddin'. I asks her to come live with me as my wife an she 'greed and she jus' moved her clothes to my room and we lived together a long time. One mornin' Nora jus' died, and there warn't no chilen, so I sets out for Texas.[43]

Slaves were sometimes deliberately bred. At least, a number of ex-slave informants insisted that was so. Elige Davison, who had been a slave in Virginia, reported:

I been marry once 'fore freedom, with home weddin'. Massa, he bring some more women to see me. He wouldn't let me have jus' one woman. I have 'bout fifteen and I don't know how many chillen. Some over a hundred, I's sho.[44]

Katie Darling, born a slave in Texas in 1849, also indicates that slaves were bred:

Niggers didn't cou't then like they do now, massa pick out a po'tly man and a po'tly gal and just put 'em together. What he want am the stock.[45]

Jeptha Choice was born in 1835 in Texas. He said:

The master was might careful about raisin' healthy nigger families and used us strong, healthy young bucks to stand the healthy nigger gals. When I was young they took care not to strain me and I was as handsome as a speckled pup and was in demand for breedin'. Late on we niggers was 'lowed to marry and the master and missus would fix the nigger and gal up and have the doin's in the big house. The white folks would gather round in a circle with the nigger and gal in the center and then master laid a broom on the floor and they held hands and jumped over it. That married 'em for good.[46]

In a recently published book entitled *Marriage and Family Among Negroes*, Professor Jesse Bernard made the following statement:

> There was a time when marriage was so uncommon among Negroes
> that almost every Negro infant in the United States was born out
> of wedlock. For few masters encouraged even unofficial marriage
> among their slaves. Thus most of the children of slaves—and probably
> a considerable proportion of those of the related few free Negroes—
> were born out of wedlock.[47]

Professor Bernard's emphasis on legal arrangements surrounding
marriage is meaningless in a discussion of slavery, a system in which
slaves had no legal rights to marry. The fact that the slaves were not
legally married is no more significant than the fact that the Sioux
Indians in 1850 had children born of parents not legally married
by the laws of the United States. No serious anthropologist would
assume that there is any meaning or significance in declaring that
Sioux children were "born out of wedlock" or that there were
few "official marriages" among the Sioux. Instead they have
described the Sioux kinship system and marriage customs in relationship to an understanding of the totality of Sioux reality, not in
reference to non-Sioux law.

Professor Bernard offers the following description of the slave
marriage and family structure:

> In no case, however, was a vow of life-long commitment required
> and, for most slaves, "marriage" was probably a fragile bond that
> depended on the way the partners felt toward one another . . . .
> Unions were based on mutual attraction. Love was important, and
> it was usually faithful—as long as it lasted. But however satisfactory
> the "companionship" pattern may have been for the men and women
> involved, it left children and old people unprotected . . . .[48]

However, she offers no evidence for the assertions that " 'marriage'
was probably a fragile bond . . . . ," that unions were based on
"mutual attraction," that children and old people were unprotected,
and that unions lasted only as long as did love, with the implication
that that was not likely to be a permanent condition. Moreover,
there is very little evidence that Professor Bernard was very interested in evidence about slave kinship relations that would do anything other than support a historical origin in a pathological relationship (slavery) for what she felt to be the pathological elements
in black kinship patterns after slavery. Very interestingly the
description of slave marriage quoted above comes after she quotes

two descriptions taken from the slave narratives this work is based on, which describe the marriage ceremony of jumping the broom and a similar ceremony in which the master was reported to have officiated. Her description of slave marriage is seemingly designed to minimize or negate the significance of these ceremonies. Such an analysis does not stand the test of empirical verification. If the slave family was so weak, how can we then account for the following facts which emerge with incessant urgency from the slave interviews?

As soon as the Civil War was over, and even in the few years before the end of the war when the discipline on the plantations was virtually destroyed, thousands of slaves went looking for and found their mothers, fathers, sisters, brothers, sons and daughters from whom they had been separated.

Hundreds of the ex-slaves interviewed knew something of their family histories, including stories about parents and grandparents who had come from Africa.

Most ex-slaves knew their precise relationship with brothers and sisters and half-brothers and half-sisters and obviously valued these relationships.

The language in which the ex-slaves describe the fairly ubiquitous marriage ceremony of jumping the broom indicates that these and similar ceremonies were not there because the masters required them but because the slaves wanted them.

What of old people and children being left unprotected? Given the fact that slaves were under the absolute authority of masters and overseers, what is amazing is how much protection children received. They were given special food—usually "taken" from the master, they were raised within the confines of a community, attended its nighttime religious meetings, and were subject to the socialization processes of the slave community. Old people, it is true, were often less well protected, but that is the case in all societies where there are extreme limitations on the availability of the means of existence. Moreover, what is most amazing is that under these circumstances, how often ex-slaves referred to grandparents and indicated that they had played a significant role in raising the children.

In a forthcoming book, Professor Herbert Gutman will give overwhelming statistical evidence of the sheer unexamined mythology involved in such views as Professor Bernard's about slave marriage and family relations. Professor Gutman has made a detailed examination of the records of the legal marriages of ex-slaves that took place at the end of the Civil War when thousands of slave husbands and wives flocked to get their already socially sanctioned marriages legally sanctioned and approved. Professor Gutman indicates that the great bulk of these marriages had a de facto standing of a number of years before the Civil War.[49]

The discussion of the sociology of slavery in the United States has been too often based on unexamined and unverified assumptions. These assumptions have been usually ones that fit in with the ways whereby middle-class white intellectuals often handle their guilt-feelings about the treatment of blacks in the United States. Most of the discussion of the black family, in particular, has seen it as being unsuited for achieving success in middle-class America, while that goal itself has been seen as having unquestioned value of the highest order.

The most significant work on the black family has been E. Franklin Frazier's *The Negro Family in the United States*, first published in 1939.[50] It was based on the most painstaking reading of the published slave autobiographies, upon material collected from black college students that tapped the oral tradition available in black families, on some of the Fisk University collection of then-unpublished slave narratives, and upon Frazier's own sensitivities as a descendant of slaves.

Frazier's book was an expansion of a long article entitled "The Negro Slave Family" published in 1930 in *The Journal of Negro History*.[51] In the article he took considerable pains to emphasize those materials which developed the theme that the black slaves struggled with some fair degree of success to maintain a coherent family structure against the opposition of the masters who often did break up slave families. In his article Frazier asserts that "Although theoretically and legally, except for some human restrictions, the slaves were not persons but utilities with no will of their own, social interaction within their own world on the plantation created a social life among them with nearly all the features of any society."[52]

Frazier carefully describes the slave family, making careful distinctions between the situation of house servants, slaves on small plantations, slaves with paternalistic masters, free blacks under slavery, the slaves on the large plantations in older, settled regions of the seacoast, and the slaves on the new frontier plantations of the Mississippi River delta in the nineteenth century. My conclusions in this book are, I believe, very close to those of Frazier's article.

However, Frazier modified his analysis somewhat in the 1939 book and in the abridgement of the book published after World War II. His later treatment of the subject suggests in language often less precise than in the 1930 article that the slave family may have been somewhat weaker than he had previously suggested. But, while there are differences in emphasis between my presentation of the black family under slavery and Frazier's 1939 treatment, I am closer to his views than I am to those of many who claim to base their views on Frazier's work. Many of these, such as Nathan Glazer, who has written an introduction to a paperback edition of the book,[53] essentially ignores all of Frazier's qualifications and his emphasis upon the existence of a wide spectrum of black families.

Thus, when Frazier emphasized tendencies that weakened the black family, lessening, for example, the authority of the father, his followers have concluded that *the* reason why the contemporary black ghetto household is often characterized by the absence of a functioning male figure stems from the supposed similar experience under slavery. While Frazier offers a reasonable and multidimensional view of the slave family, those who often claim to follow his analysis take only one side of the matter, that which emphasizes the absence of a strong black family, and suggest that that is a sufficient and accurate description.

Nevertheless, I do think a careful reading of the slave narratives collected in the 1930s modifies in some crucial ways some of Professor Frazier's conclusions. I think that there were probably more stable kinship units among slaves than he did; I think that the presence of a relatively strong male figure in that kinship unit was more common than he did; and I think that in general the slave family was better adapted to the conditions of the slaves, including their ability to struggle against those conditions, than he did.

I suspect that part of the reason for the differences lies in the fact that a very different part of the black community was probably tapped in the WPA narratives, upon which I so heavily depend, than in the materials Frazier utilized. Frazier's sources were those left by slaves unique enough to have written books, and black college students in the 1930s whom Frazier interviewed for family reminiscences. That is, his sources were people who were very likely part of that "black bourgeoisie" and their ancestors, that is, those most likely to have fully accepted a negative assessment of the black family, from which they worked so hard to distinguish themselves.[54] The largely unlettered people who were interviewed in the 1930s presented a more positive view of the black family under slavery, I believe, than did those upon whose accounts Frazier relied.

The slave community acted like a generalized extended kinship system in which all adults looked after all children and there was little division between "my children for whom I'm responsible" and "your children for whom you're responsible." I would suggest that such a generalized extended kinship system was more function-ally useful and integrative under the conditions of slavery in which both mother and father usually worked in the fields than would be one which emphasized the exclusive rights and duties of biologi-cal parents, the parents of the nuclear family. There was always some older person who would, with relative ease, take over the role of absent parents—as is usually the case today in the black community. A kind of family relationship in which older children have great responsibility for caring for younger siblings is obviously more functionally integrative and useful for slaves than the pattern of sibling rivalry and often dislike that frequently comes out of contemporary middle-class nuclear families composed of highly indi-viduated persons. While sociologists and social workers have been worrying that the black kinship structure and pattern do not pre-pare blacks for entry into middle-class American society, blacks have gone ahead realistically and rather successfully in creating ways whereby they could survive as blacks in the United States.

Indeed, the activity of the slaves in creating patterns of family life that were functionally integrative did more than merely prevent the destruction of personality that often occurs when individuals struggle unsuccessfully to attain the unattainable. It was part and parcel, as we shall see, of the social process out of which came black pride, black identity, black culture, the black community, and black rebellion in America.

## Notes

1. Kenneth Stampp, *The Peculiar Institution: Slavery in the Ante-Bellum South*, p. 292.
2. Ibid., p. 340.
3. Ibid., p. vii.
4. John Hope Franklin, *From Slavery to Freedom*, pp. 203-204.

5. E. Franklin Frazier, *The Negro in the United States,* p. 14.
6. Ibid., p. 309.
7. Ibid.
8. Ibid., pp. 309–310.
9. FWPSN, Oklahoma, pp. 27–28.
10. Ibid., pp. 30, 32.
11. Ibid., pp. 33–34.
12. Ibid., p. 38.
13. Ibid., p. 68.
14. Ibid., p. 76.
15. Ibid., p. 111.
16. Ibid., p. 124.
17. Ibid., pp. 126–127.
18. Ibid., p. 131.
19. Ibid., p. 145.
20. Ibid., p. 147.
21. Ibid., pp. 154, 156.
22. Ibid., pp. 157–158.
23. Ibid., p. 169.
24. Ibid., pp. 169, 170.
25. Ibid., p. 192.
26. Ibid., p. 195.
27. Ibid., p. 203.
28. Ibid., p. 204.
29. Ibid., p. 207.
30. Ibid.
31. Ibid., p. 212.
32. Ibid., p. 217.
33. Ibid., p. 234.
34. Ibid., pp. 295–297.
35. Ibid., p. 306.
36. Ibid., p. 325.
37. Ibid., p. 355.
38. FWPSN, Texas, Part 1, p. 156.
39. Ibid., p. 189.
40. Ibid., p. 272.
41. FWPSN, Georgia, Part 1, p. 303.
42. FWPSN, Texas, Part 1, pp. 296–297.
43. Ibid., p. 238.
44 Ibid., p. 299.
45. Ibid., p. 279.
46. Ibid., p. 218.
47 Jesse Bernard, *Marriage and Family Among Negroes,* p. 1.
48: Ibid., p. 10.
49. Based upon oral communication with Professor Gutman at the American Historical Association Convention, December 1969.
50. Frazier, *The Negro Family in the United States.*
51. Frazier, "The Negro Slave Family," *The Journal of Negro History* 15 (1930):198–259. This article relies almost exclusively upon both the published slave narratives and the Fisk University collection of unpublished autobiographies.
52. Ibid., pp. 205–206.
53. Nathan Glazer, Foreword to Frazier, *The Negro Family* 1966 abridged edition, pp. vii–xviii.
54. E. Franklin Frazier, *Black Bourgeoisie.*

# 6

# MASTER
# AND SLAVE:
# RESISTANCE

Under slavery, as under any other social system, those at the bottom were not totally dominated by the master class. They found ways of subverting the worst of the system and even at times of dominating the masters. The slaves created a unified black community in which class differences within the community, while not totally eradicated, were much less significant than the ties of blackness in a white man's world; all blacks potentially could bring into that community needed information, as well as provide extra food and protection for runaway slaves.

While blacks were oppressed and exploited, they fought back in a constant struggle by all available means. These struggles eventually led to the crucial role that blacks played in the Civil War, the war for their own liberation. As Frantz Fanon has suggested, the oppressed, in order to prevent themselves becoming total victims, lash out against their oppressors and in doing so, create their humanity.[1] Only by resistance did the slave escape becoming Sambo, the "infantile" personality of the myth. By their daily resistance they produced their Nat Turners.

We must conceive of the slave personality as an ambivalent one. On the one hand are submissiveness and a sense that one deserves to be a slave; on the other hand is a great deal of anger in ways that protect the personality and have objective results in the improvement of the slave's situation and eventual liberation, at least from chattel slavery.

Unless the slave has had a tendency to be Sambo he can never become Nat Turner. One who has never feared becoming Sambo, never *need* rebel to maintain his humanity. A pure Sambo, or a pure rebel, is a theoretical abstraction which does not concretely help us understand the behavior of living human beings. Unless we understand the contradictory nature of the rebel personality, we can never portray this reality.

Either the oppressed continuously struggle in forms of their own choosing or they are defeated by life. Only they can know what they can and must do. The black community, slave and free, South and North, made itself, and in so doing brought about the abolition of slavery. It did this not out of a belief in ideological abstractions, but out of a felt inner necessity. Only when the slaves, through their own struggles, saw the necessity and possibility of freedom, could they struggle to overcome, to transcend that bondage.

The slaves went from being frightened human beings, thrown among strange men, including fellow slaves who were not their kinsmen and who did not speak their language or understand their customs and habits, to what W. E. B. DuBois once described as the general strike whereby hundreds of thousands of slaves deserted the plantations, destroying the South's ability to supply its army.[2] The over 200,000 blacks who joined the Northern army maintained the ability of the North to mount the military initiative after the battle of Gettysburg and win the war.[3] How did this happen? How did potential Sambos become Nat Turners?

The assertion that the involuntary immigrants from Africa upon first arriving in the New World were in a state of shock, needs no extensive documentation at this point;[4] even most of the voluntary immigrants who arrived in the New World experienced a sense of profound dislocation. That the slaves were able to transform themselves into a people who played a crucial role in bringing the South to surrender requires much explanation; that they did this by the continual creation of a community whose primary function was to struggle against their oppressors needs elaboration. How were individual men and women, frightened and disoriented beyond belief by the Middle Passage across the Atlantic in the holds of slave ships and then dumped among hostile strangers as chattel slaves, transformed into a collectivity of victorious revolutionaries who performed most important roles in striking off their own shackles?

In 1935, W. E. B. DuBois summarized the process whereby blacks turned the tide of battle in the Civil War:

> Freedom for the slave was the logical result of a crazy attempt
> to wage war in the midst of four million black slaves, and trying
> the while sublimely to ignore the interests of those slaves in the
> outcome of the fighting. Yet, these slaves had enormous power in
> their hands. Simply by stopping work, they could threaten the Con-
> federacy with starvation. By walking into the Federal camps, they
> showed to doubting Northerners the easy possibility of using them
> thus, but by the same gesture, depriving their enemies of their use
> in just these fields. It was the fugitive slave who made the slaveholders
> face the alternative of surrendering to the North, or to the Negroes.
>
> It was this plain alternative that brought Lee's sudden surrender.
> Either the South must make terms with its slaves, free them, use
> them to fight the North, and thereafter no longer treat them as
> bondsmen; or they could surrender to the North with the assumption
> that the North after the war, must help them to defend slavery,
> as it had before.[5]

In a long social process the slaves developed an independent community and culture which molded the slave personality. This social
personality was kept whole by the day-to-day and night-to-night
life of the slave quarters. While the struggles that the slaves engaged
in were rarely epic, they were real and often successful in limited
terms.

In some ways insight into the essence of the slave personality produced by this community is contained in the Br'er Rabbit stories,
not as Joel Chandler Harris redid them for white audiences,[6] but
as they were carried from Africa in the oral traditions of black
people and transformed in the New World. These stories are not
childlike tales for toddlers. They contain the social insights of a
people and express a most sophisticated view of human life.

There are a variety of myths and folktales from black populations
in Africa and the New World in which a relatively weak creature
succeeds in at least surviving in his competition with the greater
beasts, usually by trickery. At times this creature wins, but he
never really loses. He is often absurd, but he is also filled with
life and keeps struggling against his situation.

In West Africa he is often identified with Legba, the trickster messenger of the gods. In these West African versions there is a sense of organic relationship between the people and Legba, or with Anansi the Spider, another form he takes, and the rest of the forces of the universe. The distance between the natural and the supernatural is not felt, but Legba or Anansi are clearly not totally of the sphere of men, although they certainly are in crucial ways like humans.[7]

In the Caribbean, Anansi the Spider reappears, and here he is most human, a symbol of man, not another type of creature inhabiting the same world. He survives by his wits, and although sometimes defeated and humiliated, he manages to survive in a tense competition with his more powerful neighbors. In the Caribbean, Anansi, the spider trickster, defeats Lion, Tiger, and Snake in great contests of wit.[8] He appears as the main figure in the famous "Tar Baby" stories in a collection made by Beckwith in Jamaica. In two of these, Anansi emerges victorious; in one there is a stand-off relationship between Anansi and those he tries to trick; and in one he is defeated, the price of defeat being shame and humiliation.[9]

Sometimes in the Caribbean he becomes Br'er Rabbit, the form in which he is also known in North America. In all cases we have a creature whose life situation is very much like that of slaves. He survives under difficult circumstances and he occasionally triumphs over the more powerful beasts. No matter what he does, even when he is defeated, he gains the sympathy of the nonpowerful everwhere and the pity and contempt of the powerful. And he always seems to have a greater share of the classic human virtues than do the Great Beasts.

Harold Courlander, an outstanding student of Haitian life, while indicating that in "the folk tales and legends of Haiti there has been a powerful assimilation from many cultures"[10] discusses the African origins and Haitian fate of the Anansi stories:

> Anansi, the spider trickster-hero and buffoon of West Africa, has survived in Haiti as well as elsewhere in the Antilles. In Jamaica and other British islands, Anansi has become Brother Anansi, Sister Nancy, or just plain Nancy. Although he usually figures in tales dealing with other animals, he has more and more come to assume a human form, as he has in Haitian tales. But in Haiti the name Anansi is only rarely heard. Anansi's cleverness and stupidity are now attributed to two characters named Ti Malice and Nonc' Bouki, both of whom are regarded as human beings.

In West Africa the spider hero directed his mischief against the great and strong creatures of the forest, now one, now another. In Haiti, Ti Malice, who has inherited Anansi's wit and guile, pits himself mostly against Bouki, who has inherited Anansi's stubborn nature and his pompous stupidities. Ti Malice (whose first name probably comes from the Spanish *tio*, uncle) has become the slick sharpy of the city, the clever and predatory "operator," the practical joker. Like his spider prototype, Ti Malice has humor as well as cunning, though he is often remorseless. Bouki is full of self-confidence but is slow-witted and an easy prey for Ti Malice. He is thought of as a clumsy peasant of the mountains. He has a constant desire to pit himself against Ti Malice, and a capacity for involving himself in utterly fantastic situations which appeal to the Haitian sense of the ridiculous.[11]

The slave narratives contain many Br'er Rabbit stories. Typical is one told by Sabe Rutledge, raised under slavery in South Carolina, in which Br'er Partridge hides from Br'er Rabbit:

How come I know all these Buh Rabbit story, Mudder spin you know. Have the great oak log, iron fire dog. Have we chillun to sit by the fireplace put the light-wood under—blaze up. We four chillun have to pick seed out the cotton. Work till ten o'clock at night and rise early! Mudder and Father tell you story to keep you eye open! Pick out cotton seed be we job every night in winter time—cept Sunday! When we grow bigger, Mudder make one card. One would spin and then Mudder go to knitting. Night time picking these cotton seed out; day time in winter getting wood!

Fall—harvest peanut, peas, 'tater!

I member all them Buh Rabbit story! Mudder tell 'em and we laugh and wake up! They was one bout Buh Rabbit and Buh Patridge. You know Buh Patridge the onliest one get the best of Buh Rabbit!

Buh Rabbit bet Buh Patridge (Buh Rabbit think he so sharp you know!). He bet Buh Patridge if he fly off down the road a piece and lit Buh Rabbit can *find 'em*. Buh Patridge bet him he *can't!* So Buh Patridge take off and fly down the road a piece and lit—like a Patridge will do—lit and turn up on he back and rake the leaves over him and kiver [cover] his body all cept he two foots sticking up like stick!

Now Buh Rabbit come! He hunt and he hunt and he hunt! Couldn't find 'em and he get so hot he take off he coat and hang it on Buh Patridge foots!

He go on hunting and after while he call out,

"Well I can't find Buh Patridge! Can't find Buh Patridge!"

And Buh Patridge sing out,

"Well, Buh Rabbit, here I is! You hang you coat on my feet!" Buh Rabbit have to pay the bet! (I don't member what the bet was.) So Buh Patridge was the onliest one I ever hear bout could get the best of Buh Rabbit![12]

It is clear that in this story there is an implied alternative ending, one where when Br'er Patridge cries out "here I is," Br'er Rabbit declares, "I found you and I win the bet."

In myth and folktale the slave not only acted out his desires, he accomplished much more than that. In his laughter and pleasure at the exploits of Anansi and Br'er Rabbit he created for himself, out of his own being, that necessary self-confidence denied to him by so much of his environment. Anansi-Br'er Rabbit is both Sambo and Nat Turner, both the victim and the revolutionary, who manages to assert himself and his humanity and overcome his own inner victimization, the internalized reflection of his objective circumstances. At least Anansi-Br'er Rabbit is not passive, if not always successful. He struggles in concrete ways through his own activity in behalf of himself to change his circumstances. These stories were part of the process whereby the slaves gained enough footing to allow them to rebel.

The slave personality was, like all other adult personalities, not one that should be described in the metaphor of static psychology as "infantile." While even wise and mature adults in any society can at times behave in an infantile manner, they are not necessarily childish and thus incapable of taking care of themselves. In any society, particularly one based upon social hierarchy and exploitation, most people at all levels of society display an extreme ambivalence of personality. In extreme cases that inner contradiction leads either to the attempt to resolve the contradictions by self-destruction through madness or self-liberation through revolution. In most situations, however, men live with the contradictions, varying their emphasis, trying to find ways to live in physical and psychic comfort.

The slave personality is an example of the "highest of the high and the lowest of the low" syndrome in which the person conceives of himself both as becoming like God (through conversion, for example) and unworthy of any recognition. It produces social greatness as well as social incompetence. Erik Erikson, for example, in *The Young Man Luther*, describes the religious revolutionary as feeling himself to be both a worthless child and a man chosen to do the Lord's work. Only in fighting the enemies of his heavenly Father would the child become a man.[13]

The slave narratives are the richest source we have ever had for a description of the slave personality. In them the same individuals describe themselves as simultaneously Objects and Subjects and tell us of the consequences of their self-transformation from one to the other. On the one hand is the Object: the man who does not receive enough food, clothing, or shelter to keep alive, and does not work well because of incompetence; the man who is whipped and humiliated; the man who calls upon those who listen to him to have pity and be merciful. On the other hand is the Subject: the man with needs and wants of his own, not only those that others can objectively and quantifiably impute to him; the man who acts as best he can to satisfy those needs and wants. He may demand better and more food, clothing, and shelter. He may demand higher status, dignity, and the time and opportunity to carry on flirtations, to laugh, dance, sing, make love, loaf, play with his children and raise them as he sees fit; he may demand the end of being the whipped Object and become the one who chooses not to work well as an act of rebellion. The Subject wants liberty and freedom and the opportunity to appropriate for himself and his family the best that is available in his time and place.

If we allow ourselves to see the slave as Subject, we need not insist that he did not laugh and dance and sing. We can see through the slave narratives that when the slave laughed and danced and sang, he celebrated life and thus resisted destruction. While it is true that a Swiss traveler to the West Indies observed that "a mournful silence"[14] pervaded the slaves at work, this does not mean that the slaves were never joyful. Indeed, the denial that the slaves did those human things that express joy, or the assertion that if they did them it was because they had been infantilized by slavery, are manifestations of the view of the slave as Victim and Object. Those who would hold this view would question: how dare they laugh and dance and sing and make us feel less sorry for them as Victims and Objects? And they would rationalize that if the slaves did so, it was not because they were amused or felt a need to dance and sing but because they were victims who had been so programmed as to be "forced" to do these things, or because they could do nothing more important. But we sometimes forget that the master, as well as "Sambo," laughes and dances and sings. And when the master does these things, no one thinks of him as an infant but rather as a full man enjoying life.

The entire view of the slave as Victim and Object is related to the matter of guilt. Only those who feel themselves innately superior can feel such guilt about the conditions of others. The Dutch student of slavery Hoetink perceptively observes:

Feelings of guilt may be emotions which one can permit oneself only in a position of superiority. True feelings of guilt are not infrequently deeply hidden: a person who speaks about his own guilt feelings may be the practicioner of "philanthropy" in the bad sense of the word: the condescending self-accusation accompanying a gratuity, which one can permit oneself only in a supposedly superior position. The feelings of guilt are then a function of the position of power, and of a doubtful ethical nature.

And Hoetink concludes, "These emotions are bound to be exposed at some later date by those to whom they related."[15]

Let us look at some descriptions of the development of the slave's social personality in the slave narratives.

We have already discussed in the previous chapter Mingo White's description of the beating of Ned White in which White was made "to pull off ever-thang but his pants an' lay on his stomach 'tween de pegs whilst . . . dey whupped him 'twell de blood run from him lack he was a hog."[16] Mingo White went on to describe the aftermath of this beating:

After ol' Ned got sech a terrible beatin' fer prayin' for freedom he slipped off an' went to de North to jine de Union Army.

After he got in de army he wrote to Marse Tom. In his letter he had dose words:

I am layin' down, marsa, and sittin' up, marsa; meaning dat he went to bed when he felt like it an got up when he pleased to. He [tells] Tom White dat iffen he wanted him he was in the army an' dat he could after him. After ol' Ned had got to de North, de yther han's began to warch for a chance to slip off. Many a one was cotched an' brung back. Dey knowed de penalty what dey would have to pay, an dis cause some of 'm, to git desp'rite. Druther dan to take a beatin' dey would choose to fight hit out 'twell dey was able to git away or die befo' dey would take de beatin'.

Lots of times when de patterollers would git after de slaves dey would have de worse fight an' sometimes de patterollers would git killed. After de war I saw Ned, an' he tol' me de night he left the patterollers come in de woods lookin' for him, so he jes' got a tree on 'em an' den followed. Dey figured he was headin' for de free states, so dey headed dat way too, and Ned jes' followed dem far as dey could go. Den he climb a tree and hid whilst dey turned 'roun' an' come back. Ned went on wide out any trouble much. De patterollers use ter be bad. Dey would whip de folks iffen dey was caught out after eight o'clock in de night, iffen dey didn' have no pass from de marsa.[17]

Slaves ran away after being whipped and then got caught. Sometimes they would commit suicide rather go back to slavery:

Ever once in a while slaves would run away to de North. Most times dey was caught an' brought back. Sometimes dey would git desp'rit an' would kill demse'ves 'fore dey would stand to be brought back. One time dat I hear of a slave that had 'scaped and when dey tried to ketch him he jumped in de creek an' drown hisse'f.[18]

Martha Bradley of Montgomery, Alabama, born in 1837, told the following story:

One day I wuz workin' in de field and de overseer he come 'round and say sumpin' to me he had no bizness say. I took my hoe and knocked him plum down. I knowed I'se done sumpin bad so I run to de bushes. Marster Lucas come and got me and started whoopin' me. I say to Marster Lucas whut dat overseer sez to me and Marster Lucas didn' hit me no more. Marse Lucas wuz allus good to us and he wouldn' let nobody run over his niggers.[19]

Anthony Abercrombie, an ex-slave born in the 1830s, indicated that sometimes an overseer would be mysteriously killed. He said that his master had about three hundred slaves and a bad overseer who was killed on the bank of the creek one night. "Dey never did find out who killed him, but Marse Jim always b'lieved de field han's done it."[20]

William Colbert, born in 1844 in Georgia, told a story of a beating in which his brother refused to cry out when whipped until he could stand it no longer. The story is worth quoting here in its entirety. The moral of the story is that while the slave was whipped, the master was eventually defeated.

Nawsuh, he [his master] warn't good to none of de niggers. All de niggers 'roun' hated to be bought by him kaze he wuz so mean. When he wuz too tired to whip us he had de overseer do it; and de overseer wuz meaner dan de massa. But, mister, de peoples wuz de same as dey is now. Dere wuz good uns and bad uns. I jus' happened to belong to a bad un. One day I remembers my brother, January wuz cotched over seein' a gal on de next plantation. He had a pass but de time on it done gib out. Well suh, when de massa found out dat he wuz a hour late, he got as mad as a hive of bees. So when brother January he come home, de massa took down his long mule skinner and tied him wid a rope to a pine tree. He strip' his shirt off and said:

"Now, nigger, I'm goin' to teach you some sense."

Wid dat he started layin' on de lashes. January was a big, fine lookin' nigger, de finest I ever seed. He wuz jus' four years older dan me, an' when de massa begin a beatin' him, January never said a word. De massa got madder and madder kaze he couldn't make January holla.

"What's de matter wid you, nigger?", he say. "Don't it hurt?"

January, he never said nothin', and de massa keep a beatin' till little streams of blood started flowin' down January's chest, but he never holler. His lips was a quiverin' and his body wuz a shakin', but his moutf it neber open; and all de while I sat on my mammy's and pappy's steps a cryin'. De niggers wuz all gathered about and some uv 'em couldn't stand it; dey hadda go inside dere cabins. Atter while, January, he couldn't stand it no longer hisself, and he say in a hoarse, loud whisper:

"Massa! Massa! have mercy on dis poor nigger . . . ."

Den . . . de war came. De Yankees come in and dey pulled de fruit off de trees and et it. Dey et de hams and cawn, but dey neber burned de houses. Seem to me lak dey jes' stay aroun' long enough to git plenty somp'n t'eat, kaze dey lef' in two or three days, an' we neber seed 'em since. De massa had three boys to go to war, but dere wuzn't one to come home. All the chillun he had wuz killed. Massa, he los' all his money and doe house soon begin droppin' away to nothin'. Us niggers one by one lef' de ole place and de las' time I seed de home plantation I wuz a standin' on a hill. I looked back on it for de las' time through a patch of scrub pines and it look' so lonely. Dere warn't but one person in sight, de massa. He was a-settin; in a wicker chair in de yard lookin' out ober a small field of cotton and cawn. Dere wuz fo' crosses in de graveyard in de side lawn where he wuz a-settin'. De fo'th one wuz his wife. I lost my ole woman too 37 years ago, and all dis time, I's been a carrin' on like de massa—all alone.[21]

The slaves would consciously plot against the masters and their agents, the patrollers.

I was at a ball one night. They had fence rails in the fire. Patroller knocked at the door, stepped in and closed it behind him. Nigger pulled a rail out of the fire and stuck it 'gainst the patroller and that patroller stepped aside and let that nigger get by. Niggers used to tie ropes across the road so that the patrollers' horses could trip up.[22]

Brutality bred brutality as well as nobility or docility. Amy Chapman, born in 1843 in Alabama, had many tales of brutality of masters and overseers to slaves. But one section about the retaliation of a slave woman stands out.

I could tell you 'bout bein' run myself wid dem nigger dogs, but I ain't gwineter do it. I will tell you dough 'bout a mean man who whupped a cullid woman near 'bout to death. She got so mad at him dat she tuk his baby chile what was playin' roun' de yard and grab him up an' th'owed it in a pot of lye dat she was usin' to wash wid. His wife come a-hollin' an' run her arms down in de boilin' lye to git de chile out, an' she near 'bout burnt her arms off, but it didn't do no good 'case when she jerked de chile out he was daid.[23]

Individual acts of rebellion were turned into collective actions very often. The Southern historian U. B. Phillips, despite his racist theories, devoted a great deal of attention to the process whereby individual acts of truancy became slave strikes. He wrote:

Truancy was a problem in somewhat the same class with disease, disability and death, since for industrial purposes a slave absent was no better than a slave sick, and a permanent escape was the equivalent of a death on the plantation. The character of the absconding was various. Some slaves merely took vacations without leave, some fled in postponement of threatened punishments, and most of the rest made resolute efforts to escape from bondage altogether.

Occasionally, however, a squad would strike in a body as a protest against severities. An episode of this sort was recounted in a letter of a Georgia overseer to his absent employer: "Sir, I write you a few lines in order to let you know that six of your hands has left the plantation—every man but Jack. They displeased me with their work and I give some of them a few lashes, Tom with the rest. On Wednesday morning they were missing. I think they are lying out until they can see you or your uncle Jack, as he is expected, daily. They may be gone off, or they may be lying round in this neighbourhood, but I don't know. I blame Tom for the whole. I don't think the rest would of left the plantation if Tom had not of persuaded them of for some design. I give Tom but a few licks, but if I ever get him in my power I will have satisfaction. There was a part of them had no cause for leaving, only they thought if they would all go it would injure me more. They are as independent a set for running of[f] as I have ever seen, and I think the cause is they have been treated too well. They want more whipping and no protector; but if our country is so that negroes can quit their homes and run of[f] when they please without being taken they will have the advantage of us. If they should come in, I will write to you immediately and let you know."

Such a case is analogous to that of wage-earning laborers on strike for better conditions of work. The slaves could not negotiate directly at such a time, but while they lay in the woods they might make overtures to the overseer through slaves on a neighbouring plantation as to terms upon which they would return to work, or they might await their master's posthaste arrival and appeal to him for a redress of grievances. Humble as their demeanor might be, their power of renewing the pressure by repeating their flight could not be ignored. A happy ending for all concerned might be reached by mutual concessions and pledges. That the conclusion might be tragic is illustrated in a Louisiana instance where the plantation was in charge of a negro foreman. Eight slaves after lying out for some weeks because of his cruelty and finding their hardships in the swamp intolerable returned home together and proposed to go to work again if granted amnesty. When the foreman promised a multitude of lashes instead, they killed him with their clubs. The eight then proceeded to the parish jail at Vidalia, told what they had done, and surrendered themselves. The coroner went to the plantation and found the foreman dead according to specifications. The further history of the eight is unknown . . . . Virtually all the plantations whose records are available suffered more or less from truancy, and the abundance of newspaper advertisements for fugitives reinforces the impression that the need of deterrence was vital.[24]

The mechanisms of individual acts of resistance, as well as those of collective actions, become clear if we focus upon the slave community. People do not individually resist in any significant degree without some sort of support and social confirmation from a community. There must be ways whereby individual acts of repression become known throughout the community, ways whereby individuals learn from each other that resistance is legitimate, and ways whereby individuals learn from each other of particular ways to resist. In order for large numbers to resist with any degree of success, slaves had to know that other slaves resisted, and how this was accomplished.

At the center of any community is a network of communications and social relations. The slave community, like other communities, was not composed of individuals living in a vacuum. The existence of the "bush-mail" or what West Indian blacks today wryly call the "niggergram," is a central part of slave resistance. Benjamin Russel, born a slave about 1854 in South Carolina, said in this connection:

> How did we get the news? Many plantations were strict about this, but the greater the precaution the alerter became the slaves, the wider they opened their ears and the more eager they became for outside information. The sources were: Girls that waited on the tables, the ladies' maids and the drivers; they would pick up everything they heard and pass it on to the other slaves.[25]

There were many ways that news traveled. Slaves were allowed passes to travel from one plantation to another; some slaves regularly worked on one plantation and slept on another if they were married to a woman on the second plantation; slaves would go off on their own to all-night prayer meetings and "frolics"; one slave commented that the church service on Sunday was the big time for gossip;

the arrival of new slaves from far away places would bring in news of the outside. We know that news got through from such evidence as the fact that David Walker's incendiary appeal to the slaves to revolt, and news of such events as Nat Turner's rebellion, were widely distributed in the South.

Not all news passed by word of mouth. On virtually every plantation there were a few slaves who knew how to read and who would read newspapers that had been left lying about. While it was illegal to teach slaves to read and write, many, both as children and as adults, learned how to read, and a few learned how to write. Some have estimated that as many as 10 percent of the slaves could read, but that figure need not have been as high for there to have been a significant amount of information via reading coming into the slave community.

On some plantations slaves were taught how to read by the master so that they could read the Bible and keep records. The very fact that slavery was presided over, as are all societies, by a diverse group of people, helped the slaves. Social classes are made up of individuals and there is no total homogeneity of behavior, only limits of possibilities. Some slaveowners took their religion seriously and encouraged the slaves' religious expression.

But while some masters taught their slaves to read and were allowed to continue in this practice, others were not. Henry Bibb, a runaway slave who wrote one of the better slave autobiographies before the Civil War, tells of a poor-white woman whose attempt to teach a Sunday school for the slaves was broken up by the patrols.[26] Another author of a slave autobiography, John Thompson, was forbidden to visit slaves on neighboring plantations because he could read and write, and was whipped for disobeying this restriction.[27] Solomon Northrup, who had been born free and kidnapped into slavery, could write, but was unable for many years to acquire a pen and ink or paper.[28] Slaves who were caught with books or writing material were usually severely punished.

That most slaves were illiterate is not particularly surprising in an era in which many masters and overseers were themselves illiterate or nearly so. What is noteworthy is the efforts made to prevent the slaves from learning how to read. Either the master class was suffering from extreme paranoia or it had good reason to suspect that slaves who were literate would spread sedition. There is every bit of evidence to indicate that the masters' reactions were rational.

It is equally noteworthy that many of the slaves did learn to read. Frederick Douglass writes in his autobiography that when his master forbade his mistress to continue teaching him to read because it would make him "unfit to be a slave," he discovered that "the pathway from slavery to freedom" was literacy. He therefore went out and found another way of learning to read:

> The plan which I adopted, and the one by which I was most successful, was that of making friends of all the little white boys whom I met in the street. As many of these as I could, I converted into teachers. With their kindly aid, obtained at different times and in different places, I finally succeeded in learning to read. When I was sent on errands, I always took my book with me, and by doing one part of my errand quickly, I found time to get a lesson before my return. I used also to carry bread with me, enough of which was always in the house, and to which I was always welcome; for I was much better off in this regard than many of the poor white children in our neighborhood. This bread I used to bestow upon the hungry little urchins, who, in return, would give me that more valuable bread of knowledge.[29]

Another slave tricked white boys into teaching him how to read by a simple game. After having learned a few letters from an old slave, he would engage in contests with white boys. He would point to a letter and say, "I know that letter; it is an A," and they would reply, "No, that's a B." Thus he learned the alphabet.[30]

The several hundred thousand black freedmen, anomalies of the slave system, also provided sources of information for the slaves with whom they had regular contact. Many of the freedmen were literate and could get access to newspapers and could even read to the slaves. It was through this route, most likely, that slaves heard of David Walker's appeal to them to rise and of Nat Turner's revolt. Moreover, through such sources the slaves heard of the activities of the abolitionists and were encouraged. John Thompson reported that he had, while a slave, picked up a piece of an old newspaper containing a speech by John Quincy Adams delivered in the House of Representatives presenting a petition from a group of Massachusetts ladies asking the end of slavery in the District of Columbia. The petition so impressed Thompson, he reported, that "This I kept hid away for some months, and read it until it was so worn that I could scarcely make out the letters."[31]

The freedmen spread ideas about abolitionism and black pride. From the very beginning, despite social class differences, there was a common unity of experience among black Americans, slave and free. Northern freedmen created the National Negro Convention movement which linked together various state freedmen's organizations. This movement forged close links to the struggle of the slaves and became the really outstanding center of the abolitionist movement. The newspaper of the white abolitionist Garrison was primarily supported by black freedmen, who made up the majority of its subscribers.

The freedmen were often the greatest victims of the system, for there was no security for them in any sense. Forced to support themselves and yet not easily able to enter the general society, they were usually relegated, particularly in the South, to the position of pariahs. Placed in this position, they learned much of the white society's ways—and how to struggle against that society.

Time after time runaway slaves were sheltered by freedmen, many of whom had previously been runaways. Freedmen made the most courageous conductors on the "underground railway." As Larry Gara has shown, there was no such regularly organized institution. Rather, the runaway slaves naturally utilized the re sources of the black community—the slave quarters and the homes of freedmen. In the border states and such states as Pennsylvania, Ohio, and Indiana, as well as all other Northern states, the runaways were most in danger of being caught because there were few large communities of slaves in these areas.[32] In the deep South, the area of the larger plantations, they could go from slave quarter to slave quarter and find shelter and food. Some runaways even found it wise neither to travel nor to remain hidden in the slave quarters during the day. Instead, particularly on very large plantations where several hundred slaves would work the fields, they would simply slip in among the field slaves and work. After all, "massa" could not tell one from the other.

Once the plantations thinned out and there were only small farms and relatively few slaves, the runaways had to rely on luck and the help of other blacks in the area and, occasionally, abolitionist whites. While we can do no more than make some informed guesses, it seems likely that it was this situation that helped John Brown decide that his major strategy would be to acquire a supply of arms at Harper's Ferry and set in motion a slave revolt; after arming the runaways, they could create in the border states, in the mountains, a base from which forays could be made into the plantation country and through which other runaways could be brought without fear of being caught. Brown thought he could weaken the South by running off slaves, setting into motion a slave revolt, and then waiting for the entire system to crumble. This strategy he learned from the activities of the freedmen and such organizers of liberation as his friend, the runaway slave Harriet Tubman, who went back into the South many times to lead bands of runaways to freedom.³³

The abolitionist movement was essentially a product of the black community, although whites played a role in it. Abolitionism was at all times dominated by Afro-American freedmen, not by whites, although the inherent racism of American ideology has obscured that fact not only for present-day Americans but for most whites— with the notable exceptions of such men as James Wentworth Higginson and Wendell Phillips—who participated in the movement. Every abolitionist movement depended upon the support of freedmen for its continuation; abolitionist lecturers were usually lodged in black homes, spoke in black churches, ate food prepared by black women, and traveled on monies in part donated by blacks with little money themselves. Indeed, many of the abolitionist speakers were black men, very often runaway slaves, the greatest of whom was Frederick Douglass.

The Northern abolitionists, black and white, received their inspiration from the realities and the struggles of their black brothers and sisters in slavery. It was the Fugitive Slave Act which mobilized some Northern whites into a movement to abolish slavery and protect the fugitives, and it was the fugitive slaves who created the need for the Fugitive Slave Act. Abolitionism would have been a dreary movement had it not been for the activities of the slaves themselves, runaways and those who stayed on the plantations. The literary genre upon which we have been so heavily depending throughout this work, the slave narratives and autobiographies, was in its pre-Civil War form, the main product of the abolitionist press. Tens of thousands of copies of these volumes were sold in the United States and Europe; hundreds of other abolitionist pamphlets drew heavily upon them for information. About the role of such runaway slaves as Henry Bibb, William Wells Brown, James Pennington, William and Ellen Craft, Anthony Burns, Frederick Douglass, Josiah Henson, John Brown, and Harriet Tubman³⁴ in the anti-slavery movement, Ralph Waldo Emerson commented, "The anti-slavery of the whole world is dust in the balance" in the presence of a man who has been enslaved.³⁵

Abolitionism was not primarily the product of the white New England Brahmin conscience many historians have claimed it to be. It was more accurately the product of the slave quarters of the plantation South, the border slaves, and the communities of Northern freedmen who helped bring into being a movement which drew into it some of the most eloquent and outstanding whites of the period. Abolitionism came from the black community and its task was to liberate that community by whatever means were found to be necessary, violence included, as the slave revolts and the Civil War would demonstrate. In liberating that black community, abolition transformed American society and took the lead in creating a new America.[36]

While the abolitionist movement required organizations, offices, officers, finances, printing presses and newspapers, public platforms and orators, writers and petitions, and lawyers to defend abolitionists persecuted by the law, its heart lay elsewhere in the movement of the slaves for their own liberation. And in turn the abolitionist movement had a profound general impact upon the slave communities. It gave the slaves the hope that enabled them to survive and to engage in the daily struggles that won for them the amount of extra living space that made more than mere continued existence possible. It provided for the slaves some objective cohesiveness for their struggles in the period between the defeat of Nat Turner's revolt and the Civil War.

The slave revolts themselves had grown out of the total black community, which included both slaves and freedmen. The slave revolts came out of that independent black religion which we have previously discussed. This was so both in terms of impetus and of organization. If we look at the accounts of the three most important slave uprisings in American history we find that two of them were led by exhorters, lay ministers who functioned in the blacks' own prayer meetings, while the third was led by a freedman who had an exhorter as second-in-command. Gabriel Prosser and Nat Turner were exhorters, both of them claiming descent from African religious leaders. The leader of the third major slave uprising, Denmark Vesey, was a freedman whose second-in-command, Peter Poyas, was a slave exhorter who some accounts indicate also claimed descent from an African religious leader. The accounts of all these uprisings indicate that they were preceded by all-night prayer meetings.[37]

These slave revolts pointed the way to the lines of attack that would have to be followed during the Civil War itself. Gabriel Prosser, the leader of one of the great revolts, was a skilled worker, a blacksmith. Aware of the modern community in which he lived, his objective was the capture of Richmond, Virginia, the main supply center for finished goods for much of the South. When Richmond was taken in the Civil War, the balance of victory was in the hands of the North, because the South's main domestic source of industrial products had been lost.

Denmark Vesey was a free Negro who had sailed in the West Indies. He chose as his target Charleston, South Carolina, that seaport that became one of the prime objects for the Northern armies in the Civil War.

Nat Turner was an exhorter, a field hand preacher. Although the number of participants in his slave revolt was the smallest of the three, his accomplishment was the greatest. He had no specific destination beyond the rallying of all the blacks in the countryside. His trial was the most effective propagandistically, and some 50,000 copies of its proceedings were sold. The rebellion followed by a few years the publication of David Walker's call to arms, *Appeal,* and thus was its counterpart in action.

The slave revolts came out of the natural development of the black community and were a stage in the development of that community. From the time of Nat Turner's defeat to the Civil War other strategies and tactics were used. During the Civil War itself there was a return to the slave revolts on a more complex and significant level.

Out of the independent black religion arose not only the slave revolts, but also the black secret fraternal organizations which, among other functions, became centers of resistance during the Civil War. In his study of the black soldier in the Civil War, Benjamin Quarles relates the activities of John Scobell, a literate Mississippi-born black. Scobell had been selected as a spy by Allan Pinkerton, the famous detective who interviewed every runaway slave that came within the lines of the Federal Army of the Potomac. On one occasion Scobell and ace spy Timothy Webster were traveling as a Southern gentleman and his slave in Confederate territory in Virginia. Having obtained some valuable papers which they wanted to return to Washington without themselves returning, Scobell took Webster to a rundown building on the edge of town. After giving the proper signal, they were allowed to enter a loft where they found about forty black men at a lodge meeting of the "Loyal

League, whose purpose was to speed runaway slaves on their journeys and to furnish information to Union commanders concerning the movement of the rebels." The Loyal League supplied a courier who took the documents through the rebel lines to Washington.[38]

The existence of an organized slave community helped the Northern war effort in other important ways. Federal soldiers who had escaped from Southern prisoner of war camps were aided by this natural organization of the slave community. In an important book of documents on blacks in the Civil War, compiled with running comment by James M. McPherson, there are excerpts from the diary kept by Lieutenant Hannibal Johnson of the Federal Third Marine Infantry during his war service. Johnson had been captured after the Battle of the Wilderness in Virginia on May 5, 1864 and was sent to a prison camp near Columbia, South Carolina, from which he and three other Union officers escaped in late November 1864. They headed for the Union lines near Knoxville, Tennessee, more than 200 miles away. They eventually made their way through the Confederate lines and rejoined their army. The diary indicates quite clearly that the major line of escape was from one slave community to another and that they relied, as Johnson put it, on "some trusty negro who will feed us and put us on the right road." Without any formal organization, the slave communities guided them to freedom. A few excerpts from the diary indicate something of the processes at work:

Nov. 23 . . . . Found a family of trusty negroes belonging to Colonel Boozier, who gave us a good supper, such as we had not had for many long months . . . . Here we remained till nearly morning, when we were taken to the woods and hid there to wait for a guide which these negroes say they would furnish at dark . . . .

Nov. 24. Still in the woods, the women coming to us twice during the day to bring us food and inform us that a guide will be ready at dark. God bless the poor slaves. At dark Frank took us seven miles, flanking Lexington Court House, striking the Augusta road five miles above. Traveled all night, making about twenty-two miles.

Nov. 25. Lay in the woods all day, and at night went to William Ford's plantation to get food. Here the negroes could not do enough for us, supplying us with edibles of a nice character . . . .

Nov. 28. Still at Ford's . . . . About midnight we got a guide by the name of Bob to take us seven miles on the Edgefield road, as the Augusta state road is too public to travel, and some of our officers were captured on that road to-day. Turned over by Bob to a guide by the name of George, who hid us in the woods.

Nov. 29. George has brought us food during the day, and will try to get us a guide to-night. At dark went to the negro quarters where a nice chicken supper was waiting us . . . .

Dec. 1. Just comfortable for a winter's day. At night after eating the usual diet of chicken, Peter, our guide, told us he was ready for the road. Went about twelve miles when Joe took us in charge and Peter started for home again. Were then hidden in the woods for the day.

Dec. 2. As soon as daylight the negroes on this place commenced coming to where we were hidden, all having something for us in the way of food; they also promise us a guide for the night. If such kindness will not make one an Abolitionist, then his heart must be made of stone. This is on the Matthews place. At dark were taken to the Widow Hardy's plantation, where chickens, etc., were served for our supper. Here Jim took us eight miles, and gave us into the care of Arthur, who, after going with us fifteen miles, gave us to Vance who hid us in the woods. At dark Vance brought us more chickens for our evening meal, then started on the road with us going eight miles, then Charles took us, he going five miles; then David took us a short distance and left us at the Preston Brooks' plantation (late United States Congressman from South Carolina) . . . .

Dec. 5. At dark we were taken four miles, when we found we were going in the wrong direction, retraced our steps, got another guide who took us to Colonel Frazier's. Distance in right direction about ten miles. During the night crossed the railroad above 96, and here Ned took us in charge. The boys on this place were good foragers, for while with them we lived on the fat of the land. At dark December 6th, two of the Frazier servants took us eighteen miles and then gave us into the hands of Ben and Harrison, who took us to Henry Jones' place. Just before we arrived at this plantation it commenced raining and we got as wet as if thrown into the Saluda River. Here we were put into a negro cabin with a fire and bed at our disposal, and took advantage of both . . . .

Dec. 9. We were hiding in the woods when it commenced snowing, the first of the season; soon a guide came for us and hid us for the day in a negro cabin. At night some negroes came six miles through the storm to bring us food. We are gaining in strength and weight, for we are eating most of the time when we are not on the road tramping. The snow being so deep it is not safe to travel to-night, so we are hidden in a fodder barn.[39]

The party continued in this way for nearly four more weeks until reaching the Union lines. McPherson comments: "Without the assistance, shelter, and food given them by scores of Negroes along the way, these Union soldiers and many others could not have made good their escape."[40] It is probably not too much to suggest that this description from the diary of an escaped prisoner of war is an accurate rendition of the experience of thousands of runaway slaves in the decades before the Civil War. Runaway slaves did not keep diaries, but if they had, it should be fair to estimate that they would have told of events similar to those recorded by this Northern officer.

The Civil War represents at its fullest the emergence of black Americans playing leading roles in the development of American society. In the war, the blacks played the decisive role. In the absence of many slaveholders, overseers, and patrollers, hundreds of thousands of the slaves worked sporadically or not at all other than for their own immediate needs. Two hundred thousand others joined the Union Army, many thousands as cooks and laborers before Lincoln's willingness to use them as combat troops; over 200,000 were in black regiments in the last year of the war.

The myth of Southern military prowess is based on romantic but futile individual acts of glory and heroism. This type of fighting is not enough to win a modern war, which relies heavily on supply. In the South, the slaves systematically sabotaged the war effort by refusing to produce. While the slave narratives indicate that body servants often accompanied Southern whites to war, there is much evidence to indicate that the slaves did not produce at home or play important work roles in the military camps and in the field. The South, so used to depending upon the slaves for all labor, simply did not produce the white volunteers necessary to supply the army with the hard daily labor required to keep a modern army in the field—and the slaves did not take up the slack. Southern yeoman farmers did not respond to the call to arms to defend a system about which they had ambivalent feelings, at least not in sufficient numbers, and thousands of others who did respond went home periodically during the war to get the crops in. The South consequently had to resort to a draft system earlier than did the North, and the morale of the Southern troops was often much lower than that of the North. In what was the last great volunteer war in history, the South, corrupted by slavery, could not muster volunteer support in sufficient quantity.

The 200,000 blacks who made their way into the ranks of the Northern army, the 29,000 blacks in the navy (one-fourth of the entire navy enrollment), and the tens of thousands of others who worked for the army as laborers and teamsters, played a crucial role in the winning of the war. In a letter to Lincoln, General Grant wrote, "By arming the negro we have added a powerful ally. They will make good soldiers and taking them from the enemy weakens him in the same proportion they strengthen us."[41] Toward the end of the war, Lincoln, too, came to believe that the participation of the blacks was the blow that defeated the South.[42]

The slave narratives have many references both to the "strike" of the slaves and their participation in the Northern army. Isaac Adams, born in the 1840s as a slave in Louisiana, said of the end of the war that "Along at the last the negroes on our place didn't put in much stuff—jest what they would need, and could hide from the Yankees, because they would get it all took away from them if the Yankees found out they had plenty of corn and oats. The Yankees was mighty nice about their manners, though."[43]

John Franklin, born a slave in South Carolina in the 1840s, said in the same connection, "That shortage begun in 1862, and it kept on gettin' worse all the time, and when Lincoln set all niggers free, there was such a shortage of food and clothing at our white folks houses, that we decided to move to a Dutch Fork plantation."[44]

Phoebee Banks, who had been born a slave among the Creek Indians about 1850, describes how slaves went off to join the Northern army:

Before the War is over some of the Berryman slaves and some from the McIntosh place fix up to run away from their masters.

My father and my uncle, Jacob Perryman, was some of the fixers. Some of the Creek Indians had already lost a few slaves who slip off to the North, and they take what was left down into Texas so's they couldn't get away. Some of the other Creeks was friendly to the North and was fixing to get away up there; that's the ones my daddy and uncle was fixing to join, for they was afraid their masters would take up and move to Texas before they could get away.[45]

George Conrad of Kentucky told of his father's enlistment in the Northern army: "When my father went to the army old Master told us he was gone to fight for us niggers freedom. My daddy was the only one that come back out of 13 men that enlisted . . . ."[46] Another slave said: "Mammy married a man named Jordan when I was a little baby. He was the overlooker and went off to de Yankees, when dey come for foraging through dat country de first time. He served in de Negro regiment in de battle at Fort Piller and a lot of Sesesh [Secessionists] was killed in dat battle . . . ."[47]

It was the fact of blacks having joined the Northern army and navy, the fact that blacks had taken guns in their own hands in their own behalf, that settled the matter of slavery. The blacks with guns gave new strength to the abolitionist movement which now pushed forward to the total abolition of slavery. When the war came to the blacks, free and slave, slavery was abolished. The Emancipation Proclamation had freed all slaves behind the Southern lines and was aimed at gaining the support of the slaves; it was only the actions of the slaves that guaranteed the Thirteenth Amendment to the Constitution which abolished slavery. It was the actions of the slaves and the freedmen fighting in their own behalf that added for many a new dimension to the war beyond the preservation of the Union. Lincoln, who had never believed that blacks would be able to become part of American society, and who was hard pushed by events to support abolition, by the end of the war had come to understand that the war was also fought for a "new birth of freedom." This, the conservative press understood, meant the abolition of slavery and the contingent transformation of American society.

The uproar in the press about the President's speech at Gettysburg is the greatest demonstration that Lincoln had come to understand that either a revolutionary war would be fought, or none at all. Thus, in the Second Inaugural Address he carried the idea forward when he declared:

Fondly do we hope—fervently do we pray—that this mighty scourge of war may speedily pass away. Yet, if God will that it continue until all the wealth piled by the bondman's two hundred and fifty years of unrequited toil shall be sunk, and until every drop of blood drawn with the lash, shall be paid by another drawn with the sword, as was said three thousand years ago, still it must be said, "the judgments of the Lord are true and righteous altogether."[48]

But the last word must not remain with the white President but with a black soldier who understood what the war and the blacks' role in it was all about. Corporal Thomas Long of Thomas Wentworth Higginson's regiment, acting as chaplain one Sunday, told the troops of his all-black regiment:

> If we hadn't become sojers, all might have gone back as it was before; our freedom might have slipped through de two houses of Congress and President Linkum's four years might have passed by & notin been done for we. But now tings can never go back, because we have showed our energy & our courage & our naturally manhood.
>
> Anoder ting is, suppose you had kept your freedom widout enlisting in dis army; your chilen might have grown up free, & been *well cultivated* so as to be equal to any business; but it would have been always flung in dere faces—"Your fader never fought for he own freedom"—and what could dey answer. *Neber can say that to dis African race any more,* (bringing down his hand with the greatest emphasis on the table.) Tanks to dis regiment, never can say dat any more, because we first showed dem we could fight by dere side.[49]

## Notes

1. Frantz Fanon, *The Wretched of the Earth* (New York, 1968), pp. 35–106.
2. W. E. B. Du Bois, *Black Reconstruction*, pp. 55–83.
3. Ibid., pp. 80, 112.
4. See Stanley Elkins, *Slavery* (Chicago, 1958), pp. 100–102, for an extremely exaggerated view of this matter. Elkins seems to believe that the shock of the "Middle Passage," reinforced by the brutality of North American slavery, led to a perpetual amnesia for millions of people whereby the "culture," the usable memory, of the Africans, was lost. This is, I suggest, an amazing intellectual feat, because it is a mystification of reality, not reality itself. Professor Elkins and those who have agreed with him (myself, in the past) are captives of words.
5. Du Bois, *Black Reconstruction*, p. 121.
6. Joel Chandler Harris, *Uncle Remus: His Songs and His Sayings.*
7. See the stories in Elphinstone Dayrell, *Folk Stories from Southern Nigeria West Africa.* Also, W. H. Barker and Cecilia Sinclair, *West Africa Folk Tales* (London, 1917).

8. Martha Beckwith, *Jamaica Anansi Stories* (New York, 1924).

9. Ibid., pp. 23–26.

10. Harold Courlander, *The Drum and the Hoe: Life and Lore of the Haitian People*, p. 170.

11. Ibid., p. 171.

12. FWPSN, South Carolina, Part 4, pp. 67–69.

13. Erik Erickson, *The Young Man Luther*.

14. As quoted in George Lamming, *The Pleasures of Exile*, p. 120.

15. Harry Hoetink, *The Two Variants in Caribbean Race Relations: A Contribution to the Sociology of Segmented Societies*. p. 77.

16. FWPSN, Alabama, p. 416.

17. Ibid., pp. 417–418.

18. Ibid., p. 390.

19. Ibid., p. 46.

20. Ibid., p. 7.

21. Ibid., pp. 81–82.

22. FWPSN, Arkansas, Part 1, p. 70.

23. FWPSN, Alabama, p. 60.

24. Ulrich B. Phillips, *American Negro Slavery*, pp. 303–304.

25. FWPSN, South Carolina, Part 4, pp. 52–53.

26. As noted in Charles H. Nichols, *Many Thousands Gone: The Ex-Slaves Account of Their Bondage and Freedom*, p. 44.

27. Ibid., p. 45.

28. Ibid.

29. Frederick Douglass, *Narrative of the Life of Frederick Douglass*, pp. 40–41.

30. Ibid., pp. 49–51.

31. Nichols, *Many Thousands Gone*, p. 45.

32. For the best discussion of the Underground Railroad, see Larry Gara, *The Liberty Line: The Legend of the Underground Railroad*. Gara demonstrates that the story of a powerful white organization that led thousands of slaves to freedom was more myth than reality. The slaves helped themselves to freedom and were aided by black freedmen more often than by whites. I suspect that Gara somewhat underestimates the number of runaways but he certainly succeeds in restoring the emancipation of the slaves before Emancipation to their own self-activity.

33. See Harriet Tubman, *Harriet, the Moses of Her People, Written by Sarah Bradford*.

34. Nichols, *Many Thousands Gone*, pp. 130–150.

35. As quoted in ibid., p. 162.

36. Du Bois in *Black Reconstruction*, and C. L. R. James in countless articles, books, and lectures have emphasized the fact that black people took the lead in the Civil War and thereafter in transforming America. I believe that thesis, if pursued throughout a study of American life and history, would provide a very useful and accurate starting point for a new and revolutionary analysis. Indeed, this book started out to be a chapter in such a volume but the task proved greater than had been anticipated. I hope to return to this theme in later books. Such a work would have to concentrate on the development of the American working class and would have to see that blacks were and are an integral, if separated, part of that working class. See Martin Glaberman, C. L. R. James et al., *Negro Americans Take the Lead* for a statement of this thesis. In two articles I attempt to develop this theme: "Potere Nero e Lotte Operaie," in *Dalle Strade Alle Fabbriche*, by George Rawick and Ed Clark, and "Race and Class in Auto," *Speak*

*Out* 2 (May–June 1969):5–7. Also see the extremely suggestive article of Harold M. Baron, "The Demand for Black Labor: Historical Notes on the Political Economy of Racism," *Radical America* 5 (1971):1–46.

37. I am indebted to William Gorman for a number of ideas in this chapter.
38. Benjamin Quarles, *The Negro in the Civil War*, pp. 84–85.
39. As excerpted in James M. McPherson, *The Negro's Civil War: How American Negroes Felt and Acted During the War for the Union*, pp. 150–153.
40. Ibid., p. 153.
41. Ibid., p. 191.
42. Ibid., pp. 234–235.
43. FWPSN, Oklahoma, p. 3.
44. FWPSN, South Carolina, Part 2, p. 222.
45. FWPSN, Oklahoma, p. 9.
46. Ibid., p. 341.
47. Ibid., p. 252.
48. Abraham Lincoln, "Second Inaugural Address, March 4, 1865," in Roy P. Basler, ed., *The Collected Works of Abraham Lincoln* p. 333.
49. McPherson, *The Negro's Civil War*, p. 213.

# PART II

## THE SOCIOLOGY
## OF EUROPEAN AND
## AMERICAN RACISM

# 7

# RACISM AND
# SLAVERY

Slavery has been accepted throughout human history as a natural and normal feature of man's existence. For most of this history, however, slavery was not racially based—black enslaved black, white enslaved white, black and white enslaved each other. Treatment of slaves varied from one culture to another and among individual owners. In some cultures slaves who were princes or scholars or who possessed valuable talents were treated as persons of high status; in the Ottoman Empire, slaves composed the officer corps of the army. There were degrees of servile status because slavery was utilized for many different human needs. It was a way of handling prisoners of war and defeated nations; a way of dealing with debts and of securing the protection of strong men; a way of attaching oneself to a family of higher class and status; a device for handling people who were out of their normal place in the social order, such as foreigners who were not kinsmen in societies in which kinship was the organizing force of social cohesiveness.

The slavery that emerged in the New World was different. Most of the slaves in the New World were Africans; slavery therefore became almost exclusively a status based on race. Usually this slavery was accompanied by ideas which defended it. In the English colonies, in particular, there emerged a fully developed theory and accompanying institutional behavior which viewed non-whites as inherently biologically inferior to whites, which tended to view northern Europeans as superior to all others, and which was fearful of miscegenation. Under these racist doctrines blacks were in fact excluded from the protection of the "natural rights of man" and the "rights of the citizen."

Such racist doctrines and extreme brutality are not necessarily linked. There can be a relatively paternalistic, non-brutal racism which considers blacks to be inferior but asserts that they ought to be well treated. While doubtless racism has a strong tendency to foster brutality, there is no reason to assume that the existence of one necessitates the other. For some time many scholars have assumed that because there was considerably less racism in Brazil, Brazilian slavery was less brutal than that of the United States. However, Philip Curtin has demonstrated that the slave population of Brazil did not reproduce itself and that Brazil had to continuously import new slaves to maintain its slave population. On the other hand, in the United States, the slave population, even after the slave trade was ended, steadily increased by natural means. This is at least prima facie evidence that North American slavery was less brutal, although it is possible that certain epidemic diseases that were present in Brazil but not in the United States played a role in the high death rate and low birth rate of Brazilian slaves.[1]

There is considerable evidence indicating that racist attitudes among the English existed before the development of slavery in the English colonies, and that their attitudes were expressed in "a loose body of prejudices and superstitions."[2] Winthrop Jordan locates the origin of these attitudes in the century before the English Revolution of 1640. This was an age "driven by the twin spirits of adventure and control . . . . [While] 'adventurous Elizabethans' embarked upon voyages of discovery overseas, many others embarked upon inward voyages of discovery." The first settlers of New England were involved in both of these trips. Jordan suggests that Englishmen "used peoples overseas as social mirrors" and that they were inclined to discover attributes in others "which they found first but could not speak of in themselves." In particular, "from the first, Englishmen tended to set Negroes over against themselves, to stress what they conceived to be radically contrasting qualities of color, religion, and style of life, as well as animality and a peculiarly potent sexuality."[3]

Others have located the source of racism in a combination of a natural aversion of people to those of different appearance and economic self-interest.[4] Still others seem to locate it in the totality of European history before the seventeenth century.[5] And still others have not found the evidence of the existence of racism in

England before the Atlantic slave trade to be important; racism was simply the ideological rationalization of self-interest.[6] Such non-concrete, free-floating interpretations are utilized when no more specific and historically concrete analysis is available.

Eugene Genovese points out that patterns of race relations in the New World varied from one part to the next and that such varying patterns must be located within the changing character of society at the beginning of the modern world. The origins of racism must be sought in sources within the changing ideological and psychological development of Europeans, developments which were closely linked with changes in social structure. An attempt must be made to link racism with this changing character of European ideology and to the psychodynamics of the situation. Such a theory can only be suggestive and illustrative at this point, not definitive. We shall try to unravel the process whereby, as Genovese has suggested, "previous ideological conditioning made possible a racially based slavery, and the growth of that kind of slavery transformed the conditioning from a loose body of prejudices and superstitions into a virulent moral disorder."[7]

Jordan's assertion that the English in this period of rapid change saw in others what they were afraid to see in themselves offers us the clue to the development of the psychodynamics of North American racism. Unfortunately Jordan did not pursue the point. After all, there must have been particular circumstances in which the English saw not only differences in color, religion, and life-style, but also an animality and a peculiarly potent sexuality in the black Africans they met. Moreover, as West African peasant peoples of the sixteenth and seventeenth centuries were not that dissimilar in life-style to European peasants, one must account for the perception on the part of northern Europeans that the West Africans were savages and very different from themselves in degree of civilization.

Racism and slavery in their modern forms were intimately linked from the beginning, and were both part of the same revolutionary process—the emergence of modern European capitalist society out of the feudal past. Racism was enforced by realities that included but also transcended the immediate profits of slavemasters, merchants, and slave-traders.

Racism took its strongest hold among those people who most thoroughly participated in the new, revolutionary developments of the modern world, and least among those where capitalist growth was curtailed. The advanced capitalist nations of the English and the Dutch created the most elaborate racist ideologies. French racism was closer to the English-Dutch brand than to the much milder variety of the Spanish and Portuguese colonies. This was no accident. France was becoming in the seventeenth and eighteenth centuries a capitalist nation, while on the Iberian peninsula pre-capitalist social relations were still dominant.

But there is more than the simple equation that the more capitalist a society, the more developed its racism. Racism fed on underground streams of sensibilities. It was embedded within the historical process itself. Both racism and slavery were part of the totality of relations that developed into modern capitalism.

Modern racism came of the process that marked the transition from feudalism to capitalism. The new society in England that came into being in the century between the reigns of Henry VIII and Oliver Cromwell required basic changes in human behavior and social personality. Capitalism required a new ethic to justify new forms of behavior and to repress the older ones. While part of this new ethic was the growth of democratic forms and processes, the other main ingredient was the separation of one human activity—work—from all others. Work was taken from its context as an organic part of life and subordinated to other social processes, becoming an abstract commodity. In the name of individualism, individual personality was subordinated to machines and the power of the market.

The kind of predominantly agricultural society that existed in Europe up to the sixteenth century had a particular kind of rhythm: work was regulated by the seasons; there was no such thing as the "work week" of a set number of days and hours for labor, followed by a period of rest, year in and year out; there were odd and unplanned hours, days, weeks, in everyone's life, when people could take time off to enjoy themselves or to vary their tasks. "Vacation time" was not accumulated to be spent all at once; many festivals and holidays were interspersed throughout the year, and during these periods all regular work stopped, except for the care of the farm animals.

But the sixteenth century saw the beginnings in England of a different kind of work, a different way of life. More and more, people worked steadily, day in and day out, with no long periods of rest. This kind of work also required new personalities: men and women who could tolerate few periods of rest and relaxation, who could adjust to working steadily and at high speed without rest, who could repress the desire to quit and relax. It required the repression of man's nonrational desires and his subordination to rationalized work and more work, accumulation and more accumulation.

The development of European capitalism during the sixteenth, seventeenth, and eighteenth centuries required vast changes in human psychology. Michel Foucault has demonstrated that with the modern world came a totally new definition of insanity, one that linked insanity with irrationality, sanity with extreme rationality and self-control. The sane man represses the nonrational and preconscious in the name of rationality, or at least relegates the nonrational to the sphere of religion. No one, of course, really manages to do this, but the sane man is the one who is most successful in keeping manifestations of the nonrational as private and secret as possible.[8]

Sexual promptings had to be carefully restrained, the human being trained to repression and sublimation of these desires except under very carefully regulated circumstances. As one of the ways whereby new people were created in the process of socialization, "childhood" was separated from other periods of life, and children were taught to be "innocent." The concept of childhood, as another French historian, Philippe Ariès, has pointed out, was actually "discovered" in the seventeenth century. Prior to that time children dressed the same as adults, played the same games, sang the same songs, and went to the same places. Infantile and childhood sexuality were taken for granted and not particularly repressed.

While it is clear that the medieval Church never exactly encouraged sexual activity per se and that the ethos of courtly love implied a repressive ideal in matters sexual, in actuality the situation was generally a non-repressive one, particularly among the peasantry. While the Church fathers and the ideologists of the cult of courtly love certainly did not encourage expression of sexuality, their power over the intimate life of the peasants was very limited. The peasants went about their daily lives without much intervention by the Church and the lords of the manor, and sexual behavior was not repressed. Compare this situation with that of the agricultural worker and the new working class of the modern era. The very rationalization and control over the lives of workers required by capitalist production made the matter of sexual repression both easier and more necessary. The worker had to keep his mind on his work. Whatever may have been the attitudes of the medieval Church on these matters, that of Puritanism and its later offshoots such as Methodism were much more repressive and reflected a much more limited actual situation in regard to sexual expression. Ideologies gain their meaning and strength from the concrete circumstances of life, and while the medieval Church may have discouraged sexuality in theory, the social relations of the emergent capitalism greatly repressed it in actuality.

Freud did not discover infantile and childhood sexuality; he rediscovered them, for in about the sixteenth century childhood had become a period set off from other periods, one in which open sexuality was not tolerated. Childhood became a time during which people learned to repress their sexuality and other natural desires. Thus, by the time they went to work they already had personalities that were adjusted to suppression and were tolerant of frustration.

At the heart of the changes that were required by the new organization of work were the changes in the nonrational behavior of the populace; in the totality of activity that we can think of as play and sexuality; in the sense of community; and in the replacement of the regulation of activity by custom with regulation by the operations of the market.[9]

Not only were there changes in the organization of work and concomitant reorganization of the personality to fit this new work arrangement; there were also important social and political changes, most important of which was the emergence of the state and of economic activity from general social life. In feudal society, relationships among people emphasized mutual dependency. People of lower status had to show deference to people of higher rank, and people of all levels had rights and obligations in regard to their relationships with all other persons in the society. While the serf lived on the lord's land and worked it, he could not be simply removed or sold at the will of his lord; the lord had rights to the land but could not sell it; the church and the lord were entitled to part of the produce of the land, in return for protecting their people. All relationships—economic, social, political, and religious—were intertwined with no easy separation among them. There were innumerable subtle gradations in status without sharp breaks and distinctions.

In the sixteenth and seventeenth centuries all of this began to change, most particularly in England. The philosophers Hobbes and Locke created a secular theology of the state and the economy which C. B. MacPhearson has called "possessive individualism."[10] With these theorists emerged a new view of man, society, and nature which was congruent with capitalist activity. The organic relationships among the individual, property, power, and the interests of the community were served. Contractual relationships replaced organic ones, as the authority of the state came to be seen as contractual. These views offered the theoretical dimension for freeing the use of property from what were now considered arbitrary restrictions, and the consequent expansion of the powers of the state. Social relations which had been governed by customary rights and duties, were now replaced by relatively unrestricted egoistic economic competition and the regulations of the state. While the state in seventeenth-century England was weak compared with the modern reality, it was much stronger than it had ever been before. Labor was no longer a customary obligation but a commodity to be bought and sold. The market and the state had replaced custom, community, kinship and man's natural affections as the nexus holding society together.

The need to suppress what had been most significant to them placed great stress and strain on human beings. Ultimately, what had to occur was not so much a changed personality as a rechanneled one. Since it was not possible to destroy totally previous behavior patterns, these had instead to become viewed as sinful and harmful and their opposites made into virtues of the highest order.

This process of repression and rechanneling of the human personality was carried forward first and more thoroughly and quickly in England than elsewhere. The more the process advanced, the more resistant the populace became. Jordan reminds us that in the sixteenth and seventeenth centuries the upper classes of England "were concerned with the apparent disintegration of social and moral controls at home; they fretted endlessly over the 'masterless men' who had once had a proper place in the social order but who were now wandering about, begging, robbing, raping."[11] What was to be called the "social question," the turbulence of the masses of men, had emerged as the central problem.

In the eighteenth century, as Karl Polaynai has demonstrated, the laws were altered so that these homeless men could be herded together into cities where they could become a pool of unskilled labor which would work for subsistence wages.[12] But as Edward

P. Thompson has demonstrated, the populace resisted. The new, emergent social order created opposition, and this opposition required new methods of social control.

Thompson gives a powerful description of the resistance of the general public to the new social relations:

> But, as industrial capitalism emerged, these rules of action appeared as unnatural and hateful restraints; the peasant, the rural labourer in the unenclosed village, even the urban artisan or apprentices did not measure the return of labour exclusively in money-earnings, and they rebelled against the notion of week after week of disciplined labour. In the way of life which Weber describes (unsatisfactorily) as "traditionalism," a man does not by nature wish to earn more and more money, but simply to live as he is accustomed to live and to earn as much as is necessary for that purpose. Even piece rates and other incentives lose effectiveness at a certain point if there is no inner compulsion; when enough is earned the peasant leaves industry and returns to his village, the artisan goes on a drunken spree.[13]

Racism came out of the context of this revolutionary rechanneling of human personality that was required by the new social, political, and economic order of modern capitalism. The extreme reactions of northern Europeans, particularly the English, to their meeting with West Africans in the sixteenth and seventeenth centuries can be understood if we comprehend the fact that West Africans of that period were in many ways very much like the Europeans had been and were trying to transcend. African economics were largely subsistence agricultural ones with customary work relations. Work was deeply embedded in ceremonial and religious practices, communities were close-knit and attitudes toward sexuality and the nonrational were comparatively nonrepressive. That is, the Africans were, whatever may have been their individual differences, very much like other non-urban peoples in societies whose life is dictated by hunting, pastoralism and farming.

The Englishman met the West African as a reformed sinner meets a comrade of his previous debaucheries. The reformed sinner very often creates a pornography of his former life. He must suppress even his knowledge that he had acted that way or even that he wanted to act that way. Prompted by his uneasiness at this great act of repression, he cannot leave alone those who live as he once did or as he still unconsciously desires to live. He must devote himself to their conversion or repression. In order to insure that he will not slip back into the old ways or act out his half-suppressed fantasies, he must see a tremendous difference between his reformed self and those whom he formerly resembled. But because he still has fantasies which he cannot accept, he must impute these fantasies to the realities of someone else. Thus, the English, who considered the Africans a "particularly libidinous people," also fantasized that they had seen African women publicly copulating with apes; and this fantasy they accepted as fact. They were actually imputing to the Africans acts which they themselves feared they might commit if they let loose the rigid controls they imposed on themselves.[14]

The English compared themselves with the Africans and congratulated themselves for being different and superior. Since they were able to resist these temptations, they reasoned they were superior to the black Africans who were apparently uncapable of such self-control. The Africans behaved as they did because of a different innate moral constitution.

What the English unconsciously realized about the Africans was not so much that they were different but that they were frighteningly similar. The Africans, while not having made the same technological advances, were obviously a functioning, creative, and perhaps even more satisfied and less gloomy people; and this the English and other northern Europeans found particularly threatening. They had to exaggerate the differences, changing them from ones of degree to ones of kind. They had, after all, to deny that about themselves which they wanted to abjure. They had, in a phrase, to "protest too much." The wild fluctuations of appropriate manners from the Elizabethan period to the Puritan period to the scandalous atmosphere of the Restoration indicate a people struggling with some major, but largely obscure, problem.

In light of such feelings among the British public, it follows that people in that offshoot of England, the American South, would manifest similar fears. Because of the constant presence of their black slaves, these fears were extended into a way of life; the imagined sexual proclivities of the African were an ever-present temptation to sin, but it was a temptation that had to be lived with because of the obvious profits to be gotten from black slavery.

Our analysis is corroborated by the slave narratives which offer revealing glimpses into the range of white reactions to blacks and to the institution of slavery in the South. We are presented with an entire gallery of Southern types, types that have appeared many times in American literature from Harriet Beecher Stowe to Mark Twain to William Faulkner and beyond.

The position of the Southern white woman was a peculiar one, and became markedly more so with the rise of the mid-nineteenth-century Victorian sensibilities. Placed by her men on a pedestal which was perhaps higher than any occupied by woman since the ladies of the medieval courts of love, the Southern woman was, for all this, only human. Sexuality, which was considered too gross a passion to merit even her passing acknowledgment, was nevertheless a fact of plantation life; and if the Southern gentlemen never mentioned it in polite society, and virtually ignored his own wife in such matters, he indulged himself with his slaves with varying degrees of discretion. The Southern lady suppressed her own sexuality and avoided this reality where she could, but under the intimate circumstances of plantation living, it was difficult. Thus we have the following story from Mom Ryer Emmanuel, who was a small child under slavery in South Carolina:

> Like I speak to you, my white folks was blessed wid a heap of black chillun, but den dere been a odd one in de crowd that wasn' noways like dem others. All de other chillun was black skin wid die here kinky hair en she was yellow skin wid right straight hair. My Lord, old Missus been mighty proud of her black chillun, but she sho been touches [touchy] bout dat yellow one. I remember, all us chillun was playing round bout de step one day whe' Miss Ross was settin en she ax dat yellow child, say, "Who your papa?" De child never know no better her right out [told] exactly de one her mammy had tell her was her papa. Lord, Miss Ross, she say, "Well, get off my step. Get off en stay off dere cause you don' noways belong to me." De poor child, she cry en she cry so hard till her mammy never know what to do. She take en grease her en black her all over wid smut, but she couldn' never trouble dat straight hair off her noway. Dat how-come dere so much different classes today, I say. Yes, man dat whe' dat old stain come from.[15]

A less specific case of cruelty was related by Jerr Hill, born a slave in 1852 on the South Carolina plantation of Jim Fernandes. Hill said that Fernandes' sister used to carry a bullwhip around her neck when she walked out on the farm, and would apply it herself to any slave she thought needed it.[16]

The capricious cruelty of such white Southern "ladies" was two-fold in its causation. On the one hand, they were jealous of the liaisons of their men with black women; on the other hand, many may have used this brutality as an outlet for their own repressed sexuality. Beating slaves was, in this case, one of the few acceptable alternatives.

The white Southern male, on the other hand, was not constrained by such attitudes, and certain lapses in correct behavior were tolerated by a society that recognized, though with some reluctance, the "animal" part of the male personality. Because his black slaves were, in the master's eye, full-time animals, they were considered suitable companions for drunken carousing as well as for sexual gratification; and if the slaves were not entirely willing to partake in the master's revels, they were in no position to disobey him. Thus the myth of the carefree slave just "a-singin' and a-dancin' " was perpetuated, as illustrated in this wonderfully grotesque picture drawn by Junius Quattlebaum, who was born into slavery in 1853:

> Marster lak to see his slaves happy and singin' bout de place. If he ever heard any of them quarrelin' wid each other, he would holler at them and say: "Sing! Us ain't got no time to fuss on dis place . . . ."
>
> [The master joined them when drunk at a corn-husking, passed the bottle around, and then commanded them:]
>
> "Everybody sing. Sing dis song: Pass 'round de bottle and we'll all take a drink." Some of them in de crowd 'jected to anything. Marster kinda scratch he head and say: "Well, let me git a pole and you all is gwine to sing." And singin' dere was, as sho' as you's born. Them niggers 'round de corn piles dat night h'isted dat song right now; dere was no waitin' for de pole or nothin' else. They wanted to sing, bad.
>
> [The next day the master was too sick to get the slaves to work, and there was a holiday.][11]

It was not an uncommon occurrence for such a master to later turn on his former companions and beat them for leading him into evil ways. Many of the narratives bear witness to the fact that the master was most dangerous just after he returned from having been "saved" at a revival meeting.

There are many accounts that deal with more successful paternalistic Southern white plantation owners. Some of the owners acted paternalistically because they were, quite literally, the fathers of some of their slaves. Stearlin Arwine, born in 1853 in Texas, had a master who owned four slave women and their children. Arwine's grandmother lived with the master and the three other women were the products of this liaison. In his will, the master freed all of them; however, the executor of his estate, a judge, took the slaves to work for himself and later sold them.[18]

Zack Herndon, born in South Carolina about 1846, said that while his master believed in slavery and owned a hundred slaves, he was a good man who allowed his slaves to marry as they pleased because he believed that God never intended "for no souls to be bred as if they was cattle, and he never practice no sech."[19]

Clearly the strains of seeing slaves, on the one hand, as mere beasts of burden and, on the other hand, of grudgingly admitting that they were human, were too great for the Southern white. Mark Twain's portrait of Huck Finn struggling between his fear of becoming implicated in the escape of Nigger Jim and his natural affections for the runaway slave illustrates the author's comprehension that, in his relationship to blacks, the white man was often a bit mad.[20]

If we can understand these strains placed upon the master class of the South, maintaining a life-style more closely resembling that of the eighteenth-century landed aristocracy than that of the nineteenth-century capitalist bourgeoisie, while at the same time viewing itself spiritually as a "democratic" bourgeoisie, we can understand its opposition to the transformation of the South into an industrial society (even one using slave labor), its romantic and fanatical opposition to abolition, and its general ineffectiveness in using its enormous social and political skills except to fight a reactionary, fratricidal war. Much of the contemporary South is still engaged in the fantastic effort to maintain the "Southern way of life," over a hundred years after the formal emancipation of the slaves.

Marvin Harris, in an essay on American racism, puzzles over the participation of poor whites who had nothing to gain by fighting for the Southern cause. "They fought because they were prejudiced," Harris writes, "but it is no ordinary prejudice that leads a man to kill another over his looks."[21]

We suggest that the answer to the problem raised by Harris and many others lies in the depth of the racism of the descendents of the seventeenth-century Englishmen, the first people to begin that perilous and difficult experience of rechanneling human personality to fit it into the necessities of the new capitalism. The very existence of organized society, of civilization, was wrapped up for these people in the maintenance of the "proper" relationships between the races. From the most reactionary and brutal to the most liberal and paternalistic, the Southern white believed that it was impossible for blacks and whites to live together on a level of equality. Not only did backcountry Mississippi redneck planters believe this, so did Thomas Jefferson.[22] Indeed, so did Abraham Lincoln and most of the leading New England white abolitionists. All were fearful that emancipation would mean miscegenation and this, they felt certain would be bad for the nation.

A leading historian of West Indian slavery, Elsa Goveia, has argued that it was difficult for the West Indian whites to conceive of the abolition of slavery because "The slave system had become more than an economic enterprise which could be abandoned when it ceased to be profitable. It had become the very basis of organized society throughout the British West Indies, and therefore it was believed to be an indispensable element in maintaining the existing social structure and in preserving law and order in the community."[23] Yet the West Indian whites could eventually accept abolition peacefully because they did not actually have to live among a population of free blacks. In the West Indies many plantations had always been owned by absentee owners and few whites thought of the West Indies as the place where they intended to live all their lives. The West Indian planters returned to England in large numbers even before slavery was abolished in the 1830s and those that remained knew they were always free to pick up and leave, transferring their capital from agriculture to British industry.[24]

But in the United States, few could conceive of such action, despite the fact that more lucrative and satisfactory industrial investments would have allowed for the economic and social development of the South at a much greater rate. Abolition of slavery would have required accepting the equal coexistence of whites and blacks in the same territory, an idea which was out of the question for almost all whites—and there was nowhere else either they or the blacks could go.

Slavery was maintained in the South even though in the long run it was not the most economically profitable method of utilizing Southern resources. There is no doubt, after the work of Eugene Genovese and others, that while individual planters certainly did make profits from slavery, American slavery was ultimately very inefficient and Southern planters were constantly in debt to Yankees and English merchants.[25]

Southern slavery was both patriarchal and paternalistic and, at the same time, a system that by the nineteenth century systematically overworked the slaves. Very often the paternalistic patriarchal master, racist to the core, but "kindly," would abdicate direct responsibility for the direction of the work of the slaves and turned it over to an overseer. Many slaves reported that their masters did not even recognize them when they met in town. This system weakened the moral defense of slavery as a means of "saving" black souls by example, and allowed for great exploitation, but on a very inefficient basis. Karl Marx wrote about this situation:

> . . . as soon as people, whose production still moves within the lower forms of slave-labour, corvee-labour, &c., are drawn into the whirlpool of an international market dominated by the capitalistic mode of production, the sale of their products for export becoming their principal interest, the civilized horrors of over-work are grafted on the barbaric horrors of slavery, serfdom, &c. Hence the negro labour in the Southern States of the American Union preserved something of a patriarchal character, so long as production was chiefly directed to immediate local consumption. But in proportion, as the export of cotton became of vital interest to these states, the overworking of the negro and sometimes the using up of his life in 7 years' of labour became a factor in a calculated and calculating system.[26]

The more slavery was incorporated into the world capitalist market, and the more paternalism became obviously limited by great exploitation, the more the slave owners tended to withdraw from reality and to build up, even for themselves, the image of patriarchal, paternalistic relations. The less true in fact it was, the more the Southern master class believed that slavery was beneficial, the more they became systematically blind to its horrors, and the more they either turned its operations over to overseers or sold their slaves to new men who were hacking plantations out of the bottom lands of the Mississippi. Slavery, many Southern gentlemen and ladies believed, saved them from becoming either stingy, narrow, money-grubbing entrepreneurs (a fate worse than death itself to gracious hostesses and paternalistic masters), or from becoming industrial proletarians instead of poor whites living on marginal lands and pretending to be grand slave owners. The "peculiar institution" of the South kept industrial capitalism and its accompanying commercial psychology from "corrupting" the South—and in so doing, corrupted it in other, more significant ways. In a quite literal sense,

Southern slavery produced a reactionary ruling class which could not move from agriculture to industry and commerce easily. Throughout the South, immigrants, often Yankees or Jews, were the merchants, it being usually beneath the dignity of a planter to descend to the operations of a business as opposed to being part of "a way of life"; external merchants, Yankee and English, profited greatly out of the trade that Southerners could have controlled if they had so wished, if they had not been so blinded by the reactionary view of the world that slavery produced in them.

Those involved in the modern, capitalist world, even those critical of it at times, often find it difficult to understand that social classes often do not, cannot, act out of rational, economic self-interest. Both Karl Marx and Max Weber understood this, but many liberal economic determinists do not. For fear of being misunderstood, it would be best to state our point of view clearly. Social classes entrenched as the rulers of reactionary social systems, ones that by their very nature do not utilize all the natural and technological resources available at a given time, do not act out of narrow economic self-interest, but, rather, out of fantasies that no longer have even the vaguest coincidence with reality.[27] *Southern planters chose to oppose industrialism precisely and only because they were entrenched in a social system whose maintenance they desired, and this social system could not exist without racism.* There is no other explanation for the fact that the great intellectual talents of such Southern spokesmen as George Fitzhugh were utilized to develop tortured ideological defenses of the enslavement of their fellow men.

While the planter class could have and to some slight extent did use slaves in industry, for the most part they did not because they chose not to do so because they feared industry itself as a threat to the Southern way of life. Moreover, they refused to acquire the skills necessary for industry and commerce. Anyone who has examined the books of Southern slave plantations knows that the methods of bookkeeping were generally much more primitive and crude than those that prevailed in the North or in England at the same period. Even such simple skills were not learned by the plantocracy.

Eugene Genovese writes that "a ruling class does not grow up simply according to the tendencies inherent in its relationship to the means of production; it grows up in relationship to the specific class or classes it rules."[28] The slave system was inefficient and the masters made this vice into a virtue. W. E. B. DuBois was not in our view at all facetious when he accounted for the lack of a suitable work ethic among the Southern blacks by suggesting that they were only following the model of Southern whites.[29]

One more point need be made here. Why did the North abolish slavery gradually before the Civil War? Why were the racist fears of Northern whites in an essentially English culture not as extreme as those of Southerners? Part of the answer is demographic, part a matter of the psychology of social class. In the old North, blacks made up a relatively small percentage of the population because the patterns of settlement and the nature of the land did not lead to the domination of the plantation system. Slavery could be replaced by other methods of social control over a relatively tiny black population—an elaborate system of segregation of churches, schools, and residences was established. Moreover, as has been recently demonstrated, prominent Northern and Midwestern whites took the lead in terrorizing the black community in a series of riots and similar acts in order to keep them under control. Blacks were largely confined to certain occupations and by the 1850s free blacks in the North had begun to be pushed out of skilled and semi-skilled artisanry. It was not that Northerners and Midwesterners were less racist, but that they were more *successfully* racist. Uncorrupted by a large slave population, the Yankee variant of the work ethic did not degenerate as it did in the South, but was greatly enhanced. The iron will and stern self-discipline of many Yankee merchants could be directed to the organization of totally non-paternalistic, repressive attacks on the black population of the North.[30]

Slavery was itself a form of social control over the black population and, consequently, Southern racism could in fact afford to be "softer" than Northern racism. Consequently, Southern whites had, and still have much more daily social contact with blacks than did and do Northern whites. W. E. B. DuBois brilliantly understood this almost seventy years ago when he declared in *The Souls of Black Folks* that with the adoption of the Thirteenth Amendment to the Constitution, abolishing slavery, racism replaced slavery as the method of social control over the black community.[31] We can see this process dramatically in operation in the reports in the slave narratives of how slavery was replaced by sharecroppers and how the Ku Klux Klan was utilized to terrorize the black population, now not controlled by slavery.

As one reads through the slave narratives, one is constantly impressed by the fact that many ex-slaves did not see any crucial difference between their pre- and post-slavery way of life. They often lived in the same slave cabin, on the same plantation, with the heirs of the old master, and worked the land on shares. Patrols to keep them in line and paternalistic relationships with certain whites existed as before. In fact, a considerable number of ex-slaves did not know that they were free until sometime after the event.

Andy Marion, an ex-slave from South Carolina, born in 1844, who had been a carriage driver, reported:

> I was free three years befo' I knowed it. Worked along just de same. One day we was in de field on Mr. Chris Brice's place. Man came along on a big, black horse, tail platted and tied with a red ribbon. Stopped, waves his hands and shouted "You is free, all of you. Go anywhere you wants to." Us quit right then and acted de fool. We ought to have gone to de white folks 'bout it. What did de Yankees do when they come? They tied me up by my two thumbs, try to make me tell where I hided de money and gold watch and silver, but I swore I didn't know . . . . Marster was mightly glad dat I was a faithful servant, and not a liar and a thief lak he thought I was. My marster was not a Ku Klux. They killed some obstreppary [obstreperous] niggers in them times.[32]

Fred James, born in South Carolina in 1856, said:

> I 'member when freedom come, old marse said, "you is all free, but you can work on and make dis crop of corn and cotton; den I will divide up wid you when Christmas comes." Dey all worked, and when Christmas come, marse told us we could get on and shuffle for ourselves, and he didn't give us anything. We had to steal corn out of de crib. We prized de ears out between de cracks and took dem home and parched dem. We would have to eat on dese for several days. We had to work all day, sun up to dark, and never nad Saturday afternoons off anytime. My mammy had to wash clothes on Saturday nights for us to wear on Sundays.[33]

Jimmie Johnson was a "faithful" servant to the end. Born in Virginia, in 1847, he went with his new master to South Carolina. His new mistress taught him to read and when he was orphaned his master made a special "pet" out of him. When he was told that he was free by his mistress, after the master died, he stayed with her and protected her until she died. He reported that he had played with his master when they both were boys and were lifelong friends.[34]

Mary Anderson, born a slave in 1851, graphically told the story of how the old social relations were virtually reestablished after the war was over. The slaves had all left the plantation with the Northern army. But it was hard for many of them to find anyway to live. Consequently,

> The second year after the surrender our marster and missus got on their carriage and went looked up all the Negroes they heard of who ever belonged to them. Some who went off with the Yankees were never heard of again. When marster and missus found any of theirs they would say, "Well, come on back home." My father and mother, two uncles and their families moved back. Several of the young men and women who once belonged to him come back. Some were so glad to get back they cried, 'cause fare had been mighty bad part of the time they were rambling around and they were hungry. When they got back marster would say, "Well you have come back home have you," and the Negroes would say, "Yes Marster." Most all spoke of them as missus and marster as they did before the surrender, and getting back home was the greatest pleasure of all. We stayed with marster and missus and went to their church, the Maple Springs Baptist church, until they died.[35]

There were many different arrangements right after slavery was abolished with the former slaves, including paying them wages for working, but the most common was sharecropping. In some instances, the ex-slaves arranged to buy the plantation as a group, as "common tenants."[36] Sometimes, the old master would divide the plantation into forty-acre plots and sell the plots, on credit, to every family. Usually, however, the ex-slaves found themselves without these small farms as, being illiterate, they had no way of assuring their title to the land and it was a very easy matter to challenge the title and get the land away from them and back into white hands.[37]

Not only were the ex-slaves very largely tied again to the land in a servile status but a new form of social control, built upon the activities of the old slave patrols, was created: the Ku Klux Klan. The Klan systematically went out to terrorize all of the ex-slaves. Claiborne Moss told of one such incident:

> The Ku Klux got after Uncle Will once. He was a brave man. He had a little mare that was a race horse. Will rode right through the bunch before they ever realized that it was him. He got on

the other side of them. She was gone! They kept on after him. They went down to his house one night. He wouldn't run for nothing. He shot two of them and they went away. Then he was out of ammunition. People urged him to leave, for they knew he didn't have no more bullets; but he wouldn't and they came back and killed him.

They came down to Hancock County one night and the boys hid on both sides of the bridge. When they got in the middle of the bridge, the boys commenced to fire on them from both sides, and they jumped into the river. The darkies went on home when they got through shooting at them, but there wasn't no more Ku Klux in Hancock County.[38]

G. W. Hawkins, an ex-slave, said of the Ku Klux Klan:

The Ku Klux Klan weren't just after Negroes. They got after white folks and Negroes both. I didn't think they were so much after keeping the Negro from voting as some other things . . . . The main thing the Ku Klux seemed to try to do, it seemed to me, was to try to keep the colored folks obedient to their former masters and to keep the white folks from giving them too much influence. And they wanted to stop the white man that ran after colored women.[39]

Other slaves reported that the Klan's main function was to make sure that black people were honest and not sexually promiscuous.

The struggle between blacks and whites after slavery was a violent, unrelenting battle for many. The sense of the harsh conflict between ex-slaves and the Ku Klux Klan comes through in one magnificent account with great force. H. B. Holloway, born in 1848 of free mixed Indian, Spanish, and black parents, told the following story:

I have been in big riots. I was in the Atlanta riots in 1891. We lost about forty men, and I don't know how many the white folks lost, but they said it was about a hundred. I used to live there. I came here in 1892.

We had a riot there when the KKK was raising so much Cain. The first Ku Klux wore some kind of hat that went over the man's head and shoulders and had great big red eyes on it. They broke open my house one night to whip me.

I was working as a foreman in the shops. One night as I was going home, some men stopped and said, "Who are you." I answered, "H. B. Holloway." Then they said, "Well, we'll be over to your house tonight to whip you."

I said, "We growed up together and you couldn't whip me then. How you 'spect to do it now. You might kill me, but you can't beat me."

And one of them said, "Well we'll be over to see you at eleven thirty tonight, and we are going to beat you."

[Holloway armed his sons and was able to drive off the attackers. One injured man was left behind.]

My eldest son said the man said, "Holloway, don't hit me no more."

I didn't, but if I had known who he was then, I would have gone out and cut his throat. He was old Colonel Troutman's son. There was just two hours difference in our birth. Me and him both nursed from the same breast. We grew up together and were never separated until we were thirteen (beginning of the war). Many people thought we were brothers. I had fought for him and he had fought for me. When he wasn't at my house, I was at his, and his father partly raised me. That's the reason I don't trust white people.

[A while later another group of white men rode up, led by Colonel Troutman.]

Colonel Troutman said, "We just wanted to talk to you Holloway."
I said, "Stand right where you are and talk."

After some talk, I let them come up slowly to a short distance from me. The upshot of the whole thing was that they wanted me to go back to town with them to "talk" over the matter. They allowed I hadn't done nothin' wrong. But Colonel Troutman's son was hurt bad, and some of the young men in the mob had had their legs broke. And they were all young men from the town, boys that knew me and were friendly to me in the daytime. Still they wanted me to go to town in their charge, and I knew I wouldn't have a chance if I did that. Finally I told Colonel Troutman, that I was going home to see my wife that evening, and that if he wanted to talk to me, he could come over there and talk.

When they left, I sent the boys along home and told them to tell my wife. That night when I got home, Colonel Troutman was in the house talking to my wife. I went in quietly. He said that they said I had forty Niggers hid in the house that night. I told him that there wasn't anybody there but me and my family, and that all the damage that was done I done myself. He said that well he didn't blame me; that even if it was his son, they broke in on me and I had a right to defend my family, and that none of the old heads was going to do anything about it. He said I was a good man and had never given anybody any trouble and that there wasn't any excuse for anybody comin' stirrin' up trouble with me. And that was the end of it.[40]

In the struggle to maintain the subordination of blacks in American society, particularly within the South, racism as a method of social control to replace slavery was strengthened. Charles S. Johnson, on the basis of a study of ex-slave narratives, some of which were collected under his direction, concluded in the mid-1930s that "The plantation technique on the side of administration was most effective in respect to discipline and policing, and this technique has survived more or less despite the formal abolition of slavery."[41] The South moved toward a steady strengthening of racism in the quarter of a century after the black struggle during Reconstruction for real freedom was lost.[42] When slavery was no longer the mark of demarcation between the races, a much more elaborate racial code which would now for the first time *segregate* blacks from whites was created. On the plantation under slavery there had been a great deal of social contact between the masters and slaves, including a great deal of sexual activity. As we have seen, one of the aims of the Ku Klux Klan was to transform white male sexual patterns from ones where relationships with black women were normal and quasi-sanctioned to a situation where such relationships were seen as abnormal and against which strong negative sanctions were enforced. Social contact between whites and blacks was increasingly prohibited by informal sanctions and by laws which went so far as to prohibit black and white workers from sharing the same factory window.[43] One ex-slave, Ambus Gray, born in 1857, summed it up quite well: "Here in the South the colored folks is free and they're not free. The white folks get it all anyway. . . ."[44]

As historians have demonstrated, the defeat of black aspirations in the South and thus throughout the nation was as much the result of the abandonment of blacks by Northern whites as of the struggles of Southern whites. One ex-slave, Henry Jenkins, born in 1850 in South Carolina, demonstrated that the insights of historians are often only the painful reconstruction of what the masses of people know directly. Speaking of Reconstruction, he said:

> When de Yankees come, what they do? They did them things they ought not to have done and they let undone de things they ought to have done. Yes, dat just 'bout tells it. One thing you might like to hear. Mistress got all de money, de silver, de gold and de jewels, and got de well digger to hide them in de bottom of de well. Them Yankees smart. When they got dere, they asked for de ve'y things at de bottom of de well. Mistress wouldn't tell. They held a court of 'quiry in de yard; called slaves up, one by one, good many. Must have been a Judas 'mongst us. Soon a Yankee was let down in de well, and all dat money, silver, gold, jewelry, watches, rings, brooches, knives and forks, butter-dishes, water goblets, and cups was took and carried 'way by a army dat seemed more concerned 'bout stealin', than they was 'bout de Holy War for de liberation of de poor African slave people.[45]

This heritage of the plantation, fundamentally unchanged from the years before the Civil War, was evident in a significant way in the South at least through the beginning of World War II and, indeed, it has only been in the 1950s and 1960s that a movement away from the plantation relationship came to fruition. It might not be too much to suggest that the beginnings of the black revolution of the 1960s were more dependent on the end of the plantation system dominating the lives of Southern blacks than upon any other single factor.

In a unique autobiography, a black automobile worker from Detroit, born and raised on a plantation in southeast Tennessee, offered the following description of the plantation system at the end of World War I. Matthew Ward, born in 1907, described a patriarchal but brutal plantation:

> There was the Harvey Place; the father was the sheriff of Leavitt County at one time. All Negroes tried to stay away from that plantation. The Harveys would insist that Negroes borrow money or get credit and then they would have to live on the Harvey farm. If they wouldn't the Harveys would force them. The Harvey's didn't allow any law enforcement on their place. They had to settle everything on the farm themselves. This farm was the farm of slavery. Everyone said slavery had been abolished everywhere in the United

States except on the Harvey Place. We called them bad white people . . . . Old Harvey had many Negroes working for him who had committed both minor and serious crimes. He'd go to court and tell the Negro he'd get him off his offense if he'd come work for him. But this meant he could never get away from Harvey again. Harvey never tried to murder a Negro who ran away, he would capture and bring him back . . . . On the Harvey plantation it was slavery and this was true.[46]

What the blacks on the Harvey place may not have been aware of was that the shadow of the slave plantation was wide enough to cover much of the South. The social relations of slavery did not disappear on a large number of farms and plantations in the American Southland until the mechanization of agriculture during the 1930s and 1940s and the drawing into the industrial working class of millions of those like Ward who had been born on old-time Southern plantations.

## Notes

1. Philip D. Curtin, *The Atlantic Slave Trade*, pp. 28–34; for a provocative, if at times questionable, comparative discussion of slavery and racism in Brazil and the United States, see Carl Degler, *Neither Black nor White: Slavery and Race Relations in Brazil and the United States*.

2. Eugene D. Genovese, *The World the Slaveholders Made*, p. 105. The first essay in Genovese's book is the essential point of departure for this chapter. Genovese offers a pioneering exploration of the subject but does not go far enough in the development of a view of the relationship between racism and capitalism.

3. Winthrop Jordan, *White Over Black: American Attitudes Toward the Negro, 1550–1812*, pp. 40–43.

4. See Degler, *Neither Black Nor White*.

5. David Brion Davis, *The Problem of Slavery in Western Culture*, seems to suggest this, although the richness and subtle treatment of his presentation indicates a much richer understanding than this. The same might be said of Jordan's equally fine book, *White Over Black*.

6. Marvin Harris, *Patterns of Race in the Americas* (New York, 1964).

7. Genovese, *The World the Slaveholders Made*, p. 105.

8. Michel Foucault, *Madness and Civilization*.

9. Philippe Ariès, *Centuries of Childhood: A Social History of Family Life*. See also Herbert Marcuse, *Eros and Civilization*, and Norman O. Brown, *Life Against Death: The Psychoanalytical Meaning of History*. Embedded in all of these works is that great underground classic of modern thought Wilhelm Reich, *Character Analysis*, 3d ed. rev., first published in German in 1933, and its less well-known but significant companion, Wilhelm Reich, *The Mass Psychology of Fascism*, first published in German in 1933. While I cannot subscribe to all of Reich's system, this chapter could not have

been written without his monumental attempt to relate Marx and Freud which loosened the ideological armouring of Western rationalism for me and many others. This chapter is conceived of as a preliminary exploration of the emergence of the ideology of the capitalist era. The complex interplay between ideology and the other activities of day-to-day life can best be understood if we ask the question, "Under what circumstances can ideas which have already been developed direct the ordinary activities of ordinary people?" For example, while there is no doubt that the Christian fathers of medieval Europe did not encourage open sexuality, their ideas did not have much power over the intimate life of peasants whose lives were much less regimented than those of modern industrial workers. The very rationalization and control over the life of the worker required by capitalist industrial production and social relations made sexual repression more necessary and easier. The worker has to keep his mind on his work, as well as his body at his machine. Puritanism developed Christian thought under the particular circumstances of the bourgeois revolution, and what had been the ideas of isolated clerics became dominant over the minds of ordinary people.

10. C. B. MacPhearson, *Possessive Individualism.*

11. Jordan, *White Over Black,* p. 42. The first chapter of Jordan's book, a work of deep scholarship, offers great insights, and in a sense this chapter is an attempt to make explicit the significance of this work, and then to suggest lines for its development. As this work was being prepared for the press, I came across an essay by Gary B. Nash in which, using Jordan's work, he comes to similar conclusions to mine about the relationship between the transformations of the sixteenth and seventeenth centuries in England and the rise of racism. After presenting the thesis, however, he does not develop it. See Gary B. Nash, "Red, White and Black: The Origins of Racism in Colonial America," in Gary B. Nash and Richard Weiss, eds., *The Great Fear: Race in the Mind of America,* p. 15.

12. Karl Polanyai, *The Great Transformation* (New York, 1949).

13. Edward P. Thompson, *The Making of the English Working Class* (London, 1963), p. 357.

14. See Jordan, *White Over Black,* p. 31. Jordan notes that Thomas Herbert, the author of a book, published in 1634, recounting travels in Africa and Asia, said that there sometimes occurred "a beastly copulation" between apes and black women.

15. FWPSN, South Carolina, Part 2, p. 14.

16. Ibid., p. 136.

17. Ibid., Part 3, pp. 283–284.

18. FWPSN, Texas, Part 1, pp. 31–33.

19. FWPSN, South Carolina, Part 2, p. 273.

20. Mark Twain, *Huckleberry Finn,* p. 125 ff.

21. Marvin Harris, "The Origins of the Descent Rule," in *Slavery in the New World,* ed. Laura Foner and Eugene D. Genovese, p. 57.

22. See Jordan, *White over Black,* pp. 429–481, for a discussion of Jefferson's views on race.

23. Elsa V. Goveia, *Slave Society in the British Leeward Islands at the End of the Eighteenth Century,* p. 329. See also Elsa V. Goveia, "The West Indian Slave Laws of the Eighteenth Century," *Revista de Ciencias Sociales* 4 (1960):75–105. This article is more easily available as reprinted in *Slavery in the New World,* ed. Foner and Genovese, pp. 113–137.

24. Eric Williams, *Capitalism and Slavery.*

25. Genovese, *The Political Economy of Slavery.* See in particular Genovese's "A Note On the Place of Economics in the Political Economy of

Slavery," ibid., pp. 275-287. This note contains Genovese's "From Economics to Political Economy: Eight Theses."

26. Karl Marx, *Capital* (Chicago, 1906), Vol. 1, p. 260.

27. It is important to note that social classes, when they are past their creative period, act in ways that indicate an increasing departure from the observation of reality. While there is more than this type of social derangement involved, for example, in the persistence of the American war in Southeast Asia, at a time when the overwhelming majority of the American population are against the continuation of the war, can it be denied that such social madness plays an important role in the continuation of the war?

28. Genovese, *The World the Slaveholders Made*, p. 5.

29. W. E. B. Du Bois, *Black Reconstruction*, p. 35.

30. See Leonard L. Richards, *"Gentlemen of Property and Standing": Anti-Abolition Mobs in Jacksonian America* (New York, 1970).

31. Du Bois, *The Souls of Black Folk*, see Chapter 2, pp. 54-78. In it, Du Bois shows how the Freedman's Bureau was transformed into an agency of social control and became the agent of a new form of exploitation—one justified by racist doctrines and given institutional form.

32. FWPSN, South Carolina, Part 3, p. 170.

33. Ibid., Part 2, p. 14.

34. Ibid., pp. 53-55.

35. FWPSN, North Carolina, Part 1, p. 26.

36. See, for example, FWPSN, South Carolina, Part 4, p. 176.

37. See, for example, FWPSN, Arkansas, Part 3, p. 106.

38. Ibid., p. 164.

39. Ibid., p. 217.

40. Ibid., pp. 298-302.

41. Charles S. Johnson, *The Shadow of the Plantation*, p. 210.

42. C. Vann Woodward, *The Strange Career of Jim Crow*.

43. Harold M. Baron, "The Demand for Black Labor: Historical Notes on the Political Economy of Racism," *Radical America* 5 (1971):24.

44. FWPSN, Arkansas, Part 3, p. 103.

45. FWPSN, South Carolina, Part 3, p. 26.

46. Matthew Ward, *Indignant Heart*, p. 20.

# RACISM AND
# THE MAKING OF
# AMERICAN SOCIETY

America was born nearly free and racist. Class division among whites and the sense of class were much less sharp than in Europe.[1] There was no extensive feudal aristocracy, although there was a degree of class privilege. There was a seemingly endless supply of land. In such a society, men could contract one with another voluntarily to construct a new society.

But almost from the beginning American Indians and ɔlacks were permanently excluded from the social contract.[2] Race and ethnic consciousness was more evident than class consciousness. As long as that has been true, the promise of American life, the full promise of the Declaration of Independence of "life, liberty, and the pursuit of happiness," has been denied for both white and nonwhite.

Social contract in America has not been mere political theory. It has been popular experience. Men fight, debate, vote, and live by the decisions they make until circumstances demand changes. The earlier contract is therefore revoked and a new one initiated.

In the seventeenth and eighteenth centuries, Americans often resorted to the contract to found governments: the Mayflower Compact of 1620; the Plantation Agreement of Roger Williams and a group of religious dissenters in the wilderness of Rhode Island; the Charter Oath of Thomas Hooker and his followers who had moved from Massachusetts to what is now Connecticut; the Albany Union Plan of 1754; the Association document of 1774 in which the colonies joined together to form a Continental Congress; and the Declaration of Independence. White Americans voluntarily constructed a free government.

With the achievement of independence, the social contract took another, even more revolutionary, turn. It became the device for the expression of the direct democracy of the people. Wave after wave of settlers moved westward, establishing new municipalities and colonies by covenant. Bringing only what they could carry in their wagons and in their heads, they created a series of havens in the wilderness. When they grew tired or dissatisfied with what they had done, they picked themselves up and moved on to repeat the process elsewhere. And as they did this, they exterminated the American Indian, discriminated against Mexicans, and preserved slavery at least in those areas in which it already existed.

One of the extraordinary offshoots of the experience of actual social contract was the hundreds of utopian socialist colonies created in the early part of the nineteenth century. Although the best known of these was the Brook Farm Association of the American Transcendentalists, with which most of the outstanding intellectual and literary figures of the day were associated, the most successful was the founding by the Latter-Day Saints of the new Zion in the Utah wilderness of the salt flats near the Great Salt Lake. And while this was a movement in which all class distinctions were to be obliterated, with rich and poor alike eligible for sainthood, blacks were excluded.

As long as the voluntary social contract was continually renewed in a society of equals—a society in which most white men could realistically hope for the opportunity to pursue happiness and had a realistic chance of material success—the state played a minimal role in human affairs. Henry David Thoreau could go up on a hill above Concord after spending a night in jail for refusing to pay his church tax, declare that "the State was nowhere" to be seen and do so without being hopelessly wrong.[3]

Yet while white people often did not feel the presence of the state, black people always did. It was present in the form of the patrollers, the local sheriffs, the operations of the Fugitive Slave Law, and potentially in every white person who might act to defend the laws that preserved slavery.

It was this difference of experience with the state that largely accounts for the conflict between white radical abolitionists like William Lloyd Garrison and black abolitionists like Frederick Douglass. Garrison could simply declare himself against union with slaveholders, and thereby oppose political struggle against slavery. Douglass, on the other hand, was black. He knew of the operations of the state. Radical as he was, he never gave up political struggle. He created something of a scandal in the abolitionist movement when he arranged to pay his old master for his freedom. The Garrisonians saw this as an unprincipled acknowledgment of the morality of slavery; Douglass, the fugitive slave, saw it as a very practical way of resisting the operations of the Fugitive Slave Act, in which all citizens were obliged to aid in the capture of runaway slaves, even in the free states.

American society in the first part of the nineteenth century had been one in which property was widely diffused and in which social mobility had been relatively easy. There was a rough egalitarianism of manners and customs, and there was neither the power of church nor state to oppress the individual. At the end of the eighteenth century, an overwhelming majority of Americans were outside of the organized churches, and very few felt the power of the state. On the frontier, the populace saw neither judge nor preachers, sheriff nor powerful entrepreneur, from almost one year to the next. There were some who were wealthier and more powerful than others, and there were those who were treated with contempt. But these social facts did not dominate reality, and there was a sense that each man had committed his destiny to the community in whose creation he had played a part.

And when that society was threatened by the extension of slavery, Lincoln said that his sole purpose was to maintain it as a free Union. This was not mere political rhetoric nor a simple method for evading the slavery issue as has often been charged. Lincoln was defending what he, along with the common people of America, believed to be the heart of the whole American experience—the social contract. When Lincoln referred to the Union as mankind's last, best hope, he was invoking the social experience of the revolutionary generation and bringing it to bear against the claim of the South that a nation formed by the will of the people could be abruptly broken by a conspiracy of slave owners.

In order to preserve the essence of that Union, the society of free men, Lincoln could become a revolutionary and fight for the natural rights of men, which, after all, were what the social contract was to preserve. He could move to emancipate the slaves and use them in the military struggle. And there is little reason to believe that if he had lived, he would not have waged a struggle for a new birth of freedom for all men, black and white. Lincoln, the common man as democrat, had in the war itself begun to overcome his racism.

The Civil War brought with it a revolution in American life—the triumph of industrial capitalism and the ending of the society of rough equality. And while the common people opposed this, their struggle was defeated by their own racism. Despite the promise of the American life, the common American white man, the perpetual innocent, allowed the egalitarianism that had been present at the beginning to get out of his grasp. The solidarity of being white limited or distorted the solidarity of being a factory worker, dirt farmer, or white-collar employee. American reform movements, agrarian populism, and working-class movements were to be checked by racism.

This has been so not due simply to an ideology of racism, but to the reality that so long as there is a socially separated nonwhite population, there seems to be a way for whites to avoid being heavily represented in the pool of unskilled workers who are the unemployed in a society that in normal times always has a core of unemployed. In the past, whites have had reason to believe that they could avoid becoming part of a classic proletariat, although there was much illusion in their belief. While in fact the majority of the poor are usually white, blacks always are very overrepresented at the bottom of the American class structure. The belief that black workers can be made to carry a greater share of unemployment, underemployment, and low wages is based on a significant amount of concrete evidence.

But it is also true that whenever blacks have advanced in America, white workers as a class have moved forward. Karl Marx observed:

> In the United States of America, every independent movement of workers was paralysed so long as slavery disfigured a part of the Republic. Labour cannot emancipate itself in the white skin where in the black it is branded. But out of the death of slavery a new life at once arose. The first fruit of the Civil War was the eight hours' agitation, that ran with seven-leagued boots of the locomotive from the Atlantic to the Pacific, from New England to California.[4]

By the 1830s, when the first evidence of a modern industrial system in the United States appeared, the relationship between white and black workers had begun to be utilized to weaken the working class. Frederick Douglass, the ex-slave who became the leader of American blacks, understood this relationship and its consequence. He wrote:

> The hostility between the whites and blacks is easily explained. It has its roots and sap in the relation of slavery and was incited on both sides by the cunning of the slave masters. These masters secured their ascendency over the poor whites and the blacks by putting emnity between them. They divided both to conquer each.[5]

In the South, the poor whites were often denied an opportunity to enter nonagricultural employment and at the same time were unable to become slave owners with large estates. On the other hand, poor whites found employment as members of the slave-patrols to keep the blacks in line.

Some poor whites were pushed onto the poor land of the Appalachians, the clay soils of northern Louisiana, northern Alabama, and Arkansas, and onto marginal lands elsewhere in the South. Others left the South and migrated into Ohio, Indiana, Illinois, Missouri, Kansas, and Nebraska.

In the North, blacks either were used to drive wages down or kept out of the labor market entirely. White artisans struggled to get blacks excluded from the skilled trades and eventually drove many from the cities after a series of riots. White and black workers were continually pitted against each other, with black workers being pushed out by white workers—and white workers accepting less from employers in return.[6]

This division between black and white workers grew during the Civil War. The war had begun with much of the white working class sympathetic to preserving the Union and keeping out slave competition. Northern white workers volunteered in unprecedented numbers to answer Lincoln's call to arms. And this support was by no means cynical, although it clearly was not purely humanitarian. Free soil and free men were inseparably linked in the minds of the white population.

But the corruption of the emerging industrial capitalism dispersed these energies. The white working class in a period in which the rich could and did buy their way out of the army by hiring substitutes, came to see the struggle as a rich man's war and a poor man's fight. Initially the Northern army was a remarkably loyal one, but the seeds of disillusionment in the rank-and-file soldier were present at the beginning. In a little-known address to Congress on July 4, 1861, Abraham Lincoln declared:

> It is worthy to note that while in this, the government's hour of
> trial, large numbers of those in the Army and Navy, who have
> been favored with the offices, have resigned, and proved false to
> the hand which had pampered them, not one common soldier, or
> common sailor is known to have deserted his flag.[1]

The very problem of the corruption of the officer corps—that
group of placemen often more interested in pelf, power, glory,
and adventure than in the actual struggle—led to massive disillusionment on the part of the Northern urban population, faced with
inflation and scarcity at home. Army officers and civilians grew
rich during the war, and the conflict dragged on. The Northern
armies could not muster the enthusiasm or spirit to pursue the enemy
very often because their officers were otherwise occupied.

The split in American society between the mass movement of
the population and the profiteering of advancing capitalism is a
crucial part of the story of the Civil War. Because there was little
attention paid to the morale and views of the soldiers, they often
became disaffected from a war that threatened to end slavery.

The draft riots of 1863 in New York City were symptomatic
of this widespread anger with the corruption of the war. The poor-
est layers of the working class, hit by wartime inflation, reacted,
often incited by Southern agents and supporters. Thousands rioted
against the draft and against blacks for days, beating up and killing
freedmen, invading the homes of the rich on Upper Broadway,
and threatening the very stability of the society and the progress
of the war.

Many thousands of whites refused to renew their enlistments,
and the fate of the army was at stake. At that point, Lincoln bowed
to the pressures of the abolitionists and called upon the slaves and
free blacks to join the army. More than 200,000 flocked to the
colors.

Some, learning from the lessons of the draft riots, tried to unite
the white abolitionists, the blacks, the working class, and the small
farmers in a single movement to turn the war into a crusade for
the preservation of the basis of egalitarian democracy. Wendell
Phillips, the son of a Boston Federalist family, Harvard educated,
a man of leisure, called for such a unity. He looked for the continuation of the struggle for the realization of the Declaration of Independence in a new working class movement that would unite black

and white. Moreover, he believed that working people would gain control over their own lives only if black rights were secured within the working class movement.[8]

But such efforts were not to be successful often enough. While, in some localities, blacks and whites did join during and after the war in common struggles, this was not to remain the case. From 1864 to the end of the century, efforts were made to link black and white in a single radical and working-class movement, but these eventually failed. Thus, despite the pleas of William Sylvis of the National Labor Union, this earliest national organization of workers remained white. A similar fate was to be that of Eugene Debs' appeal to the American Railway Union in the 1890s for the inclusion of blacks within the union.

One effort for black and white unity was partially successful—and its eventual failure marked the end of a stage of struggle in the United States. The radical agrarian populist movement, a movement with a desire to forge a link with urban, working-class discontent, was one that included blacks in significant numbers. There was a separately organized but cooperative Colored Farmers Alliance as part of Southern populism. C. Vann Woodward indicates that the history of this movement can be marked by the change from the inclusion of blacks to their exclusion. Tom Watson, who was to become the prototype of the Southern white populist demagogue, appealing to the racism of the white poor, had in the early days of populism fought side by side with black farmers, once actually leading white farmers with guns to relieve a beleaguered black populist leader.[9]

While this is not the point to develop in this analysis, it is becoming increasingly clear that one of the central issues facing the working class movement from the end of the Civil War to the turn of the century was this question of the unity of the working class. While there were moments of successful joint struggle, and blacks played prominent roles at times in the union movement, these efforts were to fail, and blacks were excluded from the union movement. It is also clear that this exclusion of blacks was to be crucial for limiting the development of this movement.[10]

Faced with its isolation from the white population, blacks in freedom turned, as they had in slavery, to the development of their own community as the source of strength and struggle for survival. The black church became the central instrument of acculturation into the big city world, just as independent religious meetings had been so central in establishing continuity and community for the slaves. The music of the slaves was further developed into modern jazz forms. The kinship structure that had emerged under slavery, where generalized extended family units allowed for children to be taken care of despite the absence of the biological parents, continued to be operative. Black ghetto children may not always live with their biological parents, but there is almost always some other adult, grandmother, aunt, uncle, or neighbor, willing to step in and raise the child.

The black community continues to be an integral social organization in the urban ghetto, although it has had to make enormous adjustments. As with most rural people who have moved into an urban environment, American blacks have resorted to the development of ideologies that have given meaning to their lives, explained to them their difficulties, and recreated the community network of relationships. For example, in the 1920s, the Universal Negro Improvement Association of Marcus Garvey recruited several million urban black people. While Garvey talked of a return to Africa, it is clear that the dominant meaning of the UNIA for those who joined was in terms of social cohesiveness and re-creation of community ties. The UNIA ran Freedom Halls in most cities where black people arriving from the South could live at a nominal charge until they found a place of their own. They could get information about jobs, churches, and other necessary matters for immigrants.[11] In addition to the UNIA, the thousands of small black churches played a similar role. They were often organized around a pastor and a congregation who had come together from the South; when later immigrants from the "old country" came, they had a core of people to help them make the adjustment to the new situation.

In the past fifteen years, with the development of a new movement for change in the urban ghettos, black people have become more and more ideological in their affiliations. For them, the various black nationalist ideologies have proven to be very useful. They have helped develop among black people a new sense of identity, a new sense of community, and new social and political organizations. They have forced certain concessions from the dominant white majority, and they have placed the black community in a stronger position to defend itself against the outside world. In an urban setting in which the official forces of government have done little but allow the central cities to rot, the black nationalist organizations have provided services to the black community that were needed and were not available from any other source. They have raised the demand for community control, reviving the American social contract.

Once again the black community has vigorously challenged the American social system. In so doing, it has had a major impact on American life. The churches and schools have been challenged to change their tone and their character; the mass media try to accommodate themselves to the feelings and social attitudes of young Americans, white as well as black, although the populace is always ahead of these concessions; city governments have tried to stimulate change and have instead revealed their weakness and corruption; institutions, such as trade unions, have been shown to be bureaucratic and inaccessible to the wishes of those who pay dues; the peace movement has learned from the experience of black movements; Puerto Ricans, American Indians, and Mexican–Americans have followed the lead of the black organizations, and a new mood has swept these communities; the mass disaffection from the values and behaviors of the older America on the part of millions of young people has taken much of its cultural apparatus from the black community. Above all, perhaps, have been the facts that the current development of life-styles far removed from the Puritanism that has hitherto completely dominated American society has borrowed much from the black community and that those younger whites of all social classes involved in this development look toward the black community for moral support.

Indeed, these changes in life-styles among young Americans, which have taken the entire world by surprise, began in the late 1950s coincident with the development of new black change movements. If racism had its roots in the Puritan–Protestant ethic, then the abandonment of this world view cannot but help limit racism. Many younger white Americans in their own search for new life-styles have been able least to recognize their own racism and attempt to do something about it. Some have even understood that racism is not simply an ideology. They have directed their criticism not simply at prejudice but at institutions that embody racism. And it must be remembered that these changes among the young are no longer largely confined to the middle class but hit large sectors of the working class who are in revolt against a merit system that threatens to leave them out. Long-haired younger factory workers are becoming increasingly common.

Can the black community raise its challenge to the white world in such fashion as to capitalize upon this willingness under certain circumstances of younger whites to follow their lead? That is a political question and only can be answered politically. However, we have seen that there has been a vibrant black community forged under slavery which has been central to struggles for change in the United States. If America is to be mankind's last, best hope, it will be because there will be found ways of releasing the creative and revolutionary force of the American people. The black community will be in the forefront of those changes if they occur.

This is the promise and the challenge of the development of the American black community from 1619 to the present—a community which has always taken the lead in the struggle for the realization of the promise of the Declaration of Independence. The vision implicit in that revolutionary document of a society in which all men are guaranteed life, liberty, and the pursuit of happiness, can have a chance of becoming a reality only through the pressures put on all institutions by those who are the most excluded from American society. The pressure of blacks for equality intensifies all social conflicts in the United States. It has already created new forces among whites who are beginning to push for basic changes in the institutional framework that makes up American capitalism. It gives hope to millions in this country and throughout the world that the black preacher's vision of a world in which men are "free at last, free at last, Great God Almighty, free at last" might become a reality.

## Notes

1. Charles Beard and other historians who have followed him misread the concern of the authors of the Federalist Papers with faction and class. The founding fathers were more concerned with dealing with future class divisions, divisions which they feared as a cause of instability on the basis of their knowledge of European history, than they were with the moderate class differences that existed in their own time.

2. While this is no place to enter into a full length discussion of the matter, it is clear that in seventeenth-century Virginia, permanent chattel slavery for blacks, as distinguished from a form of indentured servitude, did not become the universal situation until after 1660, and that, for the first forty years of slavery in Virginia, blacks found it relatively easy to become free and even to own land. However, it should be stressed that there were only a small handful of blacks in Virginia at this early date.

3. Henry David Thoreau, "Essay on Civil Disobedience," in *Walden and Other Essays*, p. 296.

4. Karl Marx, *Capital*, vol. 1, p. 329.

5. Frederick Douglass and others, "Reply of the Colored Delegation to President Johnson," in Philip S. Foner, ed., *The Life and Writings of Frederick Douglass*, vol. 4, p. 192.

6. For a general discussion of whites and blacks as workers, see W. E. B. Du Bois, *Black Reconstruction in America, 1860–1880*, pp. 3–31, and Harold M. Baron, "The Demand for Black Labor: Historical Notes on the Political Economy of Racism," *Radical America* 5 (March–April 1971): 1–46.

7. Abraham Lincoln, "Message to Congress in Special Session, July 4, 1861," in *The Collected Works of Abraham Lincoln*, ed. Roy P. Basler, vol. 4, p. 438.

8. See the essay on Wendell Phillips in Richard Hofstadter, *The American Political Tradition and the Men Who Made It*.

9. See C. Vann Woodward, *Tom Watson: Agrarian Rebel*. Also, Woodward, *The Origins of the New South* (Baton Rouge, La., 1951).

10. In the past two decades, Professor Herbert Gutman has been developing in numerous articles a history of the American working class from the Civil War to the beginning of the twentieth century, much of which deals with the complex relationship between black and white workers. A book based on this monumental body of work will soon be published, and it gives promise of being a major contribution to our understanding of the development of the American people. See, for example, Herbert G. Gutman, "The Negro and the United Mine Workers of America: The Career and Letters of Richard L. Davis and Something of Their Meaning: 1890–1900," in *The Negro and the American Labor Movement*, ed. Julius Jacobson, pp. 49–127.

11. Robert Hill, a Jamaican scholar, has been at work on a study of Marcus Garvey. This discussion of the UNIA Freedom Halls comes both from personal communications and from an address given by Hill in Montreal at a Black Writers Congress in 1968.

# APPENDIXES
# BIBLIOGRAPHY
# INDEX

# EDITOR'S
# INTRODUCTION TO
# VOLUMES 2-19

It has taken a monumental struggle on the part of black Americans to transform their status in American society to gain a place for the voices of those who had been slaves in the writing of their own history. After a century of almost total neglect, the past five years have witnessed the republication of some of the slave narratives originally published in the nineteenth century.[1] And yet the main body of the material left by those who had been slaves has not yet been published except in very abbreviated, edited, and selected form. The unpublished interviews conducted in the twentieth century with ex-slaves have simply not been made generally available (except in very selected and edited form) and yet they are the most significant source of material on the lives of the slaves, their communities, and their struggles. This volume is both a substantive essay on slavery, which makes an effort to allow the slaves to enter into the creation of their written history, and an introduction to the main body of such largely unpublished interview materials.

The material will be published in two or three series. This volume is published along with six others, which contain material from the Works Projects Administration Writers' Project interviews. A second series, with the remainder of the WPA materials, will contain twelve volumes; the second will also contain reprints of two volumes of interviews collected at Fisk University at the end of the 1920s, first published in a mimeographed small edition in

1945.[2] It is hoped that there will be further volumes in a third series containing other similar materials.

We have chosen to reprint the interviews without editing them in any way or removing from the collection interviews which might appear of only slight interest. We leave to the judgment of scholars and the general public the value and usefulness of particular interviews.

We have also retained, whenever it has not interfered with the photographic reproduction of the material, all the editorial notes made by the original editors in preparing the materials for possible publication. These notes may be of use in probing the richness of the collection. Appended to this first volume are various letters and documents found bound with the first volume of the WPA materials, the Alabama interviews, which may prove of great help to the reader in utilizing the material.

As has been suggested at the beginning of this volume, the publication of these slave narratives and this volume should lead to a vast outpouring of fresh interpretations, which will give a full, rounded, and dynamic picture of the lives of the slaves. There are many subjects which the narratives can help illuminate far beyond the boundaries that have so far been reached. Four in particular, which have been only briefly noted in this book, seem to be worthy of mention at this point. They are, I think, illustrative of the problems the interviews will help clarify.

The first of these is the question of the social structure of the slave communities. This matter has created a great deal of controversy but very little substantial research. What were the relations between house slaves and field slaves? Were house slaves necessarily, or even usually, more docile than field slaves? How were house slaves used to control field slaves? How did the house slaves act to aid the field slaves? Were house slaves usually more privileged than field slaves? Were house slaves usually able to perpetuate their class position by passing it on to their children? Were house slaves often demoted to field slaves? And were there many house slaves who were required to work in the fields as well, particularly at harvest time? The slave narratives contain much that is relevant to these questions.

Second, the narratives contain a great deal of revealing information about and accounts of Reconstruction. Some of this has been used in this volume but much more study remains to be done with the materials. In many ways, these narratives are as rich in insight into the history of black people in America for the years following the Civil War as they are in materials concerning slavery itself.

Third, an entire book could be written based primarily on the slave narratives about black American-Indian relations. The narratives from Oklahoma are particularly rich in such material. Some of the peoples of the Indian Territory, such as the Creeks and the Cherokees, were owners of black slaves who were, however, treated very differently from those black slaves owned by whites. Blacks became part of the Indian kinship structure, they were generally treated well, and they became Creek or Cherokee in culture. Runaway slaves often were sheltered in Indian communities and then sent on their way.

Finally, the narratives are a great source of black folklore and folk poetry. This volume has only scratched the surface of this material, not because it is unimportant but because it is of the greatest importance, and entire volumes ought to be based on it. There is nothing unclear or ambiguous about black folk stories or folk poetry for those willing to go beyond the literal pedantry of German historiography of the last part of the nineteenth century. As Sterling Stuckey has pointed out, the great twentieth-century American historian W. E. B. DuBois was able to relate "the music of the slaves to the total culture of America," thus emphasizing the strengths of the black slaves and the cultural weaknesses of much of white American life.[3]

This study of slavery based on the slave narratives and interviews with ex-slaves has not been able to give a precise picture of the historical development of the black community. It does not present an analysis which differentiates slave behavior of the eighteenth century from that of the nineteenth century, and it has stressed the continuity of black life before and after the Civil War. A reason for this is that the bulk of the slave narratives only present material on black life since approximately 1835. There is a need to assert the continuities in black community life that emerge from a careful reading of the narratives against a long tradition which has asserted that there was no black community or distinct behavior, that the slaves were victims tossed about by the white master class without any means of defense. Yet, even when this task is accomplished, it will still be necessary to establish methodologies to enable us to see the changes in black life since 1619. Utilizing these slave narratives and other available materials, there should be no difficulty in devising methods which can present the time sequences in black history.

Not only has this work slighted the historical development of the black community, it has not emphasized the regional differences in American slavery. That has been done in order to establish certain overall realities: there was a black community under slavery, there was the development of distinct Afro-American behavior patterns (for example, black religion), slaves were treated harshly but they were able to resist in specific ways, and so forth. But the slave narratives offer wonderfully clear material on regional differences. For example, the Texas narratives are filled with accounts of black cowboys and black slave cowboys. It is clear that the slave cowboy had much more individual autonomy than did slave field hands on cotton plantations. It is hoped that these narratives will be utilized to probe such differences, and their relationships to regional differences, as well as to develop a comprehensive picture of the changes in slave life.

This volume is an introduction to a body of material in which the slaves speak for themselves. If the volume is to have any merit beyond the presentation of the views of the author on certain matters concerning American slavery and racism, it will come from its linkage with the slave narratives—a body of material intrinsically of greater significance because it presents the reflections upon their experiences of those who were there, who suffered, and who built for themselves and those who were to come after them a way of life upon which people stand and challenge modern American society.

## Notes

1. There is, despite a flurry of recent republications of some of the slave narratives, only the beginning of an awareness of the importance of these documents. Even when the complete WPA narratives will be published, there will remain scores of items either unpublished or published in the nineteenth century in obscure places (such as church bulletins and black newspapers) not generally available.

2. Fisk University, "God Struck Me Dead," mimeographed (Nashville: Social Science Institute, 1945); Fisk University, "Unwritten History of Slavery," mimeographed (Nashville: Social Science Institute, 1945). "God Struck Me Dead" was republished, with an introduction by Clifton H. Johnson, by Pilgrim Press of Philadelphia in 1969. The "Unwritten History of Slavery" was republished by Microcard Editions of Washington, D.C., in 1968.

3. Sterling Stuckey, "Twilight of Our Past: Reflections on the Origins of Black History," *Amistad* 2 (1971):261–295.

# SLAVE NARRATIVES*

*A Folk History of Slavery in the United States
From Interviews with Former Slaves*

TYPEWRITTEN RECORDS PREPARED BY
THE FEDERAL WRITERS PROJECT
1936–1938
ASSEMBLED BY
THE LIBRARY OF CONGRESS PROJECT
WORK PROJECTS ADMINISTRATION
FOR THE DISTRICT OF COLUMBIA
SPONSORED BY THE LIBRARY OF CONGRESS

*Illustrated with Photographs*

# INDIANA NARRATIVES

WASHINGTON 1941

---

* Front matter of the Work Projects Administration Project.

FEDERAL WORKS AGENCY

WORK PROJECTS ADMINISTRATION

FOR THE DISTRICT OF COLUMBIA


Paul Edwards, Administrator
Amelfe. S. Fair, Director, Division of Community Service Programs
Mary Nan Gamble, Chief, Public Activities Programs


THE LIBRARY OF CONGRESS PROJECT
Official Project No. 165-2-26-7
Work Project No. 540


Mary Nan Gamble, Acting Project Supervisor
Francesco M. Bianco, Assistant Project Supervisor
B. A. Botkin, Chief Editor, Writers' Unit

# INTRODUCTION

## I

This collection of slave narratives had its beginning in the second year of the former Federal Writers' Project (now the Writers' Program), 1936, when several state Writers' Projects—notably those of Florida, Georgia, and South Carolina—recorded interviews with ex-slaves residing in those states. On April 22, 1937, a standard questionnaire for field workers drawn up by John A. Lomax, then National Advisor on Folklore and Folkways for the Federal Writers' Project,[1] was issued from Washington as "Supplementary Instructions #9-E to The American Guide Manual" (appended below). Also associated with the direction and criticism of the work in the Washington office of the Federal Writers' Project were Henry G. Alsberg, Director; George Cronyn, Associate Director; Sterling A. Brown, Editor on Negro Affairs; Mary Lloyd, Editor; and B. A. Botkin, Folklore Editor succeeding Mr. Lomax.[2]

On August 31, 1939, the Federal Writers' Project became the Writers' Program, and the National Technical Project in Washington was terminated. On October 17, the first Library of Congress Project, under the sponsorship of the Library of Congress, was set up by the Work Projects Administration in the District of Columbia, to continue some of the functions of the National Technical Project, chiefly those concerned with books of a regional or nationwide scope. On February 12, 1940, the project was reorganized along strictly conservation lines, and on August 16 it was succeeded by the present Library of Congress Project (Official Project No. 165-2-26-7, Work Project No. 540).

The present Library of Congress Project, under the sponsorship of the Library of Congress, is a unit of the Public Activities Program of the Community Service Programs of the Work Projects Administration

---

[1] Mr. Lomax served from June 25, 1936, to October 23, 1937, with a ninety-day furlough beginning July 24, 1937. According to a memorandum written by Mr. Alsberg on March 23, 1937, Mr. Lomax was "in charge of the collection of folklore all over the United States for the Writers' Project. In connection with this work he is making recordings of Negro songs and cowboy ballads. Though technically on the payroll of the Survey of Historical Records, his work is done for the Writers and the results will make several national volumes of folklore. The essays in the State Guides devoted to folklore are also under his supervision." Since 1933 Mr. Lomax has been Honorary Curator of the Archive of American Folk Song, Library of Congress.

[2] Folklore Consultant, from May 2 to July 31, 1938; Folklore Editor, from August 1, 1938, to August 31, 1939.

for the District of Columbia. According to the Project Proposal (WPA Form 301), the purpose of the Project is to "collect, check, edit, index, and otherwise prepare for use WPA records, Professional and Service Projects."

The Writers' Unit of the Library of Congress Project processes material left over from or not needed for publication by the state Writers' Projects. On file in the Washington office in August, 1939, was a large body of slave narratives, photographs of former slaves, interviews with white informants regarding slavery, transcripts of laws, advertisements, records of sale, transfer, and manumission of slaves, and other documents. As unpublished manuscripts of the Federal Writers' Project these records passed into the hands of the Library of Congress Project for processing; and from them has been assembled the present collection of some two thousand narratives from the following seventeen states: Alabama, Arkansas, Florida, Georgia, Indiana, Kansas, Kentucky, Maryland, Mississippi, Missouri, North Carolina, Ohio, Oklahoma, South Carolina, Tennessee, Texas, and Virginia.[1]

The work of the Writers' Unit in preparing the narratives for deposit in the Library of Congress consisted principally of arranging the manuscripts and photographs by states and alphabetically by informants within the states, listing the informants and illustrations, and collating the contents in seventeen volumes divided into thirty-three parts. The following material has been omitted: Most of the interviews with informants born too late to remember anything of significance regarding slavery or concerned chiefly with folklore; a few negligible fragments and unidentified manuscripts; a group of Tennessee interviews showing evidence of plagiarism; and the supplementary material gathered in connection with the narratives. In the course of the preparation of these volumes, the Writers' Unit compiled data for an essay on the narratives and partially completed an index and a glossary. Enough additional material is being received from the state Writers' Projects, as part of their surplus, to make a supplement, which, it is hoped, will contain several states not here represented, such as Louisiana.

All editing had previously been done in the states or the Washington office. Some of the pencilled comments have been identified as those of John A. Lomax and Alan Lomax, who also read the manuscripts. In a few cases, two drafts or versions of the same interview have been included for comparison of interesting variations or alterations.

---

[1] The bulk of the Virginia narratives is still in the state office. Excerpts from these are included in *The Negro in Virginia*, compiled by Workers of the Writers' Program of the Work Projects Administration in the State of Virginia, Sponsored by the Hampton Institute, Hastings House, Publishers, New York, 1940. Other slave narratives are published in *Drums and Shadows*, Survival Studies among the Georgia Coastal Negroes, Savannah Unit, Georgia Writers' Project, Work Projects Administration, University of Georgia Press, 1940. A composite article, "Slaves," based on excerpts from three interviews, was contributed by Elizabeth Lomax to the *American Stuff* issue of *Direction*, Vol. 1, No. 3, 1938.

## II

Set beside the work of formal historians, social scientists, and novelists, slave autobiographies, and contemporary records of abolitionists and planters, these life histories, taken down as far as possible in the narrators' words, constitute an invaluable body of unconscious evidence or indirect source material, which scholars and writers dealing with the South, especially, social psychologists and cultural anthropologists, cannot afford to reckon without. For the first and the last time, a large number of surviving slaves (many of whom have since died) have been permitted to tell their own story, in their own way. In spite of obvious limitations— bias and fallibility of both informants and interviewers, the use of leading questions, unskilled techniques, and insufficient controls and checks—this saga must remain the most authentic and colorful source of our knowledge of the lives and thoughts of thousands of slaves, of their attitudes toward one another, toward their masters, mistresses, and overseers, toward poor whites, North and South, the Civil War, Emancipation, Reconstruction, religion, education, and virtually every phase of Negro life in the South.

The narratives belong to folk history—history recovered from the memories and lips of participants or eye-witnesses, who mingle group with individual experience and both with observation, hearsay, and tradition. Whether the narrators relate what they actually saw and thought and felt, what they imagine, or what they have thought and felt about slavery since, now we know *why* they thought and felt as they did. To the white myth of slavery must be added the slaves' own folklore and folk-say of slavery. The patterns they reveal are folk and regional patterns—the patterns of field hand, house and body servant, and artisan; the patterns of kind and cruel master or mistress; the patterns of Southeast and Southwest, lowland and upland, tidewater and inland, smaller and larger plantations, and racial mixture (including Creole and Indian).

The narratives belong also to folk literature. Rich not only in folk songs, folk tales, and folk speech but also in folk humor and poetry, crude or skilful in dialect, uneven in tone and treatment, they constantly reward one with earthy imagery, salty phrase, and sensitive detail. In their unconscious art, exhibited in many a fine and powerful short story, they are a contribution to the realistic writing of the Negro. Beneath all the surface contradictions and exaggerations, the fantasy and flattery, they possess an essential truth and humanity which surpasses as it supplements history and literature.

Washington, D.C.                                        B. A. Botkin
June 12, 1941                                           Chief Editor, Writers' Unit
                                                        Library of Congress Project

# MEMORANDUM

June 9, 1937

TO: STATE DIRECTORS OF THE FEDERAL WRITERS'
PROJECT

FROM: Henry G. Alsberg, Director

In connection with the stories of ex-slaves, please send in to this office copies of State, county, or city laws affecting the conduct of slaves, free Negroes, overseers, patrollers, or any person or custom affecting the institution of slavery. It will, of course, not be necessary to send more than one copy of the laws that were common throughout the state, although any special law passed by a particular city would constitute worthwhile material.

In addition, we should like to have you collect and send in copies of any laws or accounts of any established customs relating to the admission to your State of bodies of slaves from Africa or other sections, the escape of slaves, etc. Also, we should like to see copies of advertisements of sales of slaves, published offers of rewards for fugitive slaves, copies of transfers of slaves by will or otherwise, records of freeing of slaves, etc. Public records of very particular interest regarding any transaction involving slaves should be photostated and copies furnished to the Washington office.

Furthermore, contemporary accounts of any noteworthy occurrences among the Negroes during slavery days or the Reconstruction period should be copied, if taken from contemporary newspapers. If such records have been published in books, a reference to the source would be sufficient. We have been receiving a large number of extremely interesting stories of ex-slaves. The historic background of the institution of slavery, which should be disclosed with the information we are now requesting, will be very helpful in the execution of the plans we have in mind.

Copies sent to:

| | | | | |
|---|---|---|---|---|
| Alabama | Georgia | Maryland | North Carolina | Tennessee |
| Arkansas | Kentucky | Mississippi | Oklahoma | Texas |
| Florida | Louisiana | Missouri | South Carolina | Virginia |
| | | | | West Virginia |
| | | | | Ohio |
| | | | | Kansas |

# MEMORANDUM

July 30, 1937

TO: STATE DIRECTORS OF THE FEDERAL WRITERS' PROJECT

FROM: Henry G. Alsberg, Director

The following general suggestions are being sent to all the States where there are ex-slaves still living. They will not apply *in toto* to your State as they represent general conclusions reached after reading the mass of ex-slave material already submitted. However, they will, I hope, prove helpful as an indication, along broad lines, of what we want.

## GENERAL SUGGESTIONS:

1. Instead of attempting to interview a large number of ex-slaves the workers should now concentrate on one or two of the more interesting and intelligent people, revisiting them, establishing friendly relations, and drawing them out over a period of time.

2. The specific questions suggested to be asked of the slaves should be only a basis, a beginning. The talk should run to all subjects, and the interviewer should take care to sieze upon the information already given, and stories already told, and from them derive other questions.

3. The interviewer should take the greatest care not to influence the point of view of the informant, and not to let his own opinion on the subject of slavery become obvious. Should the ex-slave, however, give only one side of the picture, the interviewer should suggest that there were other circumstances, and ask questions about them.

4. We suggest that each state choose one or two of their most successful ex-slave interviewers and have them take down some stories *word* for *word*. Some Negro informants are marvellous in their ability to participate in this type of interview. *All stories should be as nearly word-for-word as is possible.*

5. More emphasis should be laid on questions concerning the lives of the individual's since they were freed.

## SUGGESTIONS TO INTERVIEWERS:

The interviewer should attempt to weave the following questions naturally into the conversation, in simple language. Many of the interviews show that the workers have simply sprung routine questions out of context, and received routine answers.

1. What did the ex-slaves expect from freedom? Forty acres and a mule? A distribution of the land of their masters' plantation?

2. What did the slaves get after freedom? Were any of the planta-

tions actually divided up? Did their masters give them any money? Were they under any compulsion after the war to remain as servants?

3. What did the slaves do after the war? What did they receive generally? What do they think about the reconstruction period?

4. Did secret organizations such as the Ku Klux Klan exert or attempt to exert any influence over the lives of ex-slaves?

5. Did the ex-slaves ever vote? If so, under what circumstances? Did any of their friends ever hold political office? What do the ex-slaves think of the present restricted suffrage?

6. What have the ex-slaves been doing in the interim between 1864 and 1937? What jobs have they held (in detail)? How are they supported nowadays?

7. What do the ex-slaves think of the younger generation of Negroes and of present conditions?

8. Were there any instances of slave uprisings?

9. Were any of the ex-slaves in your community living in Virginia at the time of the Nat Turner rebellion? Do they remember anything about it?

10. What songs were there of the period?

The above sent to: Alabama, Arkansas, Florida, Ga., Kentucky, La., Md., Mississippi, Mo., N. Car., Okla., S. Car., Tenn., Texas, Virginia, W. Va., Ohio, Kansas, Indiana

## STORIES FROM EX-SLAVES

The main purpose of these detailed and homely questions is to get the Negro interested in talking about the days of slavery. If he will talk freely, he should be encouraged to say what he pleases without reference to the questions. It should be remembered that the Federal Writers' Project is not interested in taking sides on any question. The worker should not censor any material collected, regardless of its nature.

It will not be necessary, indeed it will probably be a mistake, to ask every person all of the questions. Any incidents or facts he can recall should be written down as nearly as possible just as he says them, but do not use dialect spelling so complicated that it may confuse the reader.

A second visit, a few days after the first one, is important, so that the worker may gather all the worthwhile recollections that the first talk has aroused.

*QUESTIONS:*

1. Where and when were you born?

2. Give the names of your father and mother. Where did they come from? Give names of your brothers and sisters. Tell about your life with them and describe your home and the "quarters." Describe

the beds and where you slept. Do you remember anything about your grandparents or any stories told you about them?

3. What work did you do in slavery days? Did you ever earn any money? How? What did you buy with this money?

4. What did you eat and how was it cooked? Any possums? Rabbits? Fish? What food did you like best? Did the slaves have their own gardens?

5. What clothing did you wear in hot weather? Cold weather? On Sundays? Any shoes? Describe your wedding clothes.

6. Tell about your master, mistress, their children, the house they lived in, the overseer or driver, poor white neighbors.

7. How many acres in the plantation? How many slaves on it? How and at what time did the overseer wake up the slaves? Did they work hard and late at night? How and for what causes were the slaves punished? Tell what you saw. Tell some of the stories you heard.

8. Was there a jail for slaves? Did you ever see any slaves sold or auctioned off? How did groups of slaves travel? Did you ever see slaves in chains?

9. Did the white folks help you to learn to read and write?

10. Did the slaves have a church on your plantation? Did they read the Bible? Who was your favorite preacher? Your favorite spirituals? Tell about the baptizing; baptizing songs. Funerals and funeral songs.

11. Did the slaves ever run away to the North? Why? What did you hear about patrollers? How did slaves carry news from one plantation to another? Did you hear of trouble between the blacks and whites?

12. What did the slaves do when they went to their quarters after the day's work was done on the plantation? Did they work on Saturday afternoons? What did they do Saturday nights? Sundays? Christmas morning? New Year's Day? Any other holidays? Cornshucking? Cotton Picking? Dances? When some of the white master's family married or died? A wedding or death among the slaves?

13. What games did you play as a child? Can you give the words or sing any of the play songs or ring games of the children? Riddles? Charms? Stories about "Raw Head and Bloody Bones" or other "hants" or ghosts? Stories about animals? What do you think of voodoo? Can you give the words or sing any lullabies? Work songs? Plantation hollers? Can you tell a funny story you have heard or something funny that happened to you? Tell about the ghosts you have seen.

14. When slaves became sick who looked after them? What medicines did the doctors give them? What medicine (herbs, leaves, or roots) did the slaves use for sickness? What charms did they wear and to keep off what diseases?

15. What do you remember about the war that brought your freedom? What happened on the day news came that you were free? What did your master say and do? When the Yankees came what did they do and say?

16. Tell what work you did and how you lived the first year after the war and what you saw or heard about the Ku Klux Klan and the Nightriders. Any school then for Negroes? Any land?

17. Whom did you marry? Describe the wedding. How many children and grandchildren have you and what are they doing?

18. What do you think of Abraham Lincoln? Jefferson Davis? Booker Washington? Any other prominent white man or Negro you have known or heard of?

19. Now that slavery is ended what do you think of it? Tell why you joined a church and why you think all people should be religious.

20. Was the overseer "poor white trash"? What were some of his rules?

The details of the interview should be reported as accurately as possible in the language of the original statements. An example of material collected through one of the interviews with ex-slaves is attached herewith. Although this material was collected before the standard questionnaire had been prepared, it represents an excellent method of reporting an interview. More information might have been obtained however, if a comprehensive questionnaire had been used.

*Notes by an editor on dialect usage in accounts by interviews with ex-slaves. (To be used in conjunction with Supplementary Instructions 9E.)*

Simplicity in recording the dialect is to be desired in order to hold the interest and attention of the readers. It seems to me that readers are repelled by pages sprinkled with misspellings, commas and apostrophes. The value of exact phonetic transcription is, of course, a great one. But few artists attempt this completely. Thomas Nelson Page was meticulous in his dialect; Joel Chandler Harris less meticulous but in my opinion even more accurate. But the values they sought are different from the values that I believe this book of slave narratives should have. Present day readers are less ready for the overstress of phonetic spelling than in the days of local color. Authors realize this: Julia Peterkin uses a modified Gullah instead of Gonzales' carefully spelled out Gullah. Howard Odum has questioned the use of goin' for going since the g is seldom pronounced even by the educated.

Truth to idiom is more important, I believe, than truth to pronunciation. Erskine Caldwell in his stories of Georgia, Ruth Suckow in stories of Iowa, and Zora Neale Hurston in stories of Florida Negroes get a truth to the manner of speaking without excessive misspellings. In order to make this volume of slave narratives more appealing and less difficult for the average reader, I recommend that truth to idiom be paramount, and exact truth to pronunciation secondary.

I appreciate the fact that many of the writers have recorded sensitively. The writer who wrote "ret" for right is probably as accurate as the one who spelled it "raght." But in a single publication, not devoted to a study of local speech, the reader may conceivably be puzzled by different spellings of the same word. The words "whafolks," "whufolks," "whi'folks," etc., can all be heard in the South. But "white-folks" is easier for the reader, and the word itself is suggestive of the setting and the attitude.

Words that definitely have a notably different pronunciation from the usual should be recorded as heard. More important is the recording of words with a different local meaning. Most important, however, are the turns of phrase that have flavor and vividness. Examples occurring in the copy I read are:

durin' of de war
outman my daddy (good, but unnecessarily put into quotes)
piddled in de fields
skit of woods
kinder chillish

There are, of course, questionable words, for which it may be hard to set up a single standard. Such words are:

| | |
|---|---|
| paddyrollers, padrollers, pattyrollers | for patrollers |
| missis, mistess | for mistress |
| marsa, massa, maussa, mastuh | for master |
| ter, tuh, teh | for to |

I believe that there should be, for this book, a uniform word for each of these.

The following list is composed of words which I think should not be used. These are merely samples of certain faults:

|  | | | |
|---|---|---|---|
| 1. | ah | for | I |
| 2. | bawn | for | born |
| 3. | capper | for | caper |
| 4. | com' | for | come |
| 5. | do | for | dough |
| 6. | ebry, ev'ry | for | every |
| 7. | hawd | for | hard |
| 8. | muh | for | my |
| 9. | nakid | for | naked |
| 10. | ole, ol' | for | old |
| 11. | ret, raght | for | right |
| 12. | snaik | for | snake |
| 13. | sowd | for | sword |
| 14. | sto' | for | store |
| 15. | teh | for | tell |
| 16. | twon't | for | twan't |
| 17. | useter, useta | for | used to |
| 18. | uv | for | of |
| 19. | waggin | for | wagon |
| 20. | whi' | for | white |
| 21. | wuz | for | was |

I should like to recommend that the stories be told in the language of the ex-slave, without excessive editorializing and "artistic" introductions on the part of the interviewer. The contrast between the directness of the ex-slave speech and the roundabout and at times pompous comments of the interviewer is frequently glaring. Care should be taken lest expressions such as the following creep in: "inflicting wounds from which he never fully recovered" (supposed to be spoken by an ex-slave).

Finally, I should like to recommend that the words darky and nigger and such expressions as "a comical little old black woman" be omitted from the editorial writing. Where the ex-slave himself uses these, they should be retained.

This material sent June 20 to states of : Ala., Ark., Fla., Ga., Ky., La., Md., Miss., Mo., N.C., Ohio, Okla., Tenn., Texas, Va., and S. Car.

*Negro Dialect Suggestions*
*(Stories of Ex-Slaves)*

Do not write:

*Ah* for I
*Poe* for po' (poor)
*Hit* for it
*Tuh* for to
*Wuz* for was
*Baid* for bed
*Daid* for dead
*Ouh* for our
*Mah* for my
*Ovah* for over
*Othuh* for other
*Wha* for whar (where)
*Undah* for under
*Fuh* for for
*Yondah* for yonder
*Moster* for marster or massa

*Gwainter* for gwineter (going to)
*Oman* for woman
*Ifn* for iffen (if)
*Fiuh* or *fiah* for fire
*Uz* or *uv* or *o'* for of
*Poar* for poor or po'
*J'in* for jine
*Coase* for cose
*Utha* for other
*Yo'* for you
*Gi'* for give
*Cot* for caught
*Kin'* for kind
*Cose* for 'cause
*Tho't* for thought

# BIBLIOGRAPHY[1]

*Primary Sources*[1]

Aaron. *Light and Truth of Slavery: Aaron's History in Virginia, New Jersey, and Rhode Island.* Worcester, Mass., n.d.

Adams, H. G. *God's Image in Ebony: Being a Series of Biographical Sketches, Facts, Anecdotes, Etc., Demonstrative of the Mental Powers and Intellectual Capacities of the Negro Race.* London, 1854.

Adams, John Quincy. *Narrative of John Quincy Adams When in Slavery and Now as a Freedman.* Harrisburg, 1872.

Aleckson, Sam. *Before the War and After the Union: An Autobiography.* Boston, 1929.

Allen, Richard. *The Life Experiences and Gospel Labors of the Right Reverend Richard Allen.* Nashville, Tenn.: Abingdon Press, [1833] 1960.

———, and Jones, Absalom. *A Narrative of the Proceedings of the Black People During the Late Awful Calamity in Philadelphia in the Year 1793.* Philadelphia, 1794.

Alexander, Archer. *The Story of Archer Alexander, from Slavery to Freedom, March 30, 1863.* Boston, 1885.

Anderson, John. *Story of John Anderson, Fugitive Slave.* London, 1863.

Anderson, Robert. *From Slavery to Affluence, Memoirs of Robert Anderson, Ex-Slave.* Hemingsford, Nebraska: Hemingsford Ledger, 1927.

Anderson, William. *Life and Narrative of William Anderson or Dark Deeds of American Slavery.* Chicago, 1857.

Aptheker, Herbert, ed. *A Documentary History of the Negro People*

---

[1] Recent editions are cited, noting in brackets the date of the original edition. Publication information for books published before 1930 has been omitted.

*in the United States.* 2 vols. New York: The Citadel Press, 1951, 1962.

Archer, Armstrong. *A Compendium of Slavery as It Exists in the Present Day.* London, 1844.

Armistead, Wilson. *A Tribute for the Negro: Being a Vindication of the Moral, Intellectual and Religious Capabilities of the Colored Portion of Mankind with Particular Reference to the African Race.* New York: Negro Universities Press, [1848] 1969.

Armstrong, Orland Kay. *Old Massa's People: The Old Slaves Tell Their Story.* Indianapolis: Bobbs-Merrill, 1939.

Arthur. *The Life and Dying Speech of Arthur, A Negro Man.* Boston, 1768.

*Aunt Sally, or the Cross the Way to Freedom: A Narrative of the Slave Life and Purchase of the Mother of Rev. Isaac Williams of Detroit, Michigan.* Miami, Fla.: Mnemosyne Publishing Co., [1858] 1969.

Ball, Charles. *Slavery in the United States: A Narrative of the Life and Adventures of Charles Ball, a Black Man.* New York: Negro Universities Press, [1853] 1969.

Barber, John Warner. *A History of the Amistad Captives: Being a Circumstantial Account of the Capture of the Spanish Schooner Amistad, by the Africans on Board.* New York: Arno, [1840] 1969.

Bayley, Solomon. *Narrative of Some Remarkable Incidents in the Life of Solomon Bayley, Formerly a Slave in the State of Delaware, North America, Written by Himself.* 2d ed. London, 1825.

Bayliss, John F., ed. *Black Slave Narratives.* New York: The Macmillan Company, 1970.

Bibb, Henry. *Narrative of the Life and Adventures of Henry Bibb, An American Slave, Written by Himself.* New York: Negro Universities Press, [1849] 1969.

Billington, Ray A., ed. *Journal of Charlotte L. Forten: A Free Negro in the Slave Era.* New York: Collier Books, 1961.

Black, Leonard. *Life and Sufferings of Leonard Black, a Fugitive from Slavery, Written by Himself.* New York, 1847.

Blake, Jane. *Memoirs of Margaret Jane Blake.* Philadelphia, 1834.

Boen, William. *Anecdotes and Memoirs of William Boen, a Colored Man Who Lived and Died Near Mount Holly, New Jersey.* Philadelphia, 1834.

Bontemps, Arna, ed. *Great Slave Narratives* (Olaudah Equiano, James Pennington, and William and Ellen Craft). Boston: Beacon Press, 1969.

Botkin, Benjamin, ed. *Lay My Burden Down.* Chicago: University of Chicago Press, 1945.

Brawley, Benjamin. *Early Negro American Writers: Selections with Biographical and Critical Introductions.* New York: Dover, [1935] 1970.

Brown, Hallie Q. *Homespun Heroines and Other Women of Distinction.* Xenia, Ohio, 1926.

Brown, Henry Box. *Narrative of the Life of Henry Box Brown, Written by Himself.* Philadelphia: Rhistoric Publishers, [1851] 1969.

Brown, Isaac. *Case of the Slave Isaac Brown: An Outrage Exposed!* n.p., 1847.

Brown, Jane. *Narrative of the Life of Jane Brown and Her Two Children.* Hartford, 1860.

Brown, John. *Slave Life in Georgia: A Narrative of the Life, Sufferings, and Escape of John Brown, A Fugitive Slave.* London, 1855.

Brown, Josephine. *Biography of a Bondsman by His Daughter.* Boston, 1855.

Brown, Sterling; Davis, Arthur; and Lee, Ulysses. *The Negro Caravan: Writings by American Negroes.* New York: Arno, [1941] 1969.

Brown, William J. *The Life of William J. Brown of Providence, R.I.* Providence, 1883.

Brown, William W. *The Black Man, His Antecedents, His Genius and His Achievements.* New York: Arno, [1863] 1969.

———. *The Narrative of William Wells Brown, A Fugitive Slave.* New York: Negro Universities Press, [1848] 1969.

Browne, Martha. *Autobiography of a Female Slave.* New York: Negro Universities Press, [1857] 1969.

Bruce, Henry Clay. *The New Man: Twenty-nine Years a Slave, Twenty-nine Years a Freeman.* New York: Negro Universities Press, [1895] 1969.

Bruner, Peter. *A Slave's Advances Toward Freedom: Not Fiction, but the True Story of a Struggle.* Oxford, Ohio: n.p., n.d.

Burton, Annie L. *Memories of Childhood's Slavery Days.* Boston, 1919.

Campbell, Israel. *Bond and Free: or Yearning for Freedom from my Green Brier House: Being the Story of My Life in Bondage and My Life in Freedom.* Philadelphia, 1861.

Catterall, Helen H., ed. *Judicial Cases Concerning American Slavery and the Negro.* 5 vols. New York: Octagon Books, 1968.

Chandler, Charles. *The Story of a Slave.* n.p., 1894.

Charlton, Dimmock. *Narratives of Dimmock Charlton, A British Subject, Taken from the Brig "Peacock" by the U.S. Sloop "Hornet," Enslaved While a Prisoner of War, and Retained Forty-five Years in Bondage.* n.p., n.d.

Child, Lydia Maria. *Authentic Anecdotes of American Slavery.* Newburyport, 1838.

———. *The Freedman's Book.* New York: Arno, [1865] 1968.

———. *Isaac T. Hopper: A True Life.* New York: Negro Universities Press, [1853] 1969.

Clarke, James Freeman. *Anti-Slavery Days.* New York: Arno, [1884] 1969.

Clarke, Lewis. *Narrative of the Sufferings of Lewis Clarke, During a Captivity of More than Twenty-Five Years Among the Algerines of Kentucky.* Boston, 1845.

———, and Clarke, Milton. *Narratives of the Sufferings of Lewis and Milton Clarke, Sons of a Soldier of the Revolution During a Captivity of More than Twenty Years Among Slaveholders of Ken-

*tucky, One of the So-Called Christian States of North America, Dictated by Themselves.* New York: Arno, [1846] 1969.

Clinkscales, John George. *On the Old Plantation: Reminiscences of His Childhood.* New York: Negro Universities Press, [1916] 1969.

Coffin, Levi. *Reminiscences of Levi Coffin, The Reputed President of the Underground Railroad.* New York: Augustus Kelly, [1880] 1969.

Coleman, Julia, ed. *Child's Anti-Slavery Book.* New York, 1859.

Cooper, Thomas. *Narrative of the Life of Thomas Cooper.* New York, 1832.

Coppin, Bishop L. J. *Unwritten History.* New York: Negro Universities Press, [1919] 1968.

Craft, William. *Running a Thousand Miles for Freedom: Or the Escape of William and Ellen Craft from Slavery.* New York: Arno, [1860] 1970.

Cugoano, Ottobah. *Thoughts and Sentiments on the Evil of Slavery.* London: Dawsons, [1787] 1969.

Curtis, Anna L. *Stories of the Underground Railroad.* New York: Island Workshop Press Co-Operative, 1941.

Davis, Noah. *A Narrative of the Life of Reverend Noah Davis, A Colored Man, Written by Himself.* Baltimore, 1859.

Dinah. *The Story of Dinah, as Related to John Hawkins Simpson, after Her Escape from the Horrors of the Virginia Slave Trade, to London.* London, 1863.

Dormigold, Kate. *A Slave Girl's Story: The Autobiography of Kate Dormigold.* Brooklyn, New York, 1898.

Douglass, Frederick. *Life and Times of Frederick Douglass, Written by Himself.* New York: Crowell, [1882] 1966.

———. *The Life and Writings of Frederick Douglass.* Edited by Philip Foner. 4 vols. New York: International Publishers, 1950.

———. *My Bondage and My Freedom.* New York: Arno, [1855] 1968.

———. *Narrative of the Life of Frederick Douglass, An American Slave, Written by Himself.* Garden City: New York: Doubleday, Dolphin Books, [1845] 1963.

Drew, Benjamin. *North-Side View of Slavery: The Refugees or The Narratives of Fugitive Slaves in Canada, Related by Themselves.* New York: Negro Universities Press, [1856] 1968.

DuBois, Sylvia. *A Biography of the Slave Who Whipt Her Mistress and Gained Her Freedom.* New Jersey, 1883.

Eldridge, Elleanor. *Memoirs of Elleanor Eldridge.* Providence, 1838.

Eliot, William Greenleaf. *The Story of Archer Alexander From Slavery to Freedom, March 30, 1863.* Westport, Conn.: Negro Universities Press, [1885] 1970.

Equiano, Olaudah. *The Interesting Narrative of the Life of Olaudah Equiano, or Gustavus Vassa, the African, Written by Himself.* New York: Negro Universities Press, [1789] 1969.

Fairchild, James H. *Underground Railroad.* Cleveland, 1877.

Fedric, Francis. *Slave Life in Virginia and Kentucky: Or Fifty Years of Slavery in the Southern States of America, by Francis Fedric, an Escaped Slave.* London, 1863.

Fisk University. "God Struck Me Dead." Mimeographed. Nashville: Social Science Institute, 1945. Reprinted with an introduction by Clifton H. Johnson, Philadelphia: Pilgrim Press, 1969.

――――. "Unwritten History of Slavery." Mimeographed. Nashville: Social Science Institute, 1945. Reprint. Washington, D.C.: Microcard Editions, 1968.

Fitzhugh, George. *Cannibals All Or Slaves Without Masters*. Cambridge, Mass.: Harvard University Press, 1960.

Franklin, Henry. *A Sketch of Henry Franklin and Family*. Philadelphia, 1887.

Frederick, Reverend Francis. *Autobiography of Reverend Francis Frederick, of Virginia*. Baltimore, 1869.

Grandy, Moses. *Narrative of the Life of Moses Grandy, Late a Slave in the United States of America*. New York: Arno, [1844] 1968.

Grant, Douglas. *The Fortunate Slave: An Illustration of African Slavery in the Early Eighteenth Century*. London: Oxford University Press, 1968.

Green, J. D. *Narrative of the Life of J. D. Green, A Runaway Slave from Kentucky*. Huddersfield, England, 1864.

Green, William. *Narrative of Events in the Life of William Green (Formerly a Slave), Written by Himself*. Philadelphia: Rhistoric Publishers, [1853] 1969.

Grimes, William. *Life of William Grimes, the Runaway Slave, Written by Himself*. New York, 1825.

Gronniosaw, James A. U. *A Narrative of the Most Remarkable Particulars in the Life of James Albert Ukawsaw Gronniosaw, an African Prince, as Related by Himself*. Leeds, 1814.

Hall, Elder Samuel. *Forty-Seven Years a Slave: a Brief Story of His Life as a Slave and After Freedom*. Washington, Georgia, 1912.

Hammon, Briton. *A Narrative of the Uncommon Sufferings and Surprising Deliverance of Briton Hammon, a Negro Man*. Boston, 1760.

Hammon, Jupiter. *An Address to the Negroes of the State of New York*. New York, 1787.

Hayden, William. *Narrative of William Hayden Containing a Faithful Account of His Travels for a Number of Years Whilst a Slave in the South, Written by Himself*. Cincinnati, 1846.

Helper, Hinton Rowan. *The Impending Crisis of the South: How to Meet It*. Westport, Conn.: Negro Universities Press, [1857] 1970.

Henson, Josiah. *An Autobiography of the Rev. Josiah Henson (Mrs. Harriet Beecher Stowe's "Uncle Tom")*. Boston, 1879.

――――. *The Life of Josiah Henson, Formerly a Slave, Now an Inhabitant of Canada, as Narrated by Himself to Samuel Eliot*. Boston, 1849.

――――. *Truth Stranger than Fiction, Father Henson's Story of His Own Life with an Introduction by Mrs. Harriet Beecher Stowe*. Chicago: Afro-American Press, [1858] 1970.

Higginson, Thomas Wentworth. *Army Life in A Black Regiment*. New York: Collier Books, [1870] 1962.

Hildreth, Richard. *Archy Moore, the White Slave: or Memoirs of a Fugitive*. New York: Negro Universities Press, [1836] 1969.

Horton, George Moses. *The Home of Liberty, Poems.* Raleigh, North Carolina, 1829.

Howe, Samuel Gridley. *The Refugees from Slavery in Canada West. Report to the Freedman's Inquiry Commission.* New York: Arno, [1864] 1969.

Hughes, Louis. *Thirty Years A Slave.* Miami, Florida: Mnemosyne Publishing Co., [1897] 1969.

Jackson, Andrew. *Narrative and Writings of Andrew Jackson* of *Kentucky: Containing an Account of His Birth and Twenty-Six Years of His Life While a Slave, Narrated by Himself, Witten by a Friend.* Miami, Florida: Mnemosyne Publishing Co., [1847] 1969.

Jacobs, Harriet. *Incidents in the Life of a Slave Girl, Written by Herself.* Edited by L. Maris Child. Detroit: Negro History Press, [1862] 1969.

James, Reverend Thomas. *Life of Reverend Thomas James, by Himself.* Rochester, 1886.

Joanna. *Narrative of Joanna, an Emancipated Slave of Surinam (From Stedman's Narrative of Five Years' Expedition Against the Revoluted Negroes of Surinam).* Boston, 1838.

Johnstone, Abraham. *The Address of Abraham Johnstone, a Black Man, Who Was Hanged at Woodbury in the County of Glochester, and State of New Jersey, on Saturday the Eighth Day of July Last.* Philadelphia, 1797.

Jones, Thomas. *The Experience of Thomas Jones Who Was a Slave for Forty-Three Years, Written by a Friend as Given to Him by Brother Jones.* Philadelphia: Rhistoric Press, [1850] 1969.

Joseph and Encoh. *Narrative of the Barbarous Treatment of Two Unfortunate Females, Natives of Concordia, Louisiana, by Joseph and Encoh, Runaway Slaves.* New York, 1842.

Katz, William L., ed. *Five Slave Narratives* (Lunsford Lane, James W. Pennington, William W. Brown, Jacob Stroyer, Moses Grandy). New York: Arno, 1969.

Keckley, Elizabeth. *Behind the Scenes by Elizabeth Keckley, Formerly a Slave, But More Recently Modiste and Friend to Mrs. Abraham Lincoln, or Thirty Years a Slave and Four Years in the White House.* New York: Arno, [1868] 1969.

Lane, Lunsford. *The Narrative of Lunsford Lane, Formerly of Raleigh, N.C.* New York: Arno, [1842] 1968.

Langston, John Mercer. *From Virginia Plantation to the National Capital.* New York: Arno, [1894] 1969.

Larison, Cornelius Wilson. *Silva DuBois (now 116 years old): A Biography.* Westport, Conn.: Negro Universities Press, 1970.

Lester, Julius, ed. *To Be a Slave.* New York: Dial, 1968.

Lewis, Joseph Vance. *Out of the Ditch: A True Story of an Ex-Slave, by J. Vance Lewis.* Boston, 1910.

Loguen, Jermain W. *The Rev. J. W. Loguen as a Slave and as a Freeman, A Narrative of Real Life.* New York: Negro Universities Press, [1859] 1968.

Maddison, Reuben. *A True Story.* Birmingham, England, 1852.

Marrant, John. *A Narrative of the Lord's Wonderful Dealings with John Marrant, a Black, by the Rev. Mr. Aldridge*. London, 1785.

Mars, James. *Life of James Mars, a Slave Born and Sold in Connecticut, Written by Himself*. Miami, Florida: Mnemosyne Publishing Co., [1866] 1969.

Mason, Isaac. *Life of Isaac Mason as A Slave*. Miami, Florida: Mnemosyne Publishing Co., [1893] 1969.

Meachum, John B. *An Address to the Colored Citizens of the United States, Prefaced by a Narrative of the Author as a Slave in Virginia*. Philadelphia, 1846.

Meltzer, Milton, ed. *In Their Own Words: A History of the American Negro 1619–1865*. 2 vols. New York: Thomas Y. Crowell, 1964.

Montejo, Estaban. *Autobiography of a Runaway Slave*. Edited by Miguel Barnet. Translated by Jocasta Innes. New York: Pantheon, 1968.

Mott, A. and Wood, M. S. *Narratives of Colored Americans*. New York, 1882.

Mountain, Joseph. *Sketches of the Life of Joseph Mountain, a Negro, Who Was Executed at New Haven, on the 20th Day of October, 1790, For a Rape, Committed on the 26th Day of May Last*. New Haven, 1790.

Northup, Solomon. *Twelve Years a Slave*. Edited by Sue Eakin and Joseph Logsdon. Baton Rouge, La.: Louisiana State University Press, [1857] 1968.

Offley, G. W. *A Narrative of the Life and Labors of the Rev. G. W. Offley, a Colored Man and Local Preacher, Who Lived Twenty-seven Years at the South and Twenty-four at the North, Written by Himself*. Hartford, 1860.

O'Neal, William. *Life and History of William O'Neal: or, The Man Who Sold His Wife*. St. Louis, 1896.

Osofsky, Gilbert, ed. *Puttin' On Ole Massa: The Slave Narratives of Henry Bibb, William Wells Brown, and Solomon Northup*. New York: Harper Torchbooks, 1969.

Parker, Jamie. *Jamie Parker, the Fugitive*. Edited by Mrs. Emily Catherine Pierson. Hartford, 1851.

Parker, William. "The Freedman's Story." *Atlantic Monthly* 17 (February–March 1866): 152–160, 276–295.

Pennington, James W. C. *The Fugitive Blacksmith, or Events in the History of James W. C. Pennington, Pastor of a Presbyterian Church, New York, Formerly a Slave in the State of Maryland, United States*. New York: Negro Universities Press, [1849] 1970.

Peterson, Danile H. *The Looking Glass: Being A True Narrative of the Life of the Reverend D. H. Peterson*. New York, 1854.

Picquet, Louisa. *Louisa Picquet, the Octroon: or, Inside Views of Southern Domestic Life*. New York, 1861.

Platt, Reverend S. H. *The Martyrs and the Fugitive, or a Narrative of the Captivity, Sufferings and Death of an African Family and the Escape of Their Son*. New York, 1859.

Pollard, Edward A. *Black Diamonds in the Darkey Houses of the South*. New York: Negro Universities Press, [1859] 1969.

186 / BIBLIOGRAPHY

Prince, Mary. *The History of Mary Prince, a West Indian Slave, Related by Herself, With a Supplement by the Editor, to Which is Added the Narrative of Asa–Asa, A Captured African.* London, 1831.

Randolph, Peter. *From Slave Cabin to the Pulpit, the Autobiography of Reverend Peter Randolph: The Southern Question Illustrated and Sketches of Slave Life.* Boston, 1893.

Redpath, James. *The Roving Editor: or, Talks with Slaves in the Southern States.* New York: Negro Universities Press, [1859] 1969.

Roberts, James. *Narrative of James Roberts, Soldier in the Revolutionary War and Battle of New Orleans.* Chicago, 1858.

Roberts, Ralph. "A Slave's Story." *Putnam's Monthly Magazine* 9 (1857):614–620.

Roper, Moses. *A Narrative of the Adventures and Escape of Moses Roper from American Slavery.* New York: Negro Universities Press, [1839] 1970.

Savannah Unit. Georgia Writers' Project. *Drums and Shadows.* Athens, Georgia: University of Georgia Press, 1940.

Seymour. *Life of Maumer Juno of Charleston, South Carolina.* Atlanta, Georgia, 1892.

Sheppard. *A Short Sketch of the Life of Mr. Sheppard While He Was in Slavery, Together with Several of the Songs Sung During the Evening of the Jubilee Club.* Bellville, Ontario, 1887.

Simpson, John Hawkins. *Horrors of the Virginia Slave Trade and of Slave Rearing Plantations.* London, 1863.

Singleton, William Henry. *Recollections of My Slavery Days.* Peekskill, New York, 1922.

*Slave Insurrections: Selected Documents.* Westport, Conn.: Negro Universities Press, 1970.

Smith, E. *Uncle Tom's Kindred: or, the Wrongs of the Lowly: Sketches and Narratives.* 10 vols. Mansfield, Ohio: Wesleyan Methodist Connection of America, 1853.

Smith, James Lindsay. *Autobiography of James L. Smith: Including also Reminiscences of Slave Life, etc.* New York: Negro Universities Press, [1881] 1969.

Smith, Venture. *A Narrative of the Life and Adventures of Venture, a Native of Africa, But Resident About Sixty Years in the United States of America, Related by Himself.* New London, 1835.

Spear, Chloe. *Memoir of Chloe Spear, a Native of Africa, Who Was Enslaved in Childhood.* Boston, 1832.

Starobin, Robert S., ed. *Denmark Vesey: The Slave Conspiracy of 1882.* Englewood-Cliffs, New Jersey: Prentice-Hall, 1970.

Stevens, Charles Emery. *Anthony Burns: A History.* New York: Arno, [1856] 1969.

Steward, Austin. *Twenty-two Years a Slave and Forty Years a Freeman; Embracing a Correspondence of Several Years, While President of Wilberforce Colony, London, Canada West.* New York: Negro Universities Press, [1856] 1968.

Still, Peter. *The Kidnapped and the Ransomed Being the Personal Recollections of Peter Still and His Wife, Vina, After Forty Years of*

*Slavery, Written by Kate Pickard*. New York: Negro Universities Press, [1856] 1968.

Still, William. *The Underground Railroad*. New York: Arno, [1871] 1968.

Stowe, Harriet Beecher. *A Key to Uncle Tom's Cabin Presenting the Original Facts and Documents Upon Which the Story Is Founded, Together with Corroborative Statements Verifying the Truth of the Work*. New York: Arno, [1853] 1968.

Stroyer, Jacob. *Sketches of My Life in the South*. New York: Arno, [1879] 1968.

Thompson, John. *The Life of John Thompson, a Fugitive Slave, Containing His History of Twenty-Five years in Bondage and His Providential Escape, Written by Himself*. New York: Negro Universities Press, [1856] 1968.

Thoreau, Henry David. *Walden and Other Writings*. Garden City: Doubleday and Company, 1970.

Tilmon, Levin. *A Brief Miscellaneous Narrative of the More Early Parts of the Life of L. Tilmon*. Jersey City, New Jersey, 1853.

Truth, Sojourner. *Narrative of Sojourner Truth, a Northern Slave, Emancipated from Bodily Servitude by the State of New York in 1828*. Boston, 1850.

Tubman, Harriet. *Harriet, the Moses of Her People, Written by Sarah Bradford*. New York: Corinth Books, [1886] 1961.

Turner, Nat. *The Confession, Trial, and Execution of Nat Turner, The Negro Insurrectionist; also a List of Persons Murdered in the Insurrection in Southhampton County, Virginia, on the 21st and 22nd of August, 1831, with Introductory Remarks by T. R. Gray, Petersburg, Virginia*. Miami, Florida: Mnemosyne Publishing Co., [1831] 1969.

Twain, Mark. *The Adventures of Huckleberry Finn*. Hartford, Conn.: The American Publishing Company, 1899.

Veney, Bethany. *The Narrative of Bethany Veney, A Slave Woman*. Worcester, 1890.

Voorhis, Robert. *Life and Adventures of Robert, the Hermit of Massachusetts, Who Has Lived Fourteen Years in a Cave, Secluded from Human Society, Taken From His Own Mouth*. Providence, 1829.

Walker, David. *Walker's Appeal, in Four Articles and an Address to the Slaves of the United States of America by Henry Highland Garnet*. New York: Arno, [1831], 1969.

Ward, Samuel Ringgold. *Autobiography of a Fugitive Negro: His Anti-Slavery Labours in the United States, Canada, and England*. New York: Arno, [1855] 1968.

Washington, Booker T. *Up From Slavery*. New York: Dell, [1900] 1966.

Washington, Madison. *The Heroic Slave, A Thrilling Narrative of the Adventures of Madison Washington in Pursuit of Liberty, Written by Frederick Douglass*. Boston, 1853.

Watson, Henry. *Narrative of Henry Watson, a Fugitive Slave*. Boston, 1850.

Webb, William, *History of William Webb, Composed by Himself.* Detroit, 1873.

Weld, Theodore. *American Slavery As It Is: Testimony of a Thousand Witnesses.* New York: Arno, [1839] 1968.

Wheatley, Phillis. *Letters of Phillis Wheatley, The Negro Slave Poet of Boston.* Boston, 1864.

Wheeler, Peter. *Chains and Freedom: of the Life and Adventures of Peter Wheeler, A Colored Man Yet Living as told by Charles Edward Lester.* New York, 1839.

White, George. *Account of Life, Experience, Travels, and Gospel Labours of an African.* New York, 1810.

White, William S. *The African Preacher, an Authentic Narrative by the Reverend Williams S. White, Pastor Presbyterian Church, Lexington, Virginia.* Philadelphia, 1849.

Wilkerson, James. *Wilkerson's History of His Travels and Labors in the United States, as a Missionary, in Particular that of the Union Seminary, Located in Franklin County, Ohio, Since He Purchased His Liberty in New Orleans, Louisiana.* Columbus, Ohio, 1861.

William. *The Negro Servant: An Authentic Narrative of a Young Negro, Showing How He Was Made a Slave in Africa, and Carried to Jamaica, Where He was Sold to a Captain in His Majesty's Navy, and Taken to America, Where He Became a Christian, and Afterwards Brought to England and Baptised.* Kilmarnock, 1815.

Williams, Isaac D. *Sunshine and Shadow of Slave Life.* East Saginaw, Michigan, 1885.

Williams, James. *A Narrative of Events Since the First of August, 1834, by James Williams, an Apprenticed Labourer in Jamaica.* London, 1837.

Williams, James. *Life and Adventures of James Williams, a Fugitive Slave, with a Full Description of the Underground Railroad.* Saratoga, California: R and E Research Associates, [1874] 1970.

Williams, James. *Narrative of James Williams, An American Slave Who was for Several Years a Driver on a Cotton Plantation in Alabama.* Dictated to J. G. Whittier. Philadelphia: Rhistoric Publishers, [1838] 1969.

Williamson, Passmore. *Narrative of Facts in the Case of Passmore Williamson.* Philadelphia, 1855.

Winks, Robin W.; Gara, Larry; Pease, Jane H.; Pease, William H., and Edelstein, Tilden, eds. *Four Fugitive Slave Narratives* (William Wells Brown, Josiah Henson, Austin Steward, Bej. Drew). Reading, Massachusetts: Addison-Wesley Publishing Co., 1969.

Woodson, Carter. *The African Background Outlined or Handbook for the Study of the Negro.* New York: Negro Universities Press, [1936] 1969.

——, ed. *The Mind of the Negro as Reflected in Letters Written During the Crisis.* New York: Negro Universities Press, [1926] 1969.

Writers Project, Louisiana. *Gumbo Ya-Ya.* Boston: Houghton Mifflin Co., 1945.

WPA. Federal Writers' Project. *The Negro in Virginia.* New York: Arno, [1940] 1969.

Yetman, Norman R., ed. *Voices from Slavery.* New York: Holt, Rinehart and Winston, 1970.

Zamba. *Life and Adventure of Zamba, an African Negro King, and His Experiences of Slavery in South Carolina.* London, 1847.

Zangara and Maquama. *Slavery Illustrated; in the Histories of Zangara and Maquama, Two Negroes Stolen from Africa and Sold into Slavery, Related by Themselves.* London, 1849.


*Secondary Sources*


Abraham, W. E. *The Mind of Africa.* Chicago: University of Chicago Press, Phoenix Books, 1967.

Abrahams, Roger D. *Deep Down in the Jungle: Negro Narrative Folklore from the Streets of Philadelphia.* Chicago: Aldine, 1970.

———. *Positively Black.* Englewood-Cliffs, N.J.: Prentice-Hall, 1970.

Ajayi, Ade J. F., and Espie, Ian, eds. *A Thousand Years of West African History: A Handbook for Teachers and Students.* Ibadan, Nigeria: Ibadan University Press, 1969.

Alpers, Edward A. *The East African Slave Trade.* Historical Association of Tanzania Paper no. 3. Nairobi: East African Publishing House, 1967.

Aptheker, Herbert. *American Negro Slave Revolts.* New York: International Publishers, 1943.

———. *Essays in the History of the American Negro.* New York: International Publishers, 1945.

Ariès, Philippe. *Centuries of Childhood: A Social History of Family Life.* Translated by Robert Baldick. New York: Vintage Books, 1962.

Baron, Harold M. "The Demand for Black Labor: Historical Notes on the Political Economy of Racism." *Radical America* 5 (1971):1–46.

Bascom, William R. "Acculturation Among the Gullah Negroes." *American Anthropologist* 63 (1941):43–50.

———. *The Yoruba of Southwestern Nigeria.* New York: Holt, Rinehart, and Winston, 1969.

———, and Herskovits, Melville, eds. *Continuity and Change in African Cultures.* Chicago: University of Chicago Press, Phoenix Books, 1959.

Basler, Roy P., ed. *The Collected Works of Abraham Lincoln.* 8 vols. New Brunswick, N.J.: Rutgers University Press, 1953.

Bassett, John S. *The Southern Plantation Overseer as Revealed in His Letters.* 1925. Reprint. New York: Negro Universities Press, 1968.

Bauer, Raymond, and Bauer, Alice. "Day-to-Day Resistance to Slavery." *Journal of Negro History* 27 (1942):388–419

Beckwith, Martha, ed. *Jamaica Anansi Stories.* New York: American Folklore Society, 1924.

Bernard, Jessie. *Marriage and Family Among Negroes*. Englewood-Cliffs, N.J.: Prentice-Hall, Inc., Spectrum Books, 1966.

Bohannan, Paul. *Africa and Africans*. Garden City, N.Y.: American Museum Science Books, 1964.

————, and Dalton, George, eds. *Markets in Africa*. Garden City, N.Y.: Anchor Books, 1965.

Bryce-Laporte, Roy S. "The Conceptualization of the American Slave Plantation as a Total Institution." Ph.D. dissertation, University of California, 1968.

Bontemps, Arna, and Conroy, Jack. *Anyplace But Here*. New York: Hill and Wang, 1966.

Bosman, William. *A New and Accurate Description of the Coast of Guinea: Divided into the Gold, the Slave, and the Ivory Coasts*. New York: Barnes and Noble, [1704] 1967.

Botkin, Benjamin A. "The Slave as His Own Interpreter." *Library of Congress Quarterly Journal* 2 (1944):37–45.

————. "We Called It Living Lore." *New York Folklore Quarterly* 14 (1968):189–201.

————, ed. *A Treasury of Southern Folklore: Stories, Ballads, Traditions, and Folkways of the People of the South*. New York: Crown Publishers, 1949.

Boxer, C. R. *Race Relations in the Portuguese Colonial Empire, 1415–1825*. Oxford: Oxford University Press, 1963.

————. *The Dutch Sea-Borne Empire, 1600–1800*. New York: Alfred A. Knopf, 1965.

Brackett, Jeffrey. *The Negro in Maryland: A Study of the Institution of Slavery*. Baltimore: The Johns Hopkins University Press, 1889.

Brown, Norman O. *Life Against Death: The Psychoanalytic Meaning of History*. New York: Random House, 1959.

Buckmaster, Henrietta. *Let My People Go: The Story of the Underground Railroad and the Growth of the Abolition Movement*. Boston: Beacon Press, 1959.

Cade, John B. "Out of the Mouths of Ex-Slaves." *Journal of Negro History* 20 (1935):294–337.

Cairnes, John E. *The Slave Power: Its Character, Career, and Probable Designs, Being an Attempt to Explain the Real Issues Involved in the American Contest*. 1862. Reprint. New York: Negro Universities Press, 1969.

Carroll, Joseph Cephas. *Slave Insurrections in the United States 1800–1865*. 1938. Reprint. New York: Negro Universities Press, 1968.

Cash, W. J. *The Mind of the South*. New York: Vintage Books, 1941.

Chametsky, Jules, and Kaplan, Sidney, eds. *Black and White in American Culture*. Amherst: University of Massachusetts Press, 1967.

Chew, Peter. "Black History or Black Mythology." *American Heritage* 20 (1969):1–10.

Courlander, Harold. *Negro Folk Music, U.S.A.* New York: Columbia University Press, 1963.

————. *The Drum and the Hoe: Life and Lore of the Haitian People*. Berkeley: University of California Press, 1960.

Curtin, Philip D. *The Atlantic Slave Trade*. Madison: The University of Wisconsin Press, 1969.

——. *The Image of Africa: British Ideas and Action, 1780–1850*. Madison: The University of Wisconsin Press, 1964.

——, and Vansina, Jan. "Sources of the Nineteenth Century Atlantic Slave Trade." *Journal of African History* 5 (1964):185–206.

Curtis, James C. and Gould, Lewis L., eds. *The Black Experience in America*. Austin: University of Texas Press, 1970.

Davidson, Basil. *Africa in History: Themes and Outlines*. New York: The Macmillan Co., 1968.

——. *The African Genius An Introduction to African Cultural and Social History*. Boston: Little, Brown, and Co., 1969.

——. *The African Past: Chronicles from Antiquity to Modern Times*. Middlesex, England: Penguin Books, 1966.

——. *The African Slave Trade: Precolonial History 1450–1850*. Boston: Little, Brown, and Co., 1961.

——, Buah, F. K.; and Ajayi, J. F. A. *The Growth of African Civilization: A History of West Africa 100–1800*. London: Longmans, 1965.

Davis, David Brion. "The Comparative Approach to American History: Slavery." In *The Comparative Approach to American History*, edited by C. Vann Woodward. New York: Basic Books, Inc., 1968.

——. *The Problem of Slavery in Western Culture*. Ithaca, New York: Cornell University Press, 1966.

Dayrell, Elphinstone. *Folk Stories from Southern Nigeria West Africa*. New York: Negro Universities Press, 1969.

Degler, Carl N. *Neither Black nor White: Slavery and Race Relations in Brazil and the United States*. New York: The Macmillan Co., 1971.

——. "Slavery in Brazil and the United States: An Essay in Comparative History." *American Historical Review* 75 (1970):1005–1028.

Dorson, Richard M. *American Folklore*. Chicago: University of Chicago Press, 1959.

Duberman, Martin, ed. *The Antislavery Vanguard. New Essays on the Abolitionists*. Princeton: Princeton University Press, 1965.

Du Bois, W. E. B. *Black Reconstruction in America: An Essay Toward a History of the Part Which Black Folk Played in the Attempt to Reconstruct Democracy in America, 1860–1880*. Cleveland: The World Publishing Co., Meridan Books, 1964.

——. *John Brown*. New York: International Publishers, 1962.

——. *The Souls of Black Folk: Essays and Sketches*. New York: Dell Publishing Company, [1903] 1969.

——. *The Suppression of the African Slave Trade to the United States of America, 1638–1870*. New York: Schocken Books, 1969.

——, ed. *The Negro American Family*. New York: Negro Universities Press, [1908] 1968.

Duff, John B., and Mitchell, Peter M., eds. *The Nat Turner Rebellion: The Historical Event and the Modern Controversy*. New York: Harper and Row, 1971.

Eaton, C. "Slave-Hiring in the Upper South: A Step Toward Freedom." *Mississippi Valley Historical Review* 68 (1960):663–678.

Edwards, Bryan. *The History Civil and Commercial of the British Colonies in the West Indies.* 2 vols. Dublin: Luke White, 1803.

Elkins, Stanley. *Slavery.* Chicago: University of Chicago Press, 1958.

Erikson, Eric. *The Young Man Luther.* New York: Norton, 1958.

Fage, J. D. *An Introduction to the History of West Africa.* Cambridge: University Press, 1955.

Fanon, Frantz. *The Wretched of the Earth.* New York: Grove Press, 1968.

Feldstein, Stanley. *Once A Slave: The Slaves' View of Slavery.* New York: William Morrow, 1971.

Fisher, Miles Mark. *Negro Slave Songs in the United States.* New York: Citidal Press, 1963.

Foner, Laura, and Genovese, Eugene D., eds. *Slavery in the New World: A Reader in Comparative History.* Englewood-Cliffs, N.J.: Prentice-Hall, 1969.

Foner, Philip. *The Life and Writings of Frederick Douglass.* 4 vols. New York: International Publishers, 1950–1955.

Forde, Daryll, and Kaberry, P. M., eds. *West African Kingdoms in the Nineteenth Century.* London: Oxford University Press, 1968.

Foucault, Michel. *Madness and Civilization.* New York: New American Library Mentor Books, 1967.

Franklin, John Hope. *From Slavery to Freedom: A History of Negro Americans.* 3d ed. New York: Alfred A. Knopf, 1967.

———. *The Emancipation Proclamation.* Garden City, N.Y.: Doubleday, 1963.

———. *The Free Negro in North Carolina, 1790–1860.* New York: Norton, 1971.

Frazier, E. Franklin. *Black Bourgeoisie.* Glencoe, Ill.: Free Press, 1956.

———. *The Negro Church in America.* New York: Schocken Books, 1966.

———. *The Negro Family in the United States.* Chicago: University of Chicago Press, 1939.

———. *The Negro Family in the United States.* Revised and abridged edition with an introduction by Nathan Glazer. Chicago: University of Chicago Press, Phoenix Books, 1966.

———. "The Negro Slave Family." *The Journal of Negro History* 15 (1930):198–259.

———. *The Negro in the United States.* New York: Macmillan, 1957.

———. *Race and Culture Contacts in the Modern World.* Boston: Beacon Press, 1965.

Fredrickson, George M., and Lasch, Christopher. "Resistance to Slavery." *Civil War History* 13 (1967):315–329.

Freyre, Gilberto. *The Mansions and Shanties: The Making of Modern Brazil.* Translated by Harriet de Onís. New York: Alfred A. Knopf, 1963.

———. *The Masters and the Slaves: A Study in the Development of Brazilian Civilization.* 2d ed., rev. Translated by Samuel Putnam. New York: Alfred A. Knopf, 1956.

———. *New World in the Tropics: The Culture of Modern Brazil.* New York: Vintage, 1963.

Gara, Larry. *The Liberty Line: The Legend of the Underground Railroad.* Lexington: University of Kentucky Press, Kentucky Paperbacks, 1967.

Genovese, Eugene. "American Slaves and Their History." *The New York Review of Books* 15 (1970):34–43.

———. "Dr. Herbert Aptheker's Retreat from Marxism." *Science and Society* 27 (1963):212–216.

———. *In Red and Black: Marxian Explorations in Southern and Afro-American History.* New York: Pantheon, 1971.

———. "Marxian Interpretations of the Slave South." In *Towards a New Past,* edited by Barton J. Bernstein. New York: Pantheon, 1968.

———. "Negro Labor in Africa and the Slave South." *Phylon* 21 (1960):343–350.

———. "Problems in Nineteenth Century American History." *Science and Society* 25 (1961):38–53.

———. "Rebelliousness and Docility in the Negro Slave: A Critique of the Elkins Thesis." *Civil War History* 13 (1967):293–314.

———. "Recent Contributions to the Economic Historiography of the Slave South." *Science and Society* 24 (1960):53–66.

———. "Significance of the Slave Plantation for Southern Economic Development." *Journal of Southern History* 28 (1962):422–437.

———. "Slave South: An Interpretation." *Science and Society* 25 (1961):320–337.

———. *The Political Economy of Slavery: Studies in the Economy and Society of the Slave South.* New York: Pantheon, 1966.

———. "The Treatment of Slaves in Different Countries: Problems in the Application of the Comparative Method." In *Slavery in the New World: A Reader in Comparative History,* edited by Laura Foner and Eugene Genovese. Englewood-Cliffs, N.J.: Prentice-Hall, 1969.

———. *The World the Slaveholders Made: Two Essays in Interpretation.* New York: Pantheon, 1969.

———, et al. "The Legacy of Slavery and the Roots of Black Nationalism." *Studies on the Left* 6 (1966):2–65.

Glaberman, Martin; James, C. L. R.; and others. *Negro Americans Take the Lead.* Detroit: Facing Reality Publishing Committee, 1964.

Gluckman, Max. *Politics, Law, and Ritual in Tribal Society.* Oxford: Basil Blackwell, 1967.

Goody, Jack, ed. *Literacy in Traditional Societies.* Cambridge: Cambridge University Press, 1968.

Gossett, Thomas F. *Race: The History of an Idea in America.* New York: Schocken Books, 1968.

Goveia, Elsa V. *Slave Society in the British Leeward Islands at the End of the Eighteenth Century.* New Haven: Yale University Press, 1965.

———. "The West Indian Slave Laws of the Eighteenth Century." *Revista de Ciencias Sociales* 4 (1960):75–105.

Gutman, Herbert. "The Negro and the United Mine Workers of America: The Career and Letters of Richard L. Davis and Something of Their Meaning, 1890–1900." In *The Negro and the American Labor Movement*, edited by Julius Jacobson. New York: Anchor Books, 1968.

Harding, Vincent. "Religion and Resistance Among Antebellum Negroes, 1800–1860." In *The Making of Black America*, edited by August Meier and Elliot Rudwick. 2 vols. New York: Antheneum, 1969.

Harris, Joel Chandler. *The Complete Tales of Uncle Remus*. Compiled by Richard Chase. Boston: Houghton Mifflin, 1955.

Harris, Marvin. *Patters of Race in the Americas*. New York: Walker, 1964.

———. "The Origin of the Descent Rule." In *Slavery in the New World: A Reader in Comparative History*, edited by Laura Foner and Eugene D. Genovese. Englewood-Cliffs, N.J.: Prentice-Hall, 1969.

Hegel, G. W. F. *The Phenomenology of Mind*. Translated by J. B. Baillie. London: S. Sonnenshein, 1970, 2 vols.

Herskovits, Frances S., and Herskovits, Melville J., eds. *The New World Negro: Selected Papers in Afro-American Studies*. Bloomington, Indiana: Indiana University Press, 1966.

Herskovits, Melville J. *Dahomey: An Ancient West African Kingdom*. 2 vols. New York: J. J. Augustin, 1938.

———. *The Myth of the Negro Past*. Boston, Beacon Press, 1958.

Hofstadter, Richard. *The American Political Tradition and the Men Who Made It*. New York: Vintage, 1948.

Hoetink, Harry. *The Two Variants in Caribbean Race Relations: A Contribution to the Sociology of Segmented Societies*. London: Oxford University Press, 1967.

Hurston, Zora Neale. *Mule and Men*. Philadelphia: J. B. Lippincott, 1935.

Jackson, Luther P. "Religious Development of the Negro in Virginia from 1760–1860." *The Journal of Negro History* 16 (1931):168–239.

James, C. L. R. *A History of Negro Revolt*. New York: Haskell House Publishers, 1969.

———. *A History of Pan-African Revolt*. Washington, D.C.: Drum and Spear Press, 1969.

———. "The Atlantic Slave Trade and Slavery: Some Interpretations of Their Significance in the Development of the United States and the Western World." *Amistad* 1. New York: Vintage, 1970.

———. *The Black Jacobins: Toussaint L'Ouverture and the San Domingo Revolution*. 2d ed., rev. New York: Vintage Books, 1963.

Johnson, Charles S. *Shadow of the Plantation*. Chicago: University of Chicago Press, Phoenix Books, 1966.

Johnson, Guion Griffis. *A Social History of the Sea Islands: With*

*Special Reference to St. Helena Island, South Carolina.* New York: Negro Universities Press, 1969.

Johnson, Samuel. *The History of the Yorubas From the Earliest Times to the Beginning of the British Protectorate.* London: Routledge, and Kegan Paul, 1966.

Johnston, Sir Harry H. *The Negro in the New World.* London: Methuen & Co., Ltd., 1910.

Jones, G. I. *The Trading States of the Oil Rivers: A Study of Political Development in Eastern Nigeria.* London: Oxford University Press, 1963.

Jordan, Winthrop D. "American Chiaroscuro: The Status and Definition Of Mulattoes in the British Colonies." *William and Mary Quarterly* 19 (1962):183–200.

――――. *White Over Black: American Attitudes Toward the Negro, 1550–1812.* Baltimore: Penguin Books, Inc., 1969.

Kent, R. K. "Palmares: An African State in Brazil." *Journal of African History* 6 (1965):161–175.

Klein, A. Norman. Introduction to *The Suppression of the African Slave Trade to the United States of America 1638–1870,* by W. E. B. DuBois. New York: Schocken Books, 1969.

――――. "West African Unfree Labor Before and After the Rise of the Atlantic Slave Trade." In *Slavery in the New World: A Reader in Comparative History,* edited by Laura Foner and Eugene D. Genovese. Englewood-Cliffs, N.J.: Prentice-Hall, Inc., 1969.

Klein, Herbert S. "Anglicanism, Catholicism, and the Negro Slave." *Comparative Studies in Society and History* 8 (1966):295–327.

――――. *Slavery in the Americas: A Comparative Study of Cuba and Virginia.* Chicago: University of Chicago Press, 1967.

Klingsberg, Frank J. *An Appraisal of the Negro in Colonial South Carolina: A Study in Americanization.* Washington, D.C.: The Associated Publishers, 1941.

Kilson, Martin D. de B. "Towards Freedom: An Analysis of Slave Revolts in the United States." *Phylon* 25 (1964):179–183.

Knight, Franklin W. *Slave Society in Cuba During the Nineteenth Century.* Madison: The University of Wisconsin Press, 1970.

Lamming, George. *The Pleasures of Exile.* London: Michael Joseph, 1960.

Lester, Julius. *Search for the New Land: History as Subjective Experience.* New York: Dell, 1969.

Litwack, Leon F. "The Abolitionist Dilemma: The Antislavery Movement and the Northern Negro." *The New England Quarterly* 34 (1961):51–59.

――――. *North of Slavery: The Negro in the Free States, 1790–1860.* Chicago: The University of Chicago Press, 1961.

McColley, Robert. *Slavery and Jeffersonian Virginia.* Urbana: University of Illinois Press, 1964.

McManus, Edgar J. *A History of Negro Slavery in New York.* Syracuse, N.Y.: Syracuse University Press, 1966.

MacPhearson, C. B. *Possessive Individualism*. Oxford: The Clarendon Press, 1962.

McPhearson, James M. *The Negro's Civil War: How American Negroes Felt and Acted During the War for the Union*. New York: Pantheon, 1965.

Mandel, Bernard. *Labor: Free and Slave. Workingmen and the Anti-Slavery Movement in the United States*. New York: Associated Authors, 1955.

Mannix, Daniel P. and Cowley, Malcolm. *Black Cargoes: A History of the Atlantic Slave Trade, 1518–1865*. New York: The Viking Press, 1962.

Marcuse, Herbert. *Eros and Civilization*. Boston: Beacon Press, 1955.

Marx, Karl. *Capital*. Volume 1. Chicago: Charles Kerr and Co., 1906.

Mays, Benjamin E. *The Negro's God As Reflected in His Literature*. New York: Atheneum, 1968.

Mintz, Sidney W. "Comments on the Socio-Historical Background to Pidginization and Creolization." In *Pidginization and Creolization of Languages*, edited by D. Hymes. London: Cambridge University Press, 1970.

———. Foreword to *Afro–American Anthropology: Contemporary Perspectives*, edited by Norman E. Whitten, Jr. and John F. Szwed. New York: Free Press, 1970.

———. "Labor and Sugar in Puerto Rico and in Jamaica, 1800–1850." *Comparative Studies in Society and History* 1 (1959):273–280.

———. "Review of Stanley M. Elkins' *Slavery*." *American Anthropologist* 63 (1961):579–587.

———. "Toward an Afro-American History." *Journal of World History* 13 (1971):317–332.

Morner, Magnus. "The History of Race Relations in Latin America: Some Comments on the State of Research." *Latin American Research Review* 1 (1966):23–44.

Morris, Richard B. *Government and Labor in Early America*. New York: Harper Torchbooks, 1965.

———. "The Measure of Bondage in the Slave States." *Mississippi Valley Historical Review* 41 (1954):219–240.

Moynihan, Daniel P. *The Negro Family: The Case for Political Action*. Washington, D.C.: Government Printing Office, 1965.

Nash, Gary B., and Weiss, Richard, eds. *The Great Fear: Race in the Mind of America*. New York: Holt, Rinehart, and Winston, 1970.

Nichols, Charles H. *Many Thousand Gone: The Ex-Slaves' Account of Their Bondage and Freedom*. Leidan, Netherlands: E. J. Brill, 1963.

———. "Who Read the Slave Narratives." *Phylon* 20 (1959):149–162.

Nieboer, H. J. *Slavery as an Industrial System: Ethnological Researches*. Hague: Martinus Nihoff, 1900.

Odum, Howard W., and Johnson, Guy B. *The Negro and His Songs: A Study of Typical Negro Songs in the South*. 1926. Reprint. New York: Negro Universities Press, 1969.

Oliver, Roland, and Atmore, Anthony. *Africa Since 1800.* Cambridge: Cambridge University Press, 1967.

Olmsted, Frederick L. *A Journey in the Back Country.* London: S. Low, Son & Co., 1860.

———. *A Journey in the Seaboard Slave States, with Remarks on Their Economy.* 1856. Reprint. New York: Negro Universities Press, 1968.

———. *Journeys and Explorations in the Cotton Kingdom: A Traveller's Observations on Cotton and Slavery in the American Slave States.* 2 vols. London: S. Low, Son & Co., 1861.

———. *A Journey Through Texas: or, A Saddle Trip on the Southwestern Frontier.* New York: Dix, Edwards, & Co., 1857.

Owens, Jesse, and Neimark, Paul G. *Blackthink.* New York: Morrow, 1970.

Patterson, Orlando. *The Sociology of Slavery: An Analysis of the Origins, Development, and Structure of Negro Slave Society in Jamaica.* Rutherford, N.J.: Fairleigh Dickinson University Press, 1969.

Phillips, Ulrich B. *American Negro Slavery: A Survey of the Supply, Employment, and Control of Negro Labor as Determined by the Plantation Regime.* New York: D. Appleton & Co., 1918.

———. *Life and Labor in the Old South.* 1925. Reprint. Boston: Little, Brown and Co., 1963.

———. *The Slave Economy of the Old South: Selected Essays in Economic and Social History.* Edited by Eugene D. Genovese. Baton Rouge, La.: Louisiana State University Press, 1968.

Phillips, Wendell. *Speeches, Lectures, and Letters.* New York: Negro Universities Press, 1968.

Pierson, Donald. *Negroes in Brazil: A Study of Race Contact at Bahai.* Carbondale, Ill.: Southern Illinois University Press, 1967.

Polanyai, Karl. *Dahomey and the Slave Trade: An Analysis of an Archaic Economy.* Seattle: The University of Washington Press, 1966.

———. *The Great Transformation.* Boston: Beacon Press, 1957.

Pope-Hennessey, James. *Sins of the Fathers, A Study of the Atlantic Slave Traders, 1441–1807.* New York: Alfred A. Knopf, 1967.

Puckett, Newbell N. *Folk Beliefs of the Southern Negro.* Chapel Hill: The University of North Carolina Press, 1926.

Quarles, Benjamin. *Black Abolitionists.* New York: Oxford University Press, 1967.

———. *The Negro in the Civil War.* Boston: Little, Brown, and Co., 1953.

Radcliffe-Brown, A. R. and Forde, Daryll. *African Systems of Kinship and Marriage.* London: Oxford University Press, 1965.

Rainwater, Lee, and Yancey, William, eds. *The Moynihan Report and the Politics of Controversy.* Cambridge, Mass.: MIT Press, 1965.

Rawick, George P. "Race and Class in Auto." *Speak Out* 2 (1969):5–7.

———. Potere Nero e Lotte Operaie." In *U.S.A. Della Strade Alle Fabbriche,* edited by Ed Clark and George Rawick. Milano, Italia: Feltrinelli, 1968.

————. "The American Negro Movement." *International Socialism* 16 (1964):16–24.

————. "The Historical Roots of Black Liberation." *Radical America* 2 (1968):1–13.

————. "West African Culture and North American Slavery: A Study of Culture Change Among American Slaves in the Ante-Bellum South with Focus upon Slave Religion." *Migration and Anthropology: Proceedings of the 1970 Annual Spring Meeting of the American Ethnological Society.* Seattle: University of Washington Press, 1970.

Reich, Wilhelm. *Character Analysis.* New York: Farrar, Strauss, and Giroux, 1970.

————. *The Mass Psychology of Fascism.* New York: Farrar, Strauss, and Giroux, 1970.

Richards, Leonard L. *Gentlemen of Property and Standing: Anti-Abolition Mobs in Jacksonian America.* New York: Oxford University Press, 1970.

Rodney, Walter. "African Slavery and Other Forms of Social Oppression on the Upper Guinea Coast in the Context of the Atlantic Slave Trade." *Journal of African History* 7 (1966):431–443.

————. *The Groundings with My Brothers.* London: The Bogle-L'Ouverture Publications, 1969.

————. *A History of the Upper Guinea Coast 1545–1800.* London: Oxford University Press, Clarendon Press, 1970.

————. *West Africa and the Atlantic Slave Trade.* Nairobi: East African Publishing House, 1969.

Rodrigues, Jose Honorio. "The Influence of Africa on Brazil and of Brazil on Africa." *Journal of African History* 3 (1962):49–67.

Rose, Willie L. *Rehearsal for Reconstruction: The Port Royal Experiment.* New York: Vintage, 1967.

Russel, John F. *The Free Negro in Virginia.* Baltimore: The Johns Hopkins Press, 1913.

Ryder, A. F. C. *Benin and the Europeans, 1485–1897.* London: Longmans, Green, and Co., Ltd., 1969.

Sanborn, F. B., ed. *The Life and Letters of John Brown, Liberator of Kansas and Martyr of Virginia.* 1885. Reprint. New York: Negro Universities Press. 1969.

Shugg, Roger W. *Origins of Class Struggle in Louisiana. A Social History of White Farmers and Laborers During Slavery and After, 1840–1875.* Baton Rouge, La.: Louisiana State University Press, 1939.

Sio, Arnold. "Interpretations of Slavery: The Slave Status in the Americas." *Comparative Studies in Society and History* 7 (1965): 289–308.

Simpson, Robert Bruce. "A Black Church Ecstasy in a World of Trouble." Ph.D. dissertation, Washington University, 1970.

Stampp, Kenneth M. *The Peculiar Institution: Slavery in the Ante-Bellum South.* New York: Alfred A. Knopf, 1956.

Starling, Marion Wilson. "The Slave Narrative: Its Place in American Literary History." Ph.D. dissertation, New York University, 1946.

Starobin, Robert. "Disciplining Industrial Slaves in the Old South." *The Journal of Negro History* 53 (1968):111–128.

———. *Industrial Slavery in the Old South.* New York: Oxford University Press, 1970.

———. "The Negro: A Central Theme in American History." *Journal of Contemporary History* 3 (1968):37–53.

Strother, Horatio T. *The Underground Railroad in Connecticut.* Middletown, Conn.: Wesleyan University Press, 1962.

Stuckey, Sterling. "Through the Prism of Folklore: The Black Ethos in Slavery." *The Massachusetts Review* 9 (1968):417–437.

———. "Twilight of Our Past: Reflection on the Origins of Black History." *Amistad* 2. New York: Vintage, 1971.

Syndor, Charles. *Slavery in Mississippi.* Baton Rouge, La.: Louisiana State University Press, 1966.

Szwed, John F., ed. *Black America.* New York: Basic Books, Inc., 1970.

Tannenbaum, Frank. *Slave and Citizen: The Negro in the Americas.* New York: Random House, 1946.

———. "Slavery, the Negro, and Racial Prejudice." In *The United States and Latin America*, 2d ed., edited by Herbert L. Mathews. Englewood-Cliffs, N.J.: Prentice-Hall, 1963.

Thompson, Edward P. *The Making of the English Working Class.* London: Gollancz, 1963.

Thorpe, Earle E. "Chattel Slavery and Concentration Camps." *Negro History Bulletin* 25 (1962):176–181.

Turner, Lorenzo D. *Africanisms in the Gullah Dialect.* Chicago: University of Chicago Press, 1949.

Valentine, Charles. *Culture and Poverty.* Chicago: University of Chicago Press, 1968.

van den Berghe, Pierre L. *Race and Ethnicity: Essays in Comparative Sociology.* New York: Basic Books, 1970.

———. *Race and Racism: A Comparative Perspective.* New York: John Wiley and Sons, 1967.

Wade, Richard C. *Slavery in the Cities: The South, 1820–1860.* New York: Oxford University Press, 1964.

Vansina, Jan; Mauny, R.; and Thomas, L. V. *The Historian in Tropical Africa.* London: Oxford University Press, 1964.

Virginia Writers' Project. *The Negro in Virginia.* New York: Hastings House, 1940.

Ward, Matthew. *Indignant Heart.* New York: New Books, 1952.

Washington, Booker T. *Frederick Douglass.* 1907. Reprint. New York: Greenwood Press, 1969.

Weinstein, Allen and Gatell, Frank O., eds. *American Negro Slavery.* New York: Oxford University Press, 1968.

Welsch, Erwin K. *The Negro in the United States: A Research Guide.* Bloomington: Indiana University Press, 1965.

Wesley, Charles. *Negro Labor in the United States, 1850–1925: A Study in American Economic History.* New York: Vanguard Press, 1927.

Whitten, Norman E., Jr., and Szwed, John F., eds. *Afro.-American*

*Anthropology: Contemporary Perspectives.* New York: The Free Press, 1970.

Wiley, Bell Irvin. *Southern Negroes, 1861–1865.* New Haven: Yale University Press, 1938.

Williams, Eric. *Capitalism and Slavery.* Chapel Hill, N.C.: University of North Carolina Press, 1944.

Woodward, C. Vann. *The Origins of the New South, 1877–1913.* Baton Rouge, La.: Louisiana State University Press, 1951.

———. *The Strange Career of Jim Crow.* New York: Oxford University Press, Galaxy Books, 1957.

———. *Tom Watson.* New York: Galaxy Books, Oxford University Press, 1963.

Writers Program, Louisiana. *Gumbo Ya-Ya.* Boston: Houghton Mifflin, 1945.

Yetman, Norman K. "The Background of the Slave Narrative Collection." *American Quarterly* 19 (1967):534–553.

# INDEX

*p.120 - Bibliog.*

*127*

# ABOUT THE AUTHOR

GEORGE P. RAWICK is Associate Professor of Sociology at Washington University, St. Louis, Missouri. He earned his A.B. from Oberlin College and his M.S. and Ph.D. in history from the University of Wisconsin. As a postdoctoral fellow, he studied sociology and an thropology at Cornell University. He has taught at several colleges and universities and is the author of numerous scholarly articles and reviews.

29,486

# Date Due